Building Peace, Rebuilding Patriarchy

Oxford Studies in Gender and International Relations

Series editors: Rahul Rao, University of St Andrews, and Laura Sjoberg, Royal Holloway University of London

Windows of Opportunity: How Women Seize Peace Negotiations for Political Change
Miriam J. Anderson

Women as Foreign Policy Leaders: National Security and Gender Politics in Superpower America
Sylvia Bashevkin

Gendered Citizenship: Understanding Gendered Violence in Democratic India
Natasha Behl

Gender, Religion, Extremism: Finding Women in Anti-Radicalization
Katherine E. Brown

Enlisting Masculinity: The Construction of Gender in U.S. Military Recruiting Advertising during the All-Volunteer Force
Melissa T. Brown

The Politics of Gender Justice at the International Criminal Court: Legacies and Legitimacy
Louise Chappell

Cosmopolitan Sex Workers: Women and Migration in a Global City
Christine B. N. Chin

Intelligent Compassion: Feminist Critical Methodology in the Women's International League for Peace and Freedom
Catia Cecilia Confortini

Complicit Sisters: Gender and Women's Issues across North-South Divides
Sara de Jong

Gender and Private Security in Global Politics
Maya Eichler

This American Moment: A Feminist Christian Realist Intervention
Caron E. Gentry

Troubling Motherhood: Maternality in Global Politics
Lucy B. Hall, Anna L. Weissman, and Laura J. Shepherd

Breaking the Binaries in Security Studies: A Gendered Analysis of Women in Combat
Ayelet Harel-Shalev and Shir Daphna-Tekoah

Scandalous Economics: Gender and the Politics of Financial Crises
Aida A. Hozić and Jacqui True

Rewriting the Victim: Dramatization as Research in Thailand's Anti-Trafficking Movement
Erin M. Kamler

Equal Opportunity Peacekeeping: Women, Peace, and Security in Post-Conflict States
Sabrina Karim and Kyle Beardsley

Gender, Sex, and the Postnational Defense: Militarism and Peacekeeping
Annica Kronsell

The Beauty Trade: Youth, Gender, and Fashion Globalization
Angela B. V. McCracken

Global Norms and Local Action: The Campaigns against Gender-Based Violence in Africa
Peace A. Medie

Rape Loot Pillage: The Political Economy of Sexual Violence in Armed Conflict
Sara Meger

Support the Troops: Military Obligation, Gender, and the Making of Political Community
Katharine M. Millar

From Global to Grassroots: The European Union, Transnational Advocacy, and Combating Violence against Women
Celeste Montoya

Who Is Worthy of Protection? Gender-Based Asylum and US Immigration Politics
Meghana Nayak

Revisiting Gendered States: Feminist Imaginings of the State in International Relations
Swati Parashar, J. Ann Tickner, and Jacqui True

Out of Time: The Queer Politics of Postcoloniality
Rahul Rao

The Other #MeToos
Iqra Shagufta Cheema

Gender, UN Peacebuilding, and the Politics of Space: Locating Legitimacy
Laura J. Shepherd

Narrating the Women, Peace and Security Agenda: Logics of Global Governance
Laura J. Shepherd

Capitalism's Sexual History
Nicola J. Smith

A Feminist Voyage through International Relations
J. Ann Tickner

The Political Economy of Violence against Women
Jacqui True

Queer International Relations: Sovereignty, Sexuality and the Will to Knowledge
Cynthia Weber

Feminist Global Health Security
Clare Wenham

Bodies of Violence: Theorizing Embodied Subjects in International Relations
Lauren B. Wilcox

Building Peace, Rebuilding Patriarchy

The Failure of Gender Interventions in Timor-Leste

MELISSA JOHNSTON

OXFORD
UNIVERSITY PRESS

Oxford University Press is a department of the University of Oxford. It furthers
the University's objective of excellence in research, scholarship, and education
by publishing worldwide. Oxford is a registered trade mark of Oxford University
Press in the UK and certain other countries.

Published in the United States of America by Oxford University Press
198 Madison Avenue, New York, NY 10016, United States of America.

© Oxford University Press 2023

All rights reserved. No part of this publication may be reproduced, stored in
a retrieval system, or transmitted, in any form or by any means, without the
prior permission in writing of Oxford University Press, or as expressly permitted
by law, by license, or under terms agreed with the appropriate reproduction
rights organization. Inquiries concerning reproduction outside the scope of the
above should be sent to the Rights Department, Oxford University Press, at the
address above.

You must not circulate this work in any other form
and you must impose this same condition on any acquirer.

Library of Congress Cataloging-in-Publication Data
Names: Johnston, Melissa (Melissa Frances), author.
Title: Building peace, rebuilding patriarchy : the failure of gender
interventions in Timor-Leste / Melissa Johnston.
Description: New York, NY : Oxford University Press, 2023. | Series: Oxford studies in gender and
international relations | Includes bibliographical references and index.
Identifiers: LCCN 2023004731 (print) | LCCN 2023004732 (ebook) |
ISBN 9780197637999 (hardback) | ISBN 9780197638019 (epub)
Subjects: LCSH: Peace-building—Timor-Leste. | Peace-building—Sex differences—Timor-Leste. |
Women in peace-building—Timor-Leste. | Women—Social conditions—Timor-Leste. |
Microfinance—Social aspects—Timor-Leste.
Classification: LCC JZ5584.T56 J65 2023 (print) | LCC JZ5584.T56 (ebook) |
DDC 959.8704—dc23/eng/20230209
LC record available at https://lccn.loc.gov/2023004731
LC ebook record available at https://lccn.loc.gov/2023004732

DOI: 10.1093/oso/9780197637999.001.0001

Printed by Integrated Books International, United States of America

Contents

List of Illustrations	ix
Associations and Organizations	xi
Acknowledgments	xix
Introduction: Gender Interventions in Context	1
1. Critical Approaches to Peacebuilding and Gender	12
2. Class Formation, Slavery, and Militarization	47
3. Class, Gender, and the Distribution of State Resources	69
4. The Political Economy of Domestic Violence	97
5. Brideprice and the Exchange of Women	116
6. Microfinance Interventions	144
7. Gendered Circuits of Debt and Violence	165
Conclusion	181
Methodological Notes	187
Glossary	197
Notes	205
References	219
Index	245

Illustrations

Figures

2.1 Timor-Leste, by district and subdistrict	49
3.1 Spending on Pensaun Veteranu and Bolsa da Mãe, 2008–2016	94
5.1 Matrilateral cross cousin marriage	135
5.2 Brideprice wealth transfer	137
5.3 Brideprice in the formal and informal economy	139
7.1 Overlapping kinship and microfinance in Mota	166

Tables

1.1 UN peacebuilding interventions in Timor-Leste, 1999–2012	14
1.2 Gender interventions in Timor-Leste, 2001–2017	16
2.1 Social rank during the Portuguese period, c. 1850–1975	52
2.2 Rank continuity during the Indonesian occupation, 1975–1998	55
2.3 Types of unfree labor during the Portuguese period	60
5.1 Types of marriage payment	117
5.2 Brideprice costs	118
5.3 Rank in Timor-Leste, by district	133
6.1 Types of microfinance in Timor-Leste	146
7.1 Interest rates, volumes, and lending to nonmembers	169
A.1 Timor-Leste interviewees, 2015, by gender	188
A.2 Cited interviewees	189

Associations and Organizations

1979 Convention on the Elimination of All Forms of Discrimination against Women	CEDAW	
A Comissão de Acolhimento, Verdade e Reconciliação	CAVR	Commission for Reception, Truth, and Reconciliation
Aliança de Maioria Parlamentar	AMP	Parliamentary Majority Alliance
Angkatan Bersenjata Republik Indonesia	ABRI	Republic of Indonesia Armed Forces during Suharto's New Order
Asian Development Bank	ADB	Regional development bank headquartered in the Philippines
Associação Popular Democrática Timorense	APODETI	Timorese pro-Indonesian integration party
Associação Social-Democrática Timorense	ASDT	Timorese Social Democratic Association, later FRETILIN
Badan Koordinasi Keluarga Berencana Nasional	BKKBN	National Family Planning Board
Banco Centro de Timor-Leste	BCTL	Central Bank of Timor-Leste
Banco Naçional Commerçio de Timor-Leste	BNCTL	National Commercial Bank of Timor-Leste
Banco Naçional Ultramarino	BNU	National Overseas Bank

ASSOCIATIONS AND ORGANIZATIONS

Bank Rakyat Indonesia	BRI	One of the largest banks in Indonesia, specializing in small-scale and microfinance- style borrowing and lending
Bolsa da Mãe		Literally, Mother's Purse, a conditional cash transfer program aimed at vulnerable women
Catholic Relief Services	CRS	
Comité Executivo da Luta		Executive Committee for the Struggle
Community Empowerment Project	CEP	World Bank project in rural Timor from 1999 to 2002
Conselho Nacional de Reconstrução de Timor	CNRT	National Council for the Reconstruction of Timor, a conservative political party founded in 2007
Conselho por Defeza Republica Demokratika Timor-Leste	CPD-RDTL	Council for the Defense of the Democratic Republic of Timor-Leste
Cooperativa Café Timor		National Timorese coffee cooperative
DD(R)R Disarmament, Demobilization, (Reinsertion) Reintegration	DDR	
Dewan Perwakilan Rakyat Daerah	DPR-D	Regional Representatives Council
Dharma Wanita		Literally, Women's Duty, an Indonesian women's association of wives of civil servants
Direçion Naçional Reinserçião Sosial	DNRS	National Directorate for Social Reinsertion
FALINTIL–Forças Defeza de Timor-Leste	F-FDTL	Defense Forces of Timor-Leste, the post-independence armed forces
Federasaun Hanai Malu		Timorese umbrella organizsiation of credit cooperatives

Forças Armadas de Libertação Naçional de Timor Leste	FALINTIL	Armed Forces for the National Liberation of Timor-Leste
Forum Kommunikasi Perempuan East Timor	FOKUPERS	East Timorese Women's Communication Forum
Frente Revolucionário do Timor-Leste Independente	FRETILIN	Revolutionary Front for Independent Timor-Leste
Fundação Pátria	Patria	Timorese women's rights NGO
Gender Affairs Unit under UNTAET	GAU	
Gender Responsive Budgeting	GRB	A public policy tool that analyses budgets to assess funding gaps, identify actions to close them and ensure commitments to gender equality and women's empowerment are properly funded
Gender Based Violence	GBV	
Gross Domestic Product	GDP	
Gerakan Pengacau Keamanan	GPK	Literally, security disturbance movement, an Indonesian armed forces term for the anti-Indonesian force FALINTIL
Grupo Mulhers Parliamentario Timor-Leste	GMPTL	Group of Women Parliamentarians in Timor-Leste, later formalized and known as the Cross-Party Caucus
Inclusive Finance for the Underserved Economy	INFUSE	UNCDF/UNDP/Australian Timorese government aid project on inclusive finance in Timor-Leste
Institut do Microfinansas de Timor-Leste	IMfTL	Institute of Microfinance of Timor-Leste
International Finance Corporation	IFC	

ASSOCIATIONS AND ORGANIZATIONS

International Financial Institution	IFI	An international organisation dealing with finance, most often the International Monetary Fund and the World Bank, or their subsidiary organisations
International Force for East Timor	INTERFET	
International Labour Organization	ILO	
International Organization for Migration	IOM	
Judicial System Monitoring Program	JSMP	
Kooperasi Unit Desa	KUD	Village Unit Cooperative, a New Order-era microfinance organization
Laksaur Militia		East Timorese militia based in Suai, Cova Lima
Lào Hamutuk		Walk Together, a Timorese NGO working on economic development monitoring
Law Against Domestic Violence	LADV	2010 Lei Contra Violensia Domestika (Tetun)
Member of Parliament	MP	
Microfinance Institution	MFI	
Ministra Solidariedade Sosiál	MSS	Ministry for Social Solidarity
Moris Rasik		Literally, independent life (i.e., self-starting), a large Timorese microfinance organization
Non Government Organisation	NGO	
Nucleos de Resistencia Popular	NUREP	The Nucleus of the Popular Resistance, a village-based network of resistance leaders
Nucleos de Resistencia Popular	NUREP	The Nucleus of the Popular Resistance, a village-based network of resistance leaders

Operasi Sapu Jagad		Operation Global Clean Sweep, an Indonesian-organized operation to destroy East Timor through deportations and killings, after its people voted to split from Indonesia in 1999
Opportunidade Timor Lorosa'e		Opportunity Timor-Leste, a Christian microfinance provider
Organização Mulher Timorense	OMT	Women's wing of the CNRT
Organização Popular da Mulher Timorense	OPMT	Popular Organization of Timorese Women, the women's wing of FRETILIN
Pembinaan Kesejahteraan Keluarga	PKK	Family Welfare Movement
Pertahanan Sipil	HANSIP	Civilian defense organization, militia
Poliçia Naçional de Timor-Leste	PNTL	National Police Force of Timor-Leste
Pramuka		Indonesian scout movement
Programa Nacional Desenvolivimentu Suku	PNDS	National Program for Village Development
PT Batara Indra Group		An Indonesian firm active in East Timor
PT Denok		An Indonesian firm active in East Timor
Pusat Koperative Unit Desa	PUSKUD	Centre for Village Cooperative Units
Rede Feto		East Timor Women's Network
Resistência Naçional dos Estudantes de Timor-Leste	RENETIL	National Resistance of the Students of Timor-Leste
Rotating Savings and Credit Association	ROSCA	Lottery finance organization also known by the Indonesian term *arisan*
Rukun Tetangga	RT	Neighborhood association
Rukun Warga	RW	Administrative unit

xvi ASSOCIATIONS AND ORGANIZATIONS

Sagrada Família		A violent group of ex-FALINTIL, banned by the state and led by Cornelio Gama
Secretariado Técnico de Administração Eleitoral	STAE	Secretary for Technical Administration of Elections Department of State Administration
Self Help Group	SHG	Self Help Group microfinance, also often called "cooperatives"
Sekretaria Estadu ba Apoiu no Promosaun Sosiu-Ekonomika ba Feto	SEM	Secretariat of State for the Support and Socio-Economic Promotion for Women (2015–2017)
Sekretaria Estadu ba Formasaun Profisionál no Empregu	SEFOPE	Secretariat of State for Vocational Training and Employment
Sekretária Estadu Promosaun Igualdade	SEPI	Secretariat of State for the the Promotion of Equality (2012–2015)
Sexual and Gender Based Violence	SGBV	
Sociedade Agricola Patria e Trabalho	SAPT	Agricultural Society for the Fatherland and Workers
Tenaga Bantuan Operasi	TBO	Military operations' assistants in the Indonesian military
Tuba Rai Metin		Literally, Stand Firmly on the Ground, a Timorese microfinance institution
UN Security Council Resolution 1325 on Women, Peace, and Security	UNSCR1325	
União Democrática Timorense	UDT	Timorese Democratic Union, a political party
United Nations	UN	
United Nations Capital Development Fund	UNCDF	
United Nations Development Fund for Women	UNIFEM	Replaced by UN Women in 2010

United Nations Development Programme	UNDP	
United Nations Entity for Gender Equality and the Empowerment of Women	UN Women	Replaced UNIFEM in 2010
United Nations High Commission for Refugees	UNHCR	
United Nations Integrated Mission in East Timor	UNMIT	
United Nations Mission in East Timor	UNAMET	
United Nations Mission of Support in East Timor	UNMISET	
United Nations Office in Timor-Leste	UNOTIL	
United Nations Office in Timor-Leste	UNOTIL	
United Nations Population Fund	UNFPA	
United Nations Transitional Administration in East Timor	UNTAET	
United States Agency for International Development	USAID	
Usaha Bersama Simpan Pinjam	UBSP	Literally, Business Together Saving Lending, a microfinance savings and loan organizations
Violence Against Women	VAW	

Vulnerable Persons' Unit	VPU	A unit in the Timorese Police Force to protect vulnerable persons such as women and children
Zona Espeçial de Economia Soçial de Mercado	ZEESM	Special Zone of Social Market Economy of Timor-Leste, the Oecusse free trade zone

Acknowledgments

The support I have received while writing this book has been fantastic. Special thanks to Jane Hutchison, Ian Wilson, Carol Warren, and Shahar Hameiri, who have been wonderful friends and mentors. Caroline Hughes's encouragement and good advice started me on the right path. I had a lot of space for my ideas at the Asia Research Centre and the Murdoch School of Political Economy. Bu Wilson—thanks so much for your insights and special expertise.

Thanks to Camille Blakely and Anna Chapman for editing.

My friends in Dili and Perth need a really special mention. Nina, you know I would have never done it without you. With you I found that research also creates extraordinary memories of dancing, gossip, weddings, births, and deaths. My gratitude to Maria Madeira for allowing me to reproduce her wonderful painting "Dili Playground—Angelica" for the cover. Tia Veronika and Tiu Arão, and my many companions during months in Timor—Anene, Nora, Afina, Afati, Akussu, and Ayu—deserve the biggest thanks. *Hau nia obrigada boot ba Familia hotu. Tau matan ba dalan. Vida naruk.* Many thanks also to all of the research assistants who helped me learn, speak, and understand Timor-Leste and West Timor, including Lina and Mina and family in Oecusse, and my favorite brother-and-sister team, Alitu and Afati. Thanks to Marzita Ardiantina for acting as research team leader throughout the fieldwork.

In Kupang, I thank from the bottom of my heart Dr. Ermi, Ita, and family. Thanks so much to Pak Dedy for your fieldwork support. Many thanks to all the team at Universitas Cendana, especially Leni Suek and Julie Kopong, as well as great insights from the amazing activists and thinkers Torry Kuswardono and Tien Riwu.

This book is dedicated to the late Chris Johnston, whose lifelong love of discovery and learning still inspires me.

Introduction

Gender Interventions in Context

In 1998, more than two decades of Indonesian occupation in East Timor began to disintegrate. The occupiers, the authoritarian Suharto regime, buckled under economic collapse and massive public demonstrations across the archipelago. In this context, the crumbling Indonesian government faced increasing public pressure to resolve the question of Timorese autonomy. But the answer was not straightforward. The occupation of East Timor had been fundamental to the identity of both the Indonesian military and Suharto's New Order, and East Timorese autonomy was therefore strongly contested.[1]

The end of Suharto's rule gave rise to internal conflict between the Indonesian Army and government, in which the Timor question played a part. At the same time, the World Bank and the International Monetary Fund, together with civil society groups, pressed the Indonesian government for a variety of liberal democratic reforms. In response, interim president B. J. Habibie allowed the East Timorese to vote to become either an autonomous part of Indonesia or fully independent. In the vote of August 31, 1999, organized by the United Nations Mission in East Timor (UNAMET), the people of East Timor decided to pursue independence.

That choice meant that the Indonesian military and militias would lose jobs, money, land, and power. Fearing material losses, and especially around the time of the referendum, Indonesian armed forces perpetrated war crimes from 1998 to 1999. The military also funded and directed Timorese militia to destroy infrastructure and engage in mass killings and sexual violence. Militia personnel, brutalized and fortified with drugs, alcohol, and blood rituals, were sent on missions of violent destruction that amounted to crimes against humanity (CAVR 2006; Tanter, Ball, and Van Klinken 2006). During the same period, more than two hundred thousand Timorese, including pro-integration militia that had supported the Indonesian occupation, fled or were removed to Indonesian West Timor. In an interview I did in Indonesian West Timor over fifteen years later, the memory of those years still burned hot for the militia members. They remembered the violence they committed against neighbours and family members, and the fracture of their communities. While large numbers of people were forced across the border into Indonesia, other militia members recalled how they were fearful of returning home because of their crimes and that they left East Timor willingly: "We came here without any order from any government and no government will order us back."[2]

The international response to the Indonesian military's scorched-earth program was inadequate. The election mission UNAMET withdrew haphazardly after some of its staff were killed on the border with Indonesia, and the mission was criticized for abandoning the Timorese.

Weeks later, on September 20, 1999, the Australian-led International Force for East Timor (INTERFET) intervened in order to secure East Timor. Australia's leading role in the force was motivated by the transnational threat posed by an arc of unstable, failing, or failed states across the region. In a later lecture on diplomacy, Alexander Downer, Australian foreign minister from 1996 to 2007, explained this view: "Australia wants to be able to look to its North and its East and see strong, stable, prosperous states. States that lack good governance and face a bleak economic future are vulnerable to the damaging effects of transnational crime. They run the risk of becoming havens for criminal gangs and others who seek to evade the law. The presence of these people in a turbulent and chaotic neighbourhood would obviously not be in our interest" (Downer 2007).

Australia participated in, led, or supported interventions in Cambodia, Timor-Leste, Bougainville, and the Solomon Islands. Its rationale for becoming involved in the Asia-Pacific region—to contain transnational risks—also arose in the context of US withdrawal from the region. Australia was left to take the lead in managing interests in Cambodia, Timor-Leste, and the Pacific more widely. Over the next thirteen years, expensive, extensive, and far-reaching peacebuilding and statebuilding interventions took place in Timor-Leste.

Men and women do not experience war, violence, peace, settlements, or justice in the same ways, and the study and the practice of peacebuilding have increasingly looked at the gender gap. Most prominently, the Women, Peace, and Security (WPS) policy agenda, which began in 2000 with United Nations Security Council Resolution 1325, called for a gender perspective to be incorporated into all UN operations, decision-making, policies, and programs for peace and security. Feminist work in security studies and international relations has greatly advanced our understanding of the gendered dimensions of war and peace. We now know that unequal gender relations mean that women and men are targeted differently and experience different outcomes from peacebuilding. Moreover, power, resources, social burdens, and violence are distributed unevenly across genders, classes, and geographic regions following peacebuilding interventions, creating substantial gender gaps.

Peacebuilding interventions—the subject of this book—began to include gender as a factor in two broad forms: gender mainstreaming within broader peacebuilding initiatives and stand-alone gender-and-development programs. Mainstreaming involves incorporating a gender perspective into all areas and levels of legislation, policies, or programs. Gender and development refers to the integration of women in (mostly economic) development programs and to the need to challenge economic power relations between men and women. Both forms of gender programming are used in conflict-affected spaces, and can be collected under the term *gender intervention*. This amalgamation of gender, security, and development has a corollary in the integration of security and development into peacebuilding itself (Duffield 2001). The official rationale behind gender mainstreaming is to make peacebuilding more effective and sustainable, and thus to facilitate the development of more stable societies and efficient economies. In this view, postconflict countries are sites on which peacebuilders can build back better, including by building more gender-equitable societies.

The case of Timor-Leste is particularly instructive, as the country was subjected to very high levels of peacebuilding and gender intervention between 1999 and 2017. These interventions have had a sustained focus on gender and women's empowerment, but, like peacebuilding generally, their results have been uneven in terms of their stated goals, such as providing redress and resources to female victims of war crimes or electing more women as village chiefs. Additionally, gender interventions have been disappointing when measured against the more ambitious goals of gender justice: "the ending of—and if necessary the provision of redress for—inequalities between women and men that result in women's subordination to men" (Goetz 2007, 31). Whereas the level of women's participation in national politics in Timor-Leste is high by international standards, deep inequalities remain overall, inequality between rural and urban areas is growing, and violence against women is endemic across the country. Why?

At the same time as the expansion of gender mainstreaming, the failure of peacebuilding to create long-lasting and equitable peace in postconflict settings as diverse as Bosnia and Herzegovina, Iraq, Afghanistan, and

Timor-Leste has prompted scholars to look for answers. Some argue that local cultures and institutions are more legitimate, authentic, and sustainable sites on which to build peace than anything that international models can provide, pushing against the notion that liberal interventions based on the rule of law, the creation of democratic institutions, and liberal market principles can fashion a lasting peace. The local turn—both in peacebuilding interventions and explanations for their shortcomings—focuses on an alleged incompatibility between international-liberal norms and "local" nonliberal norms and practices. This disjuncture is seen to result in, at best, hybrid forms of governance that combine international and local elements.

Over the past decade, the local turn has come to dominate the theory and practice of peacebuilding. Indeed, Timor-Leste has become the cause célèbre of scholars of the local turn. Initially, this was in the context of the extent and reach of peacebuilding in the country and, of particular relevance to this study, as the local turn found traction in the implementation of programs. For these two reasons—the status of Timor-Leste as a test case for local turn theories and the depth of gender interventions undertaken there—I use this nation as a case study to evaluate the outcomes of gender interventions. The implications of local-turn approaches to gender intervention are rarely explicitly drawn out, but a tacit belief has nonetheless arisen that carrying out gender interventions within a liberal peacebuilding framework does not work in postconflict societies.

Attempts to explain the unevenness of peacebuilding that are predominately associated with the local turn are nonetheless weak. Scholars of the local turn conceptualize peacebuilding as either a clash or a hybrid of liberal and local paradigms. Consequently, explanations grounded in the local turn tend to disregard contentious politics within intervened states or interveners, as some analysts have pointed out (Hughes 2009; 2015; Hameiri and Jones 2017). This lacuna limits the explanatory power of the local turn when factors beyond the interaction of local and international come into play, as they do very apparently in gender interventions. Such explanations also rely too heavily on the slippery and analytically weak concept of authenticity, assuming that domestic actors will automatically reject international interventions in favor of authentic tradition.

Some scholars of the local turn do, however, acknowledge that authenticity is constructed and malleable, and as Caroline Hughes (2015, 909) notes, this act of construction means that the nature of indigeneity itself is contested in a variety of ways within local communities. Relatedly, when it comes to explaining inconsistent and questionable benefits for women in postconflict areas, a bifurcated framework of local versus international fails to distinguish between hierarchies of gender and class power within societies, kinship groups, and households, even though all of these are key sites of violent power struggles. Therefore, scholarship and peacebuilding practice that rely on local-turn frameworks are normatively problematic because they provide justification, even a cover of legitimacy, to the continuation of highly unequal gender relations.

Finally, the local turn in peacebuilding can have adverse consequences for gender justice when put into practice. By making assumptions about authenticity—while engaging in pragmatic buyoffs of violent groups in the cause of peace—peacebuilders have inadvertently supported national and subnational groups that benefit from patriarchy and class hierarchy. Lack of analysis of local power relations makes it difficult for peacebuilders to interpret the claims of their local interlocutors, resulting in a paradox whereby peacebuilders are pressed to fix deep problems with gender relations, rights, and women's empowerment while supporting groups whose interests lie in ensuring the persistence of patriarchal relations. Compounding this paradox is that gender injustice has flow-on effects to areas as diverse as human development, education, human rights, and social justice, undermining the possibility of sustainable peace by driving society-wide grievances. Moreover, to date, little discussion has taken place about how a local turn in peacebuilding, with its emphasis on authentic institutions, cultures, and the everyday, works out for women on the ground in Timor-Leste.

Scholars working on gender and peacebuilding in Timor-Leste have sought to account for the shortcomings of interventions in a variety of ways. Feminist, historical, normative, and legal approaches have all been applied, with more or less success (Harris-Rimmer 2010; Kent 2012a; Wallis 2015; Kent 2016; Charlesworth and Wood 2001; 2002). Some focus on gender mainstreaming within the interventions themselves, under the rubric of feminist security studies (Olsson 2009; Joshi 2005). Others use a constructivist framework comparable to that of the local turn, suggesting that the disconnect between local norms, discourses, or cultures and liberal human rights are at the root of the problem (Hall and True 2008; Smith 2015b; 2015a). Still others consider the intersection of gender and budget expenditure in the Timorese economy but leave class structures unexamined (Niner 2016; Costa 2018). While building on this extensive body of work, I contend that the scholarship on gender and peacebuilding in Timor-Leste has tended to overlook a key relationship: a more comprehensive, satisfactory explanation for the failures of gender intervention lies in the historically specific and interdependent structures of gender, kinship, and class.

The Genesis of the Study

This book is my attempt to provide that fuller explanation. It has its roots in extensive fieldwork, during which I lived with Timorese families, speaking both Tetun and Indonesian and talking on frank terms with ordinary citizens. The principal fieldwork on which this study is based (see Methodological Notes for more details) happened in 2015 on my second and longer trip to Timor-Leste and Indonesian West Timor. I was a participant observer in many important kinship events: weddings, births, funerals, memorials, and engagement ceremonies. During both ordinary and extraordinary activities, I observed who spoke, who ate first, and who received deference. I asked why some people had authority and others did not, and why some people gave money and goods while others received them. Marriage, kinship, and violence were the focus of many of my interviews and daily conversations, from which emerged the themes of social structure, hierarchy, power, control, and violence. Moving out of elite spheres to live, work, and celebrate special occasions with Timorese families gave me a deep understanding of the often hidden aspects of power and hierarchy.

I based my research on two fundamental questions:

- How can the uneven outcomes of gender interventions be explained?
- How do the results of gender intervention compare with the goals of gender justice?

To answer the second question, I asked three related ones:

- What are the distributional outcomes of the interventions for different groups?
- What explains the high levels of violence against women in Timor-Leste?
- How have rural women experienced programs intended to promote women's empowerment?

Specifically, I evaluated three gender interventions: gender-responsive budgeting (GRB), the Law Against Domestic Violence (LADV), and microfinance. These three deal directly with resources, violence, and power; they have significant material consquences for power and redistribution of wealth across Timorese society; they affect large numbers of Timorese women; and they have important implications for gender justice. I chose them for these reasons.

At one level, the study measures outcomes according to the interveners' aims in each case. The first area of intervention, GRB, started in 2008 with the goal of making democratic institutions properly accountable to women. The second, the LADV was lobbied for in the period leading up to independence and passed in 2010. The law was intended to create legal protections for women's right to safety and security, and its implementation constitutes an ongoing intervention. The third area, microfinance, has as its goal the economic empowerment of women through credit markets. Microfinance has a long history in Timor-Leste, but its application from 1998 to 2018 is especially relevant to this study.

At another level, I wanted to explore how these gender interventions have worked in practice, using the concept of gender justice as a yardstick. As gender justice focuses on material relations between women and men and the redistribution of power and wealth, I needed to assess the distributional outcomes of the interventions: essentially, to determine which groups of men and women got what, when they got it, and how. To complete the evaluation, I analyzed the historical formation of various social groups and their interests, contextualizing the distributional outcomes of gender interventions within the fiscally larger distributional outcomes of peacebuilding. Finally, a full explanation of such gendered outcomes requires an assessment of the distribution of violence. As such, this book also examines how gender justice arising from peacebuilding initiatives affects violence against women.

The Political Economy of Gender Intervention

Scholars of structural political economy in Southeast Asia have long argued that international actors are just one social force among many and thus must contend with domestic social forces that compete for power and wealth. As a result of such competition, Southeast Asian states have historically been dominated by oligarchic, authoritarian, and capitalist groups, classes, and class fractions.[3] In this view, the state is a social relation, not separable from society but a structure that comprises the social power relations between groups with more or less power; the state expresses the agency, interests, and ideologies of particular social forces, especially classes. Scholars who apply a structural political economy approach to international interventions in the region argue that contests between specific social forces shape the outcomes of peacebuilding by changing or upholding the distribution and reproduction of political power (Hameiri, Hughes, and Scarpello 2017; Hughes 2009; 2015; Jones 2010).

I agree that social forces play a more significant role in the success or failure of gender interventions than does the question of local versus international agency or the existence of hybrid local/international institutions. Interveners find themselves embroiled in conflicts involving coalitions of domestic social forces that do not correspond to a division along local and international lines. Drawing on extensive qualitative data, I contend that postconflict Timor-Leste has instead been dominated by a coalition of rural and urban elites (the latter centered on the capital city, Dili), united by their membership in the kinship-based *liurai-dato* (king-noble) class. Therefore, it is essential to investigate the origins, interests, ideologies, and actions of national and local Timorese social forces—and in particular the classes and class fractions that dominate and the broader sociopolitical structures within which they are embedded—if we are to understand their attitudes toward gender interventions and thus the likelihood of success or failure.

While they are necessary, however, extant structural political economy frameworks are by themselves inadequate for an analysis of gender interventions within peacebuilding. Explanations of peacebuilding that employ such approaches have not yet explicitly examined how gender relations intersect with the social relations among oligarchic, authoritarian, and class-based fractions3. I therefore use a synthetic explanatory framework that combines structural analysis of Timorese social forces with a feminist political economy of violence against women. Specifically, in order to analyze the material power relations inherent in and instrumental to the gendered division of labor, war and militarized conflict, and neoliberal globalization, I employ a structural political economy framework but expand it to include a structural analysis of kinship.

Kinship is key to explaining the outcomes of gender intervention in Timor-Leste, because political power and kinship relations overlap in Timorese class formation. The synthetic framework I employ reveals the links between hierarchical gender relations and hierarchical class formation, highlighting the historical and material basis for gender relations and the role that gender plays in sociopolitical contests over the distribution of power and resources. Most crucially, my analysis shows how members of the liurai-dato class depend on gender and kinship relations to maintain networks of influence, legitimacy, wealth, and continuity. In that sense, gender relations and social relations are interdependent. Moreover, this overlap shapes the outcomes of gender interventions, as the liurai-dato class seeks to uphold sociopolitical and gender order in its own interests.

The Timor-Leste Context

The liurai-dato class was formed through incorporation into the Portuguese military and bureaucracy over four centuries of colonization (c. 1515–1975), and it benefited from control of a deeply gendered slave trade and tax system. Male members of the liurai-dato justified their superordination by valorizing armed masculinity, and recurrent war and conflict magnified this socially constructed distance between men and women, arming men while victimizing and denigrating women, particularly through conflict-related sexual and gender-based violence.

Thus, all gender interventions in Timor-Leste have taken place in a setting of elite dominance and must be seen in the context of the liurai-dato monopoly over state resources. Under these circumstances, the government of Xanana Gusmão—who was prime minister from 2007 to 2015—spent substantial funds on veterans as part of coalition building between city-based and rural elites. Essentially, the state used veterans' pensions to buy peace, in the process funneling resources to the liurai-dato class. Elites in Dili took the bulk of this money, but crucial resources were also directed to patrimonial networks in villages. Elite control over state resources is quite patently justified by the valorization of armed masculinity, and is one of three central themes to emerge from my study.

The second theme to emerge is control over women. In this context, my study moves beyond the level of the state to focus on gender interventions in family and gender relations, and specifically on the introduction and implementation of the LADV. This legislation took parliament ten years to pass, splitting both the liurai-dato class and those working on peacebuilding along gender-progressive and -regressive lines.[4] In line with the local turn but against the wishes of the Timorese women's movement, peacebuilders made concessions to male-dominated local authorities in a variety of areas, but particularly in traditional dispute resolution. This approach has cemented the control of village chiefs and allied men over kinship, and inadvertently supporting a political economy of domestic violence.

Staying within the thematic area of control over women, I also engage in a structural analysis of kinship to explain how the exchange of women using brideprice has laid the foundations of the liurai-dato class. Brideprice was not targeted for reform by gender interventions, yet it remains an area of profound gender injustice in Timor-Leste. Brideprice and marriage are fundamental to the kinship system, and with it, the political economy of rural areas. Thus, gender interventions that focus on legal reform come up against powerful interests and cannot address underlying unequal material relations.

The third thematic area to emerge is control over local resources and its relationship to debt, power, and neoliberal markets. In this context, I focus on the gender intervention of microfinance. Microfinance has long been part of gender and development initiatives as a way of economically empowering women, and has been subject to extensive criticism. In Timor-Leste, it has had the backing of the national elite, which has reframed microfinance as a socially focused, cooperative economy. Gender interventions for microfinance, however, have overlooked the powerful legacies of Indonesian microfinance in the country, especially the role it played in consolidating rural elites' control over resources. Microfinance on the ground has thus defied the expectations of peacebuilders; rather than producing more inclusive finance, stronger rural markets, and economic growth, it has been another tool with which the rural sections of the liurai-dato class can accumulate and control scant financial resources, strengthening their influence over social relationships through debt and market monopolization.

The argument of this book thus has four strands. First, the Timorese liurai-dato class relies on a highly gendered allocation of resources and power, comprising materially exploitative militarized and patriarchal gender relations. Second, peacebuilders have made concessions to these elites and to violent men in order to keep the peace, a tendency amplified by local-turn approaches. These approaches to security have reinforced the valorization of armed masculinity, associated most strongly with the elite, which in turn has justified the unequal distribution of state resources. Third, gender relations construct social relations through kinship relations, which also reproduce class relations. Aspects of Timorese kinship rest on the accumulation of wealth through the exploitative mechanisms of brideprice and domestic violence, making legal and political gender reforms ineffective. Last, peacebuilding programs in Timor-Leste have sought to use microfinance to empower women and grow the economy, but the primary beneficiaries have been the liurai-dato, repeating patterns of accumulation and rule through debt established during Indonesian-era microfinance.

The nature of the Timorese state has set the boundaries of gender interventions, requiring close examination of how these efforts have worked in practice and comprehensive analysis of historically specific gender and class relations. It is my hope that using the lens of feminist political economy to evaluate the outcomes of gender interventions in Timor-Leste will contribute to the study and practice of gender and peacebuilding not only in the Southeast Asian sphere but also more widely wherever these initiatives are attempted.

1
Critical Approaches to Peacebuilding and Gender

Peacebuilding expanded and deepened in the two decades following the end of the Cold War, and the number of UN peacekeeping operations increased after 1990. Initially, peacebuilding involved maintaining ceasefires, liberalizing economies, holding elections, and then leaving. And in the aftermath of the September 11, 2001, terrorist attacks on the United States, "saving failed states" came to be seen as a pressing global issue. In this view, the United States, its allies, and the Global North more generally faced risks from intrastate and transnational violence in the form of terrorism, refugees, and other nontraditional security threats. The "liberal peace"—the hypothesis that liberal markets, democratic institutions, and the rule of law are key to long-term peace, and that the presence of one liberal element strengthens the others—was used to justify these interventions. The liberal peace was also framed as an obligation of the Global North to protect and promote human rights, liberal markets, and liberal democracy. Without liberal institutions and structures, states would become "fragile" or "weak." Yet there was no straightforward way to implement the liberal peace through rapid liberalization and democratization. Thus, some scholars called for the establishment of state institutions to be prioritized over ensuring democratic elections or liberalizing markets, a position that Roland Paris (2004) has termed "institutionalization before liberalization."

As the 1990s and 2000s unfolded, international humanitarian concerns prompted a shift to more extensive peacebuilding interventions. In particular, the failure of peacekeepers to prevent the 1994 Rwandan genocide and the 1995 Srebrenica massacre resulted in recommendations for more extensive peacebuilding policies (Brahimi 2000; Williams and Bellamy 2007). International organizations, national agencies, and the militaries of various states were therefore provided with justification for intervening in other states not only to provide immediate humanitarian relief but also to achieve longer-term security and development objectives associated with the liberal peace. The UN became increasingly willing to intervene in the governance and institutions of sovereign countries, marking a departure from previous policies that had supported state sovereignty regardless of a state's record on development or human rights.[1] Subsequently, peacebuilding took on larger projects such as election monitoring, demobilizations, suppressing public violence, writing new laws, building new institutions, training staff, and establishing transparency and accountability measures. Because statebuilding became the primary means of implementing peacebuilding objectives, peacebuilding operations continued well into the postconflict period.

The first period of peacebuilding intervention in Timor-Leste occurred from 1999 to 2005, aligning precisely with the expansion and deepening of UN peacebuilding operations (see Table 1.1). The deployment of the International Force for East Timor (INTERFET) to stop the violence following the breakdown of the Suharto regime coincided with the publication of the *Report of the Panel on United Nations Peace Operations*, which recommended deepening and expanding UN roles during peacebuilding (Brahimi 2000). After international forces had gained control over the territory, the UN Transitional Administration in East Timor (UNTAET) began. It was a large, expensive, and complex transitional administration mandated to control all aspects of the state—revenue, expenditures, military, and the police—to demobilize Timorese soldiers, conduct trials, and imprison criminals. In distinction to most other peacebuilding operations in so-called failed states, UNTAET had a mandate to fund, staff, and design state institutions, not reform existing ones (Chesterman 2002, 2004).

The second phase of peacebuilding followed a 2006–2007 political crisis that began as a conflict between factions within the Timorese military and expanded to widespread violence and an attempted coup. The roots of the crisis, discussed in Chapter 3, lay in grievances over demobilization and favoritism with respect to recruitment to the military and the police, which were mobilized by politicians in intra-elite rivalry. The fieldwork for this project was carried out during the second phase of international intervention.

Since 1999 Timor-Leste has hosted six UN missions. Major projects and programs from other international organizations such as the Asian Development Bank (ADB), the World Bank, the International Labour

Table 1.1 UN peacebuilding interventions in Timor-Leste, 1999–2012

	Acronym	Purpose	Dates
United Nations Mission in East Timor	UNAMET	Facilitating the referendum on autonomy	June 1999–October 1999
International Force for East Timor	INTERFET	Multinational Australian-led "peace enforcement" military intervention to restore law and order	20 September 1999–28 February 2000
UN Transitional Administration East Timor	UNTAET	Civilian administration and peacebuilding mission	25 October 1999–20 May 2002
United Nations Mission of Support in East Timor	UNMISET	Administrative support, maintaining law and order	May 2002–May 2005
United Nations Office in Timor-Leste	UNOTIL	Political mission supporting institutional development and police building	May 2005–August 2006
United Nations Integrated Mission in East Timor	UNMIT	Assisting Timor-Leste in overcoming the consequences and underlying causes of the 2006 crisis	26 May 2006–31 December 2012

Sources: Data based on Downie (2007); UNMIT (2008); UNSCR (2012).

Organization (ILO), and the International Organization for Migration (IOM) ran concurrently with UN peacebuilding.[2] I discuss the rollout of security and peacebuilding, especially the effects of buying the peace, in more detail in Chapter 3.

Gender Interventions in Timor-Leste

These peacebuilding efforts in Timor-Leste provided the context for extensive gender intervention. In all, some fourteen interventions have been implemented in the form of either gender mainstreaming within peacebuilding operations or stand-alone gender and development programs (Table 1.2).[3]

The first, the gender mainstreaming of the UN peacekeeping operations, took place initially from 2000 to 2002 under the framework of the 1979 Convention on the Elimination of All Forms of Discrimination against Women (CEDAW) and later under UN Security Council Resolution 1325 (UNSCR 1325) on Women, Peace, and Security. Linked to this was a second intervention, establishing the Gender Affairs Unit (GAU) within UNTAET (2001–2005), initially following the provisions of CEDAW and later in line with the specific framework for dealing with gender and conflict within UNSCR 1325. The third gender intervention created the National Office for the Promotion of Women, a Timorese national institution for gender equality partially funded by the United Nations Population Fund (UNFPA) and UN Women. The office was responsible for gender mainstreaming in the Timorese government and became central to that process.[4] The fourth intervention was UNTAET's (short-lived [2000–2002]) creation of the Gender and the Law Working Group, which was composed of East Timorese judges, prosecutors, public defenders, and civil society organizations. Their mandate was to conduct gender analysis of all UNTAET regulations and drafts of proposed national legislation to aid in the gender mainstreaming process. The group lobbied for a law against domestic violence and a women's charter to influence the design of the new Timorese constitution. Fifth, after winning 26 percent of seats in the 2001 election, female politicians formed the Group of Women Parliamentarians in Timor-Leste (GMPTL) in 2002, which was formalized by a parliamentary resolution in 2007 and became known as the Women's Cross-Party Caucus. Its primary mission is to mainstream gender in the legislative process. The sixth gender mainstreaming drive constituted support given by international interveners to the caucus and the East Timorese Women's Communication Forum (FOKUPERS) in lobbying for Resolution No. 28/II in 2009, requiring gender mainstreaming, or gender-responsive budgeting (GRB), to be embedded within the Timorese national budget process.

Gender interventions also proceeded under the broader rubric of women's human rights programming, or gender and economic development programs. The women's human rights approach taken by the Commission for Reception, Truth, and Reconciliation (CAVR) from 2001 to 2005 thus formed the seventh intervention. Tasked with investigating war crimes during the Indonesian occupation, the CAVR documented the experiences

Table 1.2 Gender interventions in Timor-Leste, 2001–2017

Intervention	Timeframe	Legal framework	Type of intervention	Aims	Funders
UNSCR 1325 on Women, Peace, and Security	2000–2002	UN Security Council UNSCR 1272 forming UNTAET	Gender mainstreaming	Mainstreaming in peacekeeping operations across the four pillars of participation, prevention, protection and relief, and recovery	UN Security Council
Gender Affairs Unit (GAU) within UNTAET	2001–2005	Guidance for the unit drawing on CEDAW and later UNSCR 1325	Gender mainstreaming	To inform all peacekeeping components of the gender aspects of the mission; bimonthly gender training to all new UNTAET staff (civil and military)	No exclusive funding envelope from UNTAET
National Office for the Promotion of Women (later known as SEPI, then SEM)	2001–present	Timorese constitution, CEDAW (Timor-Leste accession 2003)	Gender mainstreaming	Responsible for leading implementation of the LADV and leading gender working groups in each ministry	UNFPA, UNIFEM (later known as UN Women), Timorese government
Gender and the Law Working Group	2001–2003	UNTAET—no specific regulation	Gender mainstreaming	Gender analysis of regulations and proposed legislation by East Timorese judges, prosecutors, public defenders, and representatives of civil society organizations. The drafting of the Women's Charter (2001) to influence the Constitution	UNTAET
Women's Cross-Party Caucus (GMPTL)	2007–present	Parliamentary Resolution No. 16/2007	Gender mainstreaming	Gender analysis of regulations and proposed legislation, and making recommendations to government	UN Women technical support, Timorese government

Gender-Responsive Budgeting	2008–2010	Resolution No. 28/II 2009 requiring gender mainstreaming in the budget	Gender mainstreaming	To ensure a gender perspective on all budget legislation; issuing recommendations to ministries to make their budgets gender sensitive	Cross Party Caucus, UN Women
Commission for Truth and Reconciliation (CAVR)	2001–2005	CEDAW UNTAET Regulation 2001/10	Gender mainstreaming	To ensure women's stories of the war were told and to lobby for justice and compensation for victims of war crimes	UNTAET, CAVR
Support to Timorese women's organizations	1997–present	UNTAET and subsequent support was guided by CEDAW, the Beijing Platform for Action, and the Timor-Leste Women's Platform for Action (2001)	Gender and development	Rede Feto: to enable information sharing across the women's network; lobbying for political empowerment; to make one out of every four candidates on the party list a woman. FOKUPERS: to address gender-based violence and human rights violations	Rede Feto, UNTAET, UNFPA, UN Women, Timorese government, and various project-based funds from international donors
Gender quotas in Parliament	2006 to the present	Law on the Election of the National Parliament No 6/2006, article 12	Gender mainstreaming	To provide a concrete incentive for the political participation of women through women's mandatory inclusion in the party lists of candidates (one in every three candidates on the list must be a woman)	–
Law Against Domestic Violence	2010–present	CEDAW, International Convention on Civil and Political Rights, Convention on the Rights of the Child, Timor-Leste Criminal Code	Gender mainstreaming	To establish the legal regime applicable to the prevention of domestic violence and set out the obligations of the state to provide protection and assistance to victims	Timorese government and its ministries, led by SEM

(continued)

Table 1.2 Continued

Intervention	Timeframe	Legal framework	Type of intervention	Aims	Funders
Vulnerable Persons' Unit	2001–2005 under UN; 2005–2017 under PNTL	UNTAET police regulations; Law Against Domestic Violence (No. 7/2010)	Gender mainstreaming	To provide police support and protection to the victims of gender-based and family violence in line with the state's obligations to its citizens	UNTAET, UNIFEM, Timorese government, National Police of Timor-Leste (PNTL)
Microfinance	1999–2017	Timor-Leste Public Instruction No. 06/2010	Gender and development	To increase women's participation in the local economy; to stimulate local economies; to provide livelihoods to vulnerable people, including victims of domestic violence	Timorese government, Banking and Payments Authority of Timor-Leste, UNCDF, IFC, ADB
Gender quotas in village leadership	2001–2017	Laws on village elections in 2004, 2009, and 2016	Gender and development	To increase women's political participation in village councils	Secretary for Technical Administration of Elections (STAE), UNDP, World Bank, Pátria, UN Women
Bolsa da Mãe	2008–2017	Constitutional right to state support for the vulnerable	Gender and development	Conditional cash transfer to vulnerable families with children to ensure school attendance and vaccination	Timorese government, Ministry of Social Solidarity

of female soldiers and *clandestinos* (resistance members and noncombatants, many of them women), of victims of sexual and gender-based violence, and of women during the war. CAVR recommended memorializing women's contributions and making reparations to war victims (CAVR 2006). Eighth—and characteristic of gender and development interventions globally—was UNTAET's support of the Timorese women's network, Rede Feto (women's network). Rede Feto held the first Timorese Women's Congress in 2000, which resulted in the drafting of the Platform for Action for Women's Rights in Timor-Leste in the same year. Via UNIFEM (later UN Women), the GAU, and UNFPA, the UN was crucial in supporting Timorese women's organizations such as the FOKUPERS and Rede Feto with money, offices, staff, technical expertise, and access to transnational networks (Grenfell and Trembath 2007). In turn, Timorese women's organizations were often the implementing partners for gender interventions and provided political information, introductions, support, guidance, and access to communities for interveners. Ninth, in the face of strong opposition, GAU, Rede Feto, and UN Women lobbied for the introduction of quotas for women in national parliament, as I discuss in more detail later. Tenth, with the support of UN Women, Timorese women's organizations and the Women's Cross-Party Caucus lobbied from 1999 to 2009 to introduce the Law Against Domestic Violence (LADV). The presence of women parliamentarians enabled the passage of this law. The LADV itself sponsored the eleventh intervention by guaranteeing funding for a Special Victims Unit within the Timorese police force and specialized services to provide support and protection to victims of violence.

The twelfth gender intervention was international support for microfinance. Microfinance, which is extended primarily to women clients, has been promoted by new national banking regulations and forms part of the Timorese government's strategic development planning for a cooperative-based rural economy. The thirteenth intervention encompasses lobbying by Timorese women's organizations and UN Women for quotas for women's leadership positions in village elections. Quotas for women and young people also formed part of the World Bank's participatory Community Empowerment Program in Timor-Leste (2000–2002). Finally, the fourteenth gender intervention was a conditional cash transfer program for vulnerable mothers, the Bolsa da Mãe (mother's purse). Gender intervention in Timor-Leste thus comprises a wide variety of policies and programming.

The Critique of the Liberal Peace, Hybridity, and the Local Turn

How have these interventions played out? As confidence in peacebuilding declined worldwide, a critique of the liberal peace gathered force after outbreaks of violence in the 2006–2007 Timorese political crisis. The resumption of violence in the country led some scholars to assert that peacebuilders had built a failed state in Timor-Leste (Goldstone 2013). More broadly with regard to Bosnia, Iraq, and Afghanistan, Paris (2004) argued that peace required strong institutions before the introduction of liberal democracy or free markets. Such neo-Weberian institutional approaches, while critical of the liberal peace, invariably attributed uneven or disappointing peacebuilding outcomes to a lack of state capacity to foster economic growth or control aggression (Hameiri 2010; Lemay-Hébert 2009).

In contrast, explanations grounded in the issue of legitimacy hinged on the apparent "ontological problem of whether the liberal peace is transferable into non-Western or non-liberal polities" (Richmond and Franks 2009, 13). Crucially, scholars argued that a mismatch between Western and non-Western models led to variable outcomes, including recurrent conflict and violence (Leonardsson and Rudd 2015, 833; Autesserre 2010). According to this view, interventions failed because they attempted to impose liberal principles that clashed with the norms, cultures, and institutions of the societies subjected to intervention (Duffield 2005, ; Richmond 2007). Some suggested that peacebuilding was a colonial "empire lite," and thus illegitimate (Ignatieff 2003). On this basis, scholars such as Roger Mac Ginty and Oliver Richmond called for what they termed a "local turn" in peacebuilding to enable local institutions, agencies, ideas, and cultures to be able to "form peace locally" (Mac Ginty and Richmond 2013, 769–771). They and others suggested that international peacebuilders had ignored or devalued the local dynamics of conflict-affected societies (Belloni 2012; Mac Ginty 2015; Paffenholz 2011; Richmond 2011).

The local turn in peacebuilding aimed to reorient research from the "high politics" of international intervention to "everyday" local realities (Randazzo 2016, 1355). Of particular concern was the interaction of international and local, a dynamic that scholars sought to capture in the notion of hybridity: "a state of affairs in which liberal and illiberal norms, institutions and actors coexist" (Belloni 2012, 22). For some, the local was where "resistance, agency and autonomy" could be found, and activated, by everyday peacebuilding agency, including through group interactions and organization, negotiation, networking, counter-organization, and discussion of the policies in question (Richmond and Mitchell 2012, 1–3).

This type of "critical localism" is qualitative, involving interviews and focus groups, often using narrative or discursive analysis (Mac Ginty 2015). (It is worth noting, however, that such interviews were often conducted with elites.) Such methods mimic postcolonial narrative and discursive analytical approaches, uncovering moments of so-called hybridization in a "colonial encounter," as Homi Bhabha terms it, between interveners and intervened (Bhabha 2004; see also Peterson 2012; Richmond 2011, 116). Postcolonial approaches draw on poststructural or postmodern theory by "deconstructing" accepted views of language, culture, narrative, identity, and gender in an investigation of the relationships of knowledge and power between former colonies and European colonial powers (Mishra and Hodge 2005). Bhabha argues that postcolonial subjects use the language and discourse of the colonizer (termed "mimicry"), but with a crucial difference: repetition of the discourse *by* the colonized creates a hybrid that is emancipatory rather than repressive (Bhabha 2004; Mishra and Hodge 2005).

In the peacebuilding context, Jenny Peterson (2012, 10) maintains that hybridity can provide a clearer picture of how aid functions in practice by focusing on the interaction of local and international, not just on the peacebuilding missions themselves. However, although hybridity could be merely a descriptive term, a significant proportion of the critical literature uses "hybrid peace" as a prescriptive goal (Millar 2014, 504). At the heart of this approach is an equation of the local with the authentic. Kumar and de la Haye (2012), for example, argue that integrating local cultural forms into "hybrid governance" ought to increase peacebuilding's legitimacy and therefore its effectiveness. Some local-turn scholars have objected, however, on the ground that interveners cannot engineer a top-down hybrid peace (Mac Ginty 2010; Wallis, Jeffery, and Kent 2016).

Nonetheless, in the Timor-Leste case, hybrid peace was prescribed in a large number of works (Boege et al. 2008; Boege, Brown, and Clements 2009; Brown and Gusmão 2009, 2012; Brown 2012a; Cummins 2010; Cummins and Leach 2012; Mearns and Farram 2008; Richmond 2007). At the same time, interveners applied hybrid programming in the country, implementing a hybrid court on war crimes, hybrid local governance, and hybrid approaches to conflict resolution, including resolution of domestic violence. Thus, in dialogue with debates within intervening organizations, the local turn and hybridity—in their criticism of the liberal peace—altered peacebuilding in practice, particularly in areas associated with tradition and authenticity, such as marriage, divorce, residence, inheritance, burial, traditional leadership, land ownership and management, and dispute arbitration and resolution.

Adding support to local-turn approaches was a significant crossover of personnel between academic and practitioner roles in Timor-Leste during this period. Academics participated in workshops on transitional justice, for example, and wrote monitoring reports and evaluations of peacebuilding programs (Mearns 2002; Fox and Soares 2003; Trembath, Grenfell, and Noronha 2010; Grenfell and Trembath 2007). By way of example, Chopra and Hohe, who both worked within UNTAET, also published in academic journals and recommended a "participatory intervention."[5] They envisaged that only contentious and abusive local structures were to be "reinvented" by international peacebuilders, whereas interventions should reinforce local political structures that were resilient and not grossly in breach of human rights (Chopra and Hohe 2004, 299–302). As a result, later iterations of local government laws officially incorporated local political roles such as *lia nain* (elder) into elected village councils (Democratic Republic of Timor-Leste 2009).

The Limits of the Critique of the Liberal Peace

As a critique of the liberal peace, the local turn bumps up against certain limits, and the first of these is found within the term *local* itself. Across the critical literature, this slippery and contested word can denote more than one thing. It is shorthand for the people who are subject to interventions, in this case Timorese citizens; it can mean a subnational jurisdiction or area; it can describe a site of resistance and alternatives to the state and the international; and it can identify "cultural appropriateness" (Hughes, Öjendal, and Schierenbeck 2015, 818). This inability to capture the meaning of *local* creates problems for analysis. For one thing, to make a binary distinction between *local* and *international* misses important social and political coalitions across these groups. In gender interventions specifically, a binary analysis overlooks political coalitions formed among gender-progressive international, national, and citizens' groups, as well as gender-regressive backlashes across these boundaries.

Nonetheless, as Caroline Hughes, Joakim Öjendal, and Isabell Schierenbeck (2015, 819) argue, "the local" offers some analytical purchase for critics of the liberal peace as a "reminder of the undemocratic nature of intervention itself" and the need for accountability to those undergoing it. In the process, the authenticity of the local is generally assumed to prevail over the international. Second, to avoid essentializing a binary opposition between local and international, writers using local turn frameworks have formulated degrees or types of local-international interaction. As Shahar Hameiri and Lee Jones point out, however, these frameworks still rely on a dichotomy, which is why binaries are always reinstated. Most compellingly, Hameiri and Jones argue that hybridity cannot explain why particular institutions emerge and function or, crucially, who benefits from them, because social groups support or resist interventions according to their own interests or normative agendas (2017, 58–59). Thus, frameworks that locate the source of peacebuilding weaknesses in the interaction of reified notions of local and international may not see local inequalities in and contests for power and resources before, during, and after intervention.

Despite their commitment to unearthing the "everyday and subaltern," thus far local-turn scholars have relied for evidence on a few Timorese interlocutors—generally from the *liurai-dato* class. Of the researchers who have gone beyond Dili, many have focused on interviewing village chiefs and lineage heads, as these men are, in the eyes of Timorese society, the keepers of tradition. Reliance on these few sources has proved to be a mutually reinforcing loop, whereby particular interlocutors have emphasized the importance of preserving the position of the elite liurai-dato. Richmond, for instance, used the opinion of Viqueque district administrator Francesco da Silva to argue that top-down approaches and democracy were ineffective (Richmond 2011, 120). The same administrator was quoted elsewhere arguing for the retention of liurai-dato leadership in villages because, if village chiefs are not "descendants of the *Liurai*, they have a lot more problems" (Cummins and Leach 2012, 101). In another example, Timorese researchers Fidelis Magalhães and Jose "Josh" Trindade both worked for Xanana Gusmão in the Office of the Prime Minister (2007–2015) and Taur Matan Ruak in the Office of the President (2012–2017).[6] Scholars of the local turn have drawn heavily on interviews with and writing by these two key Timorese researcher advocates of the local turn (Freire and Lopes 2013, 209n19; Cummins and Leach 2012, 90; McWilliam, Palmer, and Shepherd 2014, 305; Hicks 2012, 131; Wallis 2012, 760n228 and 230; Richmond 2011, 120).

As both Elisa Randazzo (2016, 1358–1359) and Meera Sabaratnam (2013) observe, local-turn scholars make normative choices about who is local and who is not. The bias also mitigates against describing contentious politics, in that neither interveners nor national governments generally consider martial arts gangs or militias or even feminist organizations to be authentic or legitimate local groups (Scambary 2013; Smith 2015b). These choices affect analyses of intervention outcomes, particularly when academics make assumptions that homogenize politics, ideology, and the power of local groups (and nations).

The implications of deciding who is local become more apparent when we turn to the issue of gender in peacebuilding interventions. As a key theorist of the local turn, Richmond sees gender issues and human rights as arising out of liberal peacebuilding but criticizes how such rights have been rolled out in various postconflict settings, suggesting that formal rights have been emphasized to the exclusion of material or welfare aspects of peace settlements (Richmond 2014, 456). It is not correct to say that gender interventions arise only from liberal frameworks (ignoring transnational and local feminism) or that liberal peace interventions have focused on gender and rights to the exclusion of other issues.

Most significant, however, is how local or hybrid frameworks have been used to interpret the results of gender intervention. Richmond presupposes a dichotomy between international liberal peacebuilding (which prioritizes individual rights) and local societies (which prioritize group rights). To illustrate, in the *Transformation of Peace,* he proposes that tension between individual and group rights exists in part because humanitarian decisions are "hegemonic acts" that third parties make in relation to others' interests (Richmond 2005, 137–140). This analysis overlooks the composition of rights-bearing groups and fails to determine who has power within those groups. The present study instead highlights that citizens experience peacebuilding along ethnic, class, and gender lines, as Peterson argues with respect to Kosovo, with some groups experiencing "the interface with the international as emancipatory, others as politically expedient and yet others as regressive or debilitating" (Peterson 2012, 19).

Although critique of the liberal peace offers important appraisals, in the final analysis, power, gender, and hierarchy continue to prevail at the local level (Paffenholz 2011, 150). Explanations based on clashes, friction, or hybridity between local and international do not take into account how crucial structural factors within recipient societies, such as class and gender, shape the outcomes of peacebuilding.

In the case of Timor-Leste, assumptions about the authenticity of the liurai has caused a fossilization of tradition in both studies and policymaking (Kammen 2017). "Local" societies, institutions, culture, and so on are naturalized in local-turn accounts because their focus is on describing the international-local hybrid. This view accepts the authenticity and legitimacy of power relations that take the form of class and gender inequalities, rather than uncovering how they have emerged. On that basis, uneven outcomes for gender intervention are understood as arising from incompatibility between international and local institutions, cultures, or practices.

Development practitioner and anthropologist Deborah Cummins uses a mix of hybridity and institutionalism to explain the disappointing results of gender quotas in village elections in Timor-Leste. Like numerous other scholars, she asserts that democratization has built "liberal-democratic institutions over existing customary governance structures and norms," creating "political hybridity" in village governance (Cummins 2013, 144, 148; see also Kirk 2015; Wallis 2012; Boege, Brown, and Clements 2009). Thus, women's lack of political participation in village governance can be explained by the fact that traditional institutions are authentically male-dominated: "The major difficulty for the women was that many community needs continue to be met through various aspects of *lisan*, which in patriarchal areas is led by male authority figures" (Cummins 2013, 151).[7] According to Cummins, hybridity helped to improve the situation for women because a new practice grew whereby a woman representative accompanied the village chief during traditional dispute resolution in cases of domestic violence.

Although individual outcomes may indeed have improved, female representation does not alter the *material* outcomes of traditional dispute resolution, as I explain in Chapter 4. Moreover, the description of such a system as "hybrid" does not explain the persistence of certain men's control over village institutions, the use of traditional dispute resolution, or the stubbornly high levels of domestic violence in Timor-Leste. Even more important to this study, because international interveners constitute a series of powerful groups with the ability to change outcomes, their alliances matter. Sections of the donor community have made concessions to and inadvertently supported gender-regressive actors. Significantly, traditional dispute resolution processes materially benefit village elites, whose control over resources at the local level and over women sets conditions that lead to high levels of re-victimization.

Advocates of the local turn criticize the *liberal* peace, yet their approach is often not as far removed from conventional liberal approaches as is assumed. For instance, local-turn approaches overlap with so-called participatory ones, which regard the engagement of civil society as essential. Participatory programming is an orthodoxy in neoliberal second-generation, market-led development strategies: the initiatives that, following (or sometimes concomitant with) reforms intended to stabilize the postconflict society, are designed to sustain economic growth and that are the focus of the current study. The World Bank and other interveners referred to programs such as participatory budgeting, local governance reform, decentralization, and microfinance in terms of being "local," "emancipatory," and "empowering," whereas local-turn scholars criticized them for forcing neoliberal market relations, with origins in Western capitalism, onto non-Western communities that were organized according to nonmarket relations such as kinship. Local-turn advocates Mac Ginty and Richmond made a distinction between a "genuine" local and the "expedient and shallow" local of the World Bank, which is part of the liberal peace (Mac Ginty and Richmond 2013). Nevertheless, prescriptive hybridity and local approaches blur with those of participatory development on the ground.

Feminist approaches to the hybrid model have retained its concepts and the focus on discourse and discursive methods while adding a feminist concern with power. It is worth pointing out that such approaches are distinct from my own focus on material power. Laura McLeod, for example, considers hybridity to be a useful analytical tool to highlight the complex interactions of local and international actors, recognizing that their diversity means neither category is "clear-cut." She broadens hybridity by adding a feminist concern that encompasses "the personal" rather than simply "macro-political processes" (McLeod 2015, 51–52). This translates into a concern for the diversity of bodily and emotional responses to war—and how these shape political choices. Also employing a hybrid framework, Sarah Smith uses a constructivist approach to argue that gender equality norms were associated with international interveners, which led to mistrust of these norms because Timorese saw interveners as part of a colonial legacy. This association with colonialism "intertwined" with national and international patriarchal barriers to the legitimacy of NGOs working on gender (Smith 2015b, 67).

One problem with constructivist approaches to gender in Timor-Leste overlaps conceptually with an issue I find in local-turn approaches: constructivist scholars take women's rights as a largely foreign or transnational norm. In this view, the norms of women's rights crossed national boundaries through international intervention and subsequently "cascaded" into society (Hall 2009; Allden 2007; Ottendörfer 2013). On the one hand, constructivist approaches fail to accommodate the idea of contentious gender relations arising independently of outside norms as women and girls resist patriarchal domination and seek to advance their interests within the gender order. On the other, they reduce the visibility of struggles over resources between women and men of different classes, which shape how gender interventions turn out in practice.

Evaluating Gender Intervention in Timor-Leste

The shortcomings of gender mainstreaming efforts in Timor-Leste are well documented. Jacqui True (2009) has argued that the mandate of gender mainstreaming under UNSCR 1325 has been left "unfulfilled," including in the Timor-Leste case.[8] Hilary Charlesworth and Mary Wood (2002, 346–347), Vijaya Joshi (2005), and Louise Olsson (2009) all point out not only that gender mainstreaming encountered resistance from Timorese national leaders but also that it was underfunded, understaffed, and marginalized within the UN operation itself. With respect to Australian aid, too, Ann Wigglesworth describes a systemic lack of commitment among the staff to gender mainstreaming (2010, 137).

Initial planning for peacebuilding in Timor-Leste included a GAU to conduct gender mainstreaming, but the budget for the unit was reduced. After deployment, the head of UNTAET, Sergio Vieira de Mello, supported cutting GAU entirely because he did not see what role gender mainstreaming could play in reconstruction. Senior women at UN headquarters—including Angela King, special adviser to the UN Secretary-General on Women's Advancement, and high-level gender consultant Sherrill Whittington—intervened to ensure that the unit would be established. King and Whittington facilitated a meeting between de Mello and Timorese women's organizations that convinced him of the importance of gender mainstreaming (Olsson 2009, 80; Charlesworth 2008, 354).

International institutions also obstructed gender intervention in Timor-Leste on the issue of quotas. UNTAET's electoral affairs office and the UN Department of Political Affairs opposed the introduction of quotas for women in national parliament (Olsson 2009, 129; Hall 2009; Hall and True 2008). As a result, there was no quota in the 2001 election. With financial and technical support from UNIFEM, Timorese women's organizations nonetheless ran electoral campaigns for female candidates, who took 26 percent of the seats. In 2006 the law was changed to require one female candidate in four (Democratic Republic of Timor-Leste 2006, art. 12). After the 2007 election, 27 percent of parliamentarians were women, marking almost no change. This prompted another legislative amendment to increase the quota to one in every three parliamentary candidates. Under those circumstances, women won 38.8 percent of seats in the 2012 election, very high by global standards. Thus, after some adjustments, the quota has been a successful gender intervention.

In the aftermath of the first wave of violence in East Timor, a Women's Congress was held in 2001. From that point on, Timorese women's organizations made the introduction of a law criminalizing domestic violence a key demand (Hynes et al. 2004; Swaine 2003). In response, the GAU, UNIFEM, and UNFPA provided staff and expertise to help draft the LADV, but a number of scholars have shown that within UNTAET itself, protection for women in cases of domestic violence was not a priority (Olsson 2009, 152; Groves, Resurreccion, and Doneys 2009). After ten years of lobbying, the LADV was passed in 2010 and can therefore be considered a successful gender intervention, but its introduction, implementation, and outcomes have been contested and uneven, as I discuss in Chapters 4 and 5. Likewise, GRB faced opposition during its introduction and implementation. Since the change in government in 2012, the Timorese parliament has not issued a gender budget statement, and bureaucrats have obstructed implementation and misappropriated funds.

In the study of peace and conflict, the gaps between the aims and outcomes of gender mainstreaming have met with various explanations. In the first place, as others have documented, gender mainstreaming was opposed within the UN and by other interveners, and some areas of the UN mission in Timor-Leste were vulnerable to gender bias as well. Because gender mainstreaming was perceived to be "all about women," UN programs and decision making left male patterns of behavior unexamined and unreformed.

In general, interveners misrecognized the relationship between gender and power.

Scholars have also drawn attention to the relative marginality of gender within peacebuilding in Timor-Leste despite criticism for overemphasizing women and gender. For instance, the late creation of GAU meant that some gender mainstreaming measures were not part of the initial peacekeeping operation. It also left GAU without a discrete funding envelope and, with just six staff out of eleven thousand in UNTAET, too small to properly carry out its mandate to mainstream gender in all peacebuilding and train hundreds of UN staff in gender mainstreaming (Charlesworth 2008; Olsson 2009, 80–81). This initial obstruction limited GAU's effectiveness and that of the gender intervention more broadly.

Another crucial factor was opposition from the Timorese parliament, notably in areas such as domestic violence legislation and GRB. The law criminalizing domestic violence faced opposition from within the Timorese leadership, evidenced quite convincingly by the ten years it took for the parliament to pass the LADV.

Some critics view gender mainstreaming as inappropriate, regarding it as enforced by Western aid conditionality (True 2009, 45). In other words, gender mainstreaming has faced a backlash within peacebuilding missions, in scholarship on peacebuilding, and from targets of intervention who have sought to paint it as externally imposed, Westernized, liberal, and thus unsuitable (Hodžić 2009). Such backlash has been conspicuous in Timor-Leste. National leaders and international commentators have criticized gender programming as illegitimate, inauthentic, marginal, or overly focused on what they perceive to be "hot-button" and marginal issues such as gender-based violence (Hicks 2013, 31; for a critique, see Niner 2011). Some Timorese elites saw gender interventions to be at odds with national goals or culture and tied to Western interests. The influential Timorese leader Xanana Gusmão, for example, argued that Timorese were obliged during UN rule to acculturate gender and human rights to please the UN, their "masters of independence" (Niner 2011, 431; Hughes 2009). As such, it is important to realize that sections of the Timorese elite found common cause with the local turn in peacebuilding on specific, often gender-based, issues.

Additionally, gender mainstreaming in Timor-Leste often lacked a feminist lens. In this view, interventions were guided by a narrow vision that privileged physical security and elections over social and economic security—a perspective insufficiently attentive to the unequal power relations between states (True 2009). As it became part of mainstream development, the received meaning of *gender* also began to shift. Feminist analysts initially used the term *gender relations* to describe unequal material relations of power between women and men and the unequal social construction of masculine and feminine norms. As the concept gained traction within the study and practice of development, however, it became an accepted euphemism that, as Andrea Cornwall remarks, "softened 'harder' talk about rights and power" (2007, 70).

Gender mainstreaming in Timor-Leste was thus not always positioned to connect women's rights with broader economic demands on the state, such as the right to housing, education, health, and safety (True 2009). For example, although GRB sought to remedy gendered state budgets, in some senses GRB has allowed the Timorese government to self-promote their actions on "women positive" policies without admitting shortcomings (Sharp and Broomhill 1990), particularly the gaps between planning and outcomes. Attention to the uneven distributional effects of international peacebuilding intervention is not new. It is commonly acknowledged that gender justice has more purchase on political and civil rights than on economic rights and entitlements (Goetz 2007, 24).

Other scholars precede me in analyzing the shortcomings of peacebuilding interventions for women in Timor-Leste, convincingly arguing that peacebuilding has failed to promote socioeconomic rights (Harris-Rimmer 2010) and that it has damaged women's entitlements and rights by relying on a postconflict "politics of memory" that privileged veterans and war victims (Kent 2016; Kent and Kinsella 2015). Nonetheless, these authors have had different concerns from mine, seeking to examine how (trans)national actors have tried to build gender perspectives into laws and institutions (Hall 2009; Costa, Sawer, and Sharp 2013; Harris-Rimmer 2010; Graydon 2016).

In contrast, I contend that rights-based approaches contain a fundamental flaw: the assumption that formal institutions rule behaviors and guarantee rights. For example, the intervention on gender-based violence was attentive to legal reform, especially via the LADV, but it did not address the material relations that set the conditions for high levels of violence against women. Similarly, measures put forward early on by the Gender and the Law Working Group to combat material factors, such as brideprice, that contributed to domestic violence were unsuccessful. In that sense, gender intervention within a peacebuilding framework in Timor-Leste lacked in-depth consideration of social relations and material conditions, and especially the connections between material conditions and violence against women.

A Structural Feminist Political Economy of Gender Intervention

The various critiques of and approaches to peacebuilding just described, in particular with respect to gender interventions, thus raise but do not fully address key aspects of the Timorese case. Structural political economy acknowledges the importance of power relations between competing social forces, while the feminist political economy developed by Jacqui True (2009) crucially explains the drivers of violence against women. A synthesis of the two—in other words, a structural feminist political economy framework—must be employed to explain the uneven outcomes of gender interventions in terms of gender and class, and specifically the role of dominant classes in shaping the postconflict order in Timor-Leste.

My framework comprises six elements: material relations and social forces; gender justice; gender divisions of labor; war, militarized conflict, and violence; kinship; and neoliberal globalization. All these factors must be taken into account if we are to arrive at a comprehensive and nuanced analysis of the Timorese case.

Material Relations and Social Forces

Structural political economy prioritizes the role of material relations among individuals in villages, households, and the state, and the role of material relations in contests between social forces over the sociopolitical order. As Lee Jones (2010) explains, this contestation between social forces can, of course, be violent. Material relations govern the distribution and use of resources, benefits, privileges, and authority both in the home and at large, and are the basis of power: "All forms of power—including the use of violence—are understood as having a material basis, often founded on material relations of inequality within and across societies and cultures" (True 2012, 9, 29).

Material relations that arise over time out of economic processes define key social forces—elements in society with the capacity to cause or resist social change—by their shared or divergent material interests (Cox 1981). Social forces can be grouped along class, class fraction (a subclass or class stratum; see Poulantzas 1975), religious, geographic, or ethnic lines that govern the distribution and use of resources, and as such they have the potential to shape and dominate social structures. Importantly, state institutions are the focus of much political struggle because of their pivotal role in access to power and resources (Jones 2013, 73). The environment within which politics operates, along with the pressures that shape political and institutional outcomes, is established by structural factors based on material relations between economically stratified social forces (Hewison, Robison, and Rodan 1993, 4). The composition of social forces is historically contingent; it establishes state and nonstate institutions and the rules that give rise to the social order and underlying ideologies, such as who has the right to rule and other forms of legitimacy.

Structural political economy thus takes material relations to be causal mechanisms that shape institutions. In this view, states and state institutions are themselves composed of competing social forces with specific material interests in upholding or contesting a political order, rather than constituting an abstract and separate apparatus (Jones 2010). Most significant to this study, those who own or control wealth-generating property directly or indirectly shape the principal institutions that move ideology in gender-progressive or gender-retrogressive directions (Agarwal 1994, 16). Different social forces have divergent interests that can motivate them to either uphold or challenge the gender order—and gender relations are a crucial aspect of the broader process through which the dominant class secures its position.

For these reasons, it is important to ask who benefits from peacebuilding. When we understand this, we understand "what kind of power was awarded by the peace and to whom" (Hughes 2009, 41). I argue that the decisions, policies, institutions, and operations on which gender interventions are based are in turn aspects of "social and political domination, as a system in which the state takes a critical, partisan role" (Hewison, Robison, and Rodan 1993, 17). For instance, after the war's end, the leaders of the Revolutionary Front for Independent Timor-Leste (FRETILIN), both from the armed resistance and its diplomatic wing played decisive roles in the national government, facilitated by international interventions. Founded in 1974 FRETILIN was the largest and most significant pro-independence party and is associated with Timor-Leste's struggle for self-rule. Postindependence, the country was integrated into the global economy through an influx of capital and the entrenchment of elites as gatekeepers of these flows, limiting the economic opportunities of a large proportion of the population and enforcing market competitiveness (Hughes 2009, 72). Thus, gender interventions that modify the sociopolitical order depend on which social forces—local, international, or coalitions of both—can successfully claim legitimacy, often in cultural and gendered terms. In addition, interveners play a significant role in supporting some groups over others in attempts to form or renew a particular social order. Or, as Hughes puts it, rather than locating results of peacebuilding in local-liberal divides or hybrids, an analysis of the intersection between political economy and the politics of culture offers a more accurate picture: "Outcomes are better understood as emerging from the intersection between, on the one hand, a politics of culture in a postconflict context, couched as a claim to power and status advanced against "outsiders" and interlopers; and on the other, the business of constructing new economic, political and social orders and making claims for their authority—a project in which local actors are significantly engaged" (Hughes 2015, 909).

Like Hughes, I am concerned with identifying the social origins, interests, and ideologies of various social forces, including women's organizations, in order to describe outcomes of gender interventions. Distinct from Hughes, however, I focus on the complex intersection of social forces and gender relations. In my view, structural factors in Timor-Leste, particularly elite dominance, have stymied the goals of gender justice, partly because gender interventions have focused on transnational actors and organizations—such as nongovernmental organizations (NGOs) with links to donors—and assumed that these actors are inherently progressive, while in reality they are middle class and may or may not be progressive in gender terms.

Gender quotas and a vibrant civil society have not resulted in the extension of gender justice to the majority of Timorese women. This reflects international experience, whereby the extension of civil and political rights to excluded groups—in this case including increased political participation and representation—does not, in fact, produce equal levels of political participation, and even less so equal levels of economic reward (Goetz 2007, 28). Nor does the entrenchment of political representation result in progress in women's social and economic status. In Timor, as elsewhere, a significant gap exists between the goals of gender interventions and their outcomes, which arise in part from a focus on narrow areas of political and economic rights and market access.

As Anne-Marie Goetz also rightly observes, because they cannot be identified as a coherent group, and gender cuts across all social forces, women's interests and conceptions of justice will differ (Goetz 2007, 18). Yet women's movements can galvanize women of varying social origins around issues of bodily autonomy, reproduction, and the gender division of labor.

Gender Justice

The normative yardstick of gender justice allows me to look at uneven outcomes of gender interventions beyond their sometimes narrowly defined aims. Further, because I am concerned with structural features, I apply the concept of gender justice to distributive and material features. The differences between and overlaps among material interests, particularly the intersection of class and gender, complicates both the definition and the enactment of gender justice (Goetz 2007, 18). Thus, I use this term because it encompasses a variety of areas, including redistribution and redress at multiple levels.

Gender justice is also amenable to a structural feminist political economy approach because it embodies a normative goal for gender relations at the level of the individual, the family, the community, the state, or the world. The local is often taken to denote ideas, institutions, cultures, and people at subnational, community, kinship, and household levels. Relationships between men and women in these arenas are crucial to the distribution of power and resources, and they are also the prime sites of gender-specific injustice. At the level of kinship or family, gender injustice hollows out democracy because what Goetz terms "continuities between patriarchy in the private sphere, and in governmental, non-governmental and market sphere" strip so many citizens—women, youth, socially derided racial or ethnic groups—of legitimacy and authority. Also, where these deep continuities exist, power holders or their constituents may have little desire to reform gender relations. Gendered inequalities in access and control over resources go unchallenged "because standards of accountability do not necessarily consider gender iniquities to be intolerable or require official remedy" (Goetz 2007, 16, 18, 27, 39, 30 [quote]).

I use gender justice to evaluate the outcomes of gender intervention in security; distribution of resources, wealth, and power; and legal reform. Perceptions of the state as having more pressing security and economic priorities than gender justice are linked to the general problem of gendered notions of security. As interveners make concessions to various groups, they mitigate against gender reform and multiply the exceptions allowed within areas of personal and family law, such as marriage, divorce, inheritance, adoption, burial, and clan-based property management (Goetz 2007, 37). These concessions can have negative outcomes for gender justice even as they link gender relations to the state. As Goetz points out, many states have ceded "control over women and children in periods of state formation to traditional patriarchal groups, excluding many forms of injustice in private relationships from the purview of formal law as a form of compensation to those authorities for their surrender of power to the state" (Goetz 2007, 35).

For example in Timor-Leste, the use of traditional dispute resolution in cases of gender-based violence is common, despite the LADV. De facto legal pluralism is not unusual internationally, and state rulings on justice are often ignored because family and community relationships between men and women are seen as legitimate, natural, biological, or cultural and thus outside the remit of the state (Goetz 2007, 35; Grenfell 2006). Rather than view this as exemplifying the persistence of traditional institutions, I understand it to involve the persistence of structural relations, of which resolution processes are but a part. Personal laws governing kinship, gender, and the family are a product of historically specific conflictual power relations at the local level, and they are influenced by transnational and international forces and regimes (Hughes 2015, 910).

In sum, my feminist political economy approach using gender justice as a benchmark in my analysis allows me to look at gender relations across time while remaining focused on outcomes for women. It permits me to examine structural relations beyond the sometimes narrow legal, political, and security-focused remits of the gender interventions I evaluate. In its attention to redistribution, gender justice gestures toward the political economy approach I employ, while revealing the tenacity of unjust gender relations between the individual, the family, and the state. Lastly, kinship and family are key sites of gender injustice and linked to my critique of the local turn in peacebuilding.

Gender Division of Labor

Sex and gender are conceptually distinct. In contrast to characteristics associated with biological sex, gender is a socially constructed set of expectations related to binary sex difference. *Gender relations* thus refers to the unequal relations between socially constructed categories of masculine and feminine. The term was coined in the 1970s to convey a new analytical engagement with what Andrea Cornwall (2007, 70) calls "the relations of power that reproduced an unequal and inequitable status quo," the locus in which female subordination and male domination were produced and sustained. Many societies devalue women and phenomena that are connoted "feminine," in favor of men and phenomena connoted "masculine." A *feminist political economy* perspective draws particular attention to ways in which gender relations in many societies often accord women a greater share of (unrecognized) burdens, and less access to and control over resources and benefits (True 2012). Unequal access and control with respect to power and resources, combined with asymmetries in gender ideology, reproduce unequal gender relations. Because gender relations are socially and historically constructed, however, they vary across time, space, and social groups, requiring investigation within the specific context.

A relational view of gender should also avoid conflating gender and women, as this can obscure the role of gender in all social relationships and typically relationships of power. Thus, I situate the gender interventions I evaluate within the context of specific gender relations in Timor-Leste, paying attention to men and militarized masculinities. Even so, because the interventions focused primarily on women—and because I am concerned with inconsistently beneficial outcomes for women—my analysis centers the gendered experiences of women and the unjust circumstances that gender interventions sought to ameliorate (Chappell 2016, 8).

Gender relations encompass the gender division of labor, a system whereby women are held to be primarily responsible for the unremunerated and often invisible work within the household.[9] This division of labor is a manifestation of different social valuations of work by men and women. Crucially, the devaluation of women reduces the perceived value of their labor, and work performed by women is thus generally undervalued relative to work done by men (Pearson 2004; Sweetman 2008). As a result of this systematic devaluation, the gender division of labor entails inequalities in bargaining power between men and women within the household, which is a site of "negotiation, even contestation, over gender norms and the distribution of resources among family members" (Pearse and Connell 2016, 32). Household bargaining thus involves contests over material resources and work. At the broadest level, men benefit from women's unpaid work and the devaluation of women's labor, receiving a "patriarchal dividend" (Walby 1989, 21; Connell 2005).

The gender division of labor can be subject to both resistance and violent enforcement. Relatedly, inequalities between women and men with respect to income, property, employment, and control over resources best explain the magnitude of violence against women in various contexts globally (True 2012, 18, 30–31). In Timor-Leste, the gender division of labor hinges on a distinction between domestic work in the household and *public* work, rather than unpaid domestic work and *paid* work, and it is this division between household and public work that I take forward.[10]

Gendered material relations are also underpinned by ideologies of male authority that justify women's greater burden of labor and their lack of control over resources in the household and beyond. Within ideological male authority, the notion of masculinity does the "rhetorical work of valorisation, denigration, and exclusion . . . *regardless of the substantive qualities in question*" (Hutchings 2008, 24, emphasis added). In other words, it rationalizes the control of women by husbands, fathers, brothers, and uncles, regardless of the particular qualities that the society ascribes to masculinity and femininity (Rubin 1975, 168). What's more, male authority permeates institutions outside the household. Male power in one sphere justifies and reinforces authority in others, including in the state. Thus, although the household and kinship are key sites of gender injustice, men's disproportionate capture of power and resources saturates all areas. In Goetz's words, "The patriarchal mindsets and social relations that are produced in the private sphere are not contained there but infuse most economic, social and political institutions" (2007, 18).

Some argue that criticism of Timorese society as patriarchal is misplaced because Timorese belief systems valorize women as the source of life (Hicks 2004, 2015). However, valorizing *reproduction* reinforces gender differences, which are ultimately harmful to women. In societies using brideprice, women's socially constructed role in reproduction and as the lynchpin of kinship systems means that their fecundity is at once both "repressed and revered" (Meillassoux 1975, 78; Fishburne Collier and Rosaldo 1981, 279). In the Timor case, this is manifested in what anthropologists have termed a "maternal religion," which places fertility at the center of ritual. Some scholars thus advocate a "return" to woman-centered religion as more culturally legitimate than "Western" gender mainstreaming (Trindade 2008).

But the valorization of women's role in reproduction reduces their value to a function of their fertility—as a function of biology—to the exclusion of other features. Moreover, as in many human societies, although Timorese women are celebrated as the source of life, menstruation and birth are considered polluting and dangerous, tainting women by association (Nguyen 2015, 26–28). Thus, worship of women's fecundity does not lead to female authority or an increase in women's ability to control material resources. An emphasis on motherhood complements rather than contradicts the ideology of male authority because men's power lies in the more highly valued material world, whereas women have a sacred place in the spiritual world (Niner 2012; Fishburne Collier and Rosaldo 1981). The disjuncture between dogma and practice arises because cultural gender notions rarely reflect actual male-female relations.

War, Militarized Conflict, and Violence

In the case of gender intervention in Timor-Leste, a feminist political economy needs to encompass war and militarized conflict, which formed social classes and established certain social forces. The interests of these forces were served by an ideology that celebrated armed masculinity, which was thus used to shape the relationships between state and society.

The ideologies of male authority and armed masculinity hold political and economic orders together at every level (True 2015, 421). For example, even prior to the Indonesian invasion, Timorese elite classes were militarized; because elites were themselves members of the military, they became dependent on the military for resources and were motivated by militaristic ideas. The celebration of armed masculinity was also crucial to Indonesian rule, holding together the New Order. Indonesia's war in Timor "gave an aura of unity and heroic purpose to an organisation that otherwise may have appeared bloated and fat" (Hughes 2009, 38). Violence against East Timorese justified the Indonesian military's dominant position in the Indonesian state, and promotion within the Indonesian military was often tied to an individual's facility with violence in Timor (Anderson 1993).

In the postconflict era, glorification of armed masculinity that originated with the Timorese elites has been extended into wider society through the valorization of veterans. Social forces that were constituted during war have captured the bulk of state resources, at the same time constraining most women's access to state and household resources. Relatedly, denial of resources has set the conditions for continued high levels of sexual and gender-based violence.

Violence against women, often referred to as VAW, is rooted in gendered and historically specific social structures rather than in random individual acts. As UN Women (2013) makes clear, VAW cuts across age and socioeconomic, educational, and geographic boundaries.[11] Sexual and gender-based violence is more prevalent during conflicts because the means of violence (especially arms) are more widely available, and because of ideologies that extol armed masculinity, men's entitlement to sex, and rape as a weapon of war. In these respects, war and militarized conflict shape social relations in gender-retrogressive directions.

Because of its focus on material relations, scholars of feminist political economy have tended to see violence against women as arising from some other, more major social process, such as war or capitalism (True 2010, 44). I do not take this approach, believing that feminist structural political economy can help to explain how material relations, the state, ideologies, the gender division of labor and kinship, and their distributional outcomes set the conditions for high rates of violence against women. VAW occurs around the world, among all social classes, arising because of patriarchal relations between men and women that are often enforced through violence. At the same time, there is a relationship between women's exclusion from productive resources and men's control over these resources on the one hand and violence against women on the other (True 2010, 39).

War and militarization often create the conditions for high levels of VAW, which gender interventions seek to reduce. When we refocus attention away from the security of the state to the insecurity of women, we can see structural continuities between domestic violence, the structural violence of poverty and deprivation, and sexual and gender-based violence (True 2012, 4). Thus, the division between public war and private violence is a gendered one. War and VAW are not separate but exist on a continuum of violence (True 2010, 38). In Timor-Leste, domestic violence has not decreased since the end of the conflict, although incidents of violence committed by an unknown perpetrator have (Hynes et al. 2004). Indeed, the overall prevalence of violence against women seems to have increased, but this could be because of more accurate translations and measurements.

During war, male deaths often exceed female deaths, but in postconflict contexts the numbers of women dying from war-related food, health, and personal insecurity may increase (Ormhaug, Meier, and Hernes 2009). Thus, feminists define postwar security as not just the cessation of public fighting between men but also the satisfaction of human needs, including the safety of women in their homes (Cockburn 2013). As such, VAW must be taken into account in any evaluation of peacebuilding.

Further, the use of sexual and gender-based violence (SGBV) as a military strategy to secure political and economic power and resources affects outcomes in gender interventions. Wartime SGBV committed by belligerent forces can "taint" female victims and exclude them from communities and resources. Victims of wartime SGBV perpetrated by "the good guys" are often not counted or reported. This can normalize nonreporting of sexual violence more widely within families and communities and contribute to a culture of impunity for perpetrators, creating the conditions for high levels of SGBV to continue (True 2012, 127; Meger 2015, 417).

In sum, war and militarization shape institutions and social classes, which in turn gender distributional outcomes. Postconflict reconstruction does not prioritize women, even though protection of women (from enemy violence) often justifies war or military intervention (Young 2003, 146; True 2012). Methodologically, my attempt to account for uneven outcomes of gender intervention involved problematizing ideologies that were taken for granted or considered simple common sense, such as the valorization of male authority, militarization, or women-centered religious practice. I also applied a feminist political economy approach to anthropological material, examining the disjuncture between rhetoric about women's value in motherhood, fertility, and birth and the lack of control and access to resources experienced by women in practice.

Kinship

Kinship is another key site of gender relations and social inequality in Timor-Leste and thus requires elaboration. In particular, determining who benefits from kinship relations can help explain high levels of VAW, the entrenchment of harmful practices, and gaps between the aims and outcomes of gender intervention.[12] Moreover, kinship plays a crucial role in class formation, most notably through the mechanism of brideprice. This contention—that kinship organizes social relations—is in line with feminist critiques of anthropological studies (Peletz 1995). In this vein, I apply Jane Fishburne Collier's argument (1988, 145) that paying brideprice in exchange for women causes social inequality, particularly in creating and reproducing *ranks*, the anthropological term used to describe kin-based lineages based on subordinate and superordinate groups.

At a basic level, all kinship systems prohibit some sexual relations and prefer others. Wide variations in these preferences and prohibitions illustrate that kinship is not biologically determined but a moral and legal code governing sex and marriage (Rubin 1975, 169; Meillassoux 1975, 11). The centrality of marriage in patrilineal kinship systems led early theorists such as Claude Lévi-Strauss to describe them as based chiefly on the exchange of women, which in turn determines "sexual access, genealogical structures, lineage names and ancestors, rights and people—men, women, and children—in concrete systems of social relationships" (Rubin 1975, 177). Gayle Rubin asserts that the exchange of women comprises and reproduces types of socially organized gender relations, and anthropologists Jane Fishburne Collier and Claude Meillassoux have convincingly argued that marriage in kinship-based societies organizes social inequality. To put it another way, marriage is the basis of kinship, and kinship organizes social relations. In this sense, control over marriage equates to control over political power (Rubin 1975, 169; Fishburne Collier 1988, vii; Meillassoux 1975, 45).

Kinship remains crucial in many areas of Timorese social and political life, intersecting with electoral politics, cash, the finance market, the state, and social classes. The mutual constitution of kinship and access to political power in the Timor case is not unexpected, because kinship systems are socially constructed and thus shaped by historical and material conditions. Indeed, the politicization of kin groups is a significant part of class formation and state formation (Meillassoux 1975; Peletz 1995, 355; Musisi 1991). Timorese male lineage heads became politicized as they leveraged militarization, slavery, and gender relations to control resources and form the currently dominant liurai-dato class.

Turning to the contemporary period, we see that brideprice—through which kinship and capital are mutually constitutive—is a significant part of the Timorese political economy, requiring definition and explication. Brideprice is a form of marriage payment and refers to the valuables that the bride's family receives from the groom's family before, during, and after marriage. In Timor-Leste, the exchange of women for a marriage payment is a "brideprice" because it is asymmetric; that is, net assets move from the groom's family to bride's family in exchange for the bride. Timor is not unique; brideprice is common in Africa, the Pacific, Central Asia, East Asia, and Southeast Asia and is the most widespread type of marriage payment globally.

Brideprice and the exchange of women affect gender justice because they exclude women from the political and economic benefits of their own economic circulation. Political authority and alliances that are created through brideprice have been the focus of much anthropological work on Timor-Leste, but such work implicitly assumes that because the exchange of women creates and cements beneficial alliances between patrilineages, it also confers benefits to women (McWilliam 2007, 2011, 2005; Hicks 2004, 2013, 2015). It tends to minimize or overlook the gendered aspects of, and gender injustices within, the exchange of women.

Gender analysis demonstrates that because women effectively function as the "conduit of a relationship, rather than the partner to it," they do not benefit from their own exchange (Rubin 1975, 174). Besides, after marriage a wife's loyalties belong to her husband's kin, her children belong to her husband's kin, and she works on land belonging to her husband's kin. Most crucially to my feminist political economy analysis, male family members—not female ones—receive and control brideprice. The use of cash and buffalo to exchange women between groups of men has a negative outcome for women because they essentially become equivalent to livestock.

Neoliberal Globalization

Gender interventions in Timor took place during second-generation neoliberal reforms. First-generation reforms were about minimizing the role of the state in regulating markets, while second-generation ones are characterized by greater attention to the efficacy of the state in harnessing social relations for the benefit of the market and of society. In particular, the regulation of economic transactions is prioritized, principally in the form of protection for property and other investor rights. Economic growth and social inclusion are seen as complementary, rather than exclusive, and legal, regulatory, and institutional reform are used to effect the latter (Rittich 2006, 210).

Second-generation neoliberalism has major implications for the conceptualization of gender—and gender justice—in gender interventions. For instance, interventions that promised "growth with equity" combined poverty reduction with the economic inclusion of women, which was to be effected through financial inclusion—in other words, through microfinance

(Hughes 2009, 52). Approaches that emphasize women's agency in the market instrumentalize an ideology of empowerment, self-help, and self-actualization, yet they do little to overturn hierarchical social and gender relations (Goetz and Gupta 1996; Rankin 2002; Ferguson 2010; Elyachar 2005).

Peace scholars who advocate local approaches have overlooked critiques of these second-generation types of participatory development by scholars such as Bill Cooke (2003), Kanishka Jayasuriya and Garry Rodan (2007), and Toby Carroll (2010), who demonstrate that locally focused initiatives can still promote a liberal agenda "to harness the ambition of each and every individual in local resources, labour and markets" (Hughes, Öjendal, and Schierenbeck 2015, 819). In another relevant critique, Meagher (2012, 8) argues that hybrid governance resembles the subcontracting of government services to private and informal spaces that was prevalent during neoliberal policymaking of the 1980s and 1990s.

In like manner, I argue that hybrid programming in local governance reform has coincided with the Timorese central government's interest in divesting itself of fiscal responsibilities that exceed its capacity. Reliance on legitimacy or capacity explanations for government use of local or hybrid approaches ignores the interest that governments can have in liberal approaches to spending and cost saving through local, individualized participatory development.

Specifically, donors to peacebuilding interventions in Timor-Leste have been instrumental in promoting the use of microfinance for women's economic empowerment, making the inclusion of neoliberal globalization an important factor in an accurate evaluation of gender interventions. First, microfinance promotes new forms of gendered economic governance. Legal reform spearheaded by the World Bank's International Finance Corporation (IFC), government and donor subsidies, and national policymaking have together shaped microfinance in Timor-Leste, with troubling outcomes. Second, microfinance in the country is a part of a new and global "deep marketization" of development, reaching beyond the state and institutionalizing debt relations in the social sphere.

In practice, then, despite a focus on the social and the idea that "institutions matter" in second-generation reforms, international development agencies have still seen development as synonymous with economic growth, only now, "good governance" is seen as guaranteeing markets (Rittich 2006, 210).

Conclusion

I draw on True's and Hughes's theoretical insights on neoliberal globalization in my methods and analysis of gender interventions (True 2012; Hughes 2015, 2012). First—and related to the gender division of labor—I concentrate on household work and budgets: who works, who is paid, and crucially, who owes debts to whom. This reveals the kinds of economic and social stratification at the village and national levels. Where possible, I connect labor and debt to historical relations of power and to current gender relations. I look at class, gender, and age stratification, and the reasons and ideologies accompanying them.

Second, I analyze people's explanations for the frequency, severity, causes, and solutions for violence against women in interviews and participant observation, using a feminist framework of analysis. The economic conditions and causes delineated in these narratives warrant explanation.

Third, I problematize the narrative of local versus international, or local versus neoliberal, in Timorese policymaking. By examining advocacy, opposition, contestation, and interests, I identify complex, strategic alliances of social groups at multiple levels, cutting across easy associations of peacebuilders with neoliberalism or local actors with an antiliberal stance.

Fourth, I link my fieldwork on village work and debts to an examination of the history of microfinance in Timor-Leste. Again, this moves beyond the narrative of microfinance as an international initiative, locating its real history in documents describing economic life under the Indonesian occupation and in Indonesian-introduced microfinance.

Relatedly, my use of structural feminist political economy involves analyzing the gendered distribution of state resources in the postconflict era by comparing the distributional outcomes for political coalitions, spending policies, veterans, victims of wartime violence, and vulnerable women in the community. For my examination of the relationships between sexual violence and material interests, I rely on documentation of sexual and gender-based violence during the war (CAVR 2006).

A range of explanations for uneven results for peacebuilding in Timor-Leste, and for gender interventions specifically, have dominated both academic and practitioner work. Many analyses suggest that the statebuilding efforts of interveners created institutions without legitimacy or capacity.

One particular critique of the liberal peace, the local turn, emphasizes the lack of authenticity, or a clash of cultural paradigms, but an explanation that relies on binaries between local or international, or hybrids of them, cannot explain the differential impact of intervention on different groups within a society. Some groups support interventions, while others repel them, according to their own interests and ideology. Coalitions of interests and struggles between them shape the outcomes of international programming. Thus, analyses based on the local turn do not give enough consideration to other relations of power within target societies, especially gender and class.

Feminist analyses of gender mainstreaming, while adding a valuable dimension to debates, have also often paid insufficient attention to class factors. Gender intervention in Timor-Leste must be evaluated in terms of gender justice, because gender justice encompasses political economy concerns with redistribution along gender *and* class lines. The gender division of labor is an important tool to analyze material relations between men and women because it results in unequal bargaining power between men and women within households, and these relations are subject to violent enforcement.

A comprehensive analysis must also include investigation of how war and militarization have shaped Timorese sociopolitical life. Specifically, it has been crucial in the interrelated process of class formation and accumulation through the material effects of war and the valorization of armed masculinity. War and militarization set the conditions for high levels of violence against women because of the availability of arms, a culture of impunity for perpetrators of sexual and gender-based violence, and the securitization of men and masculinity. Of particular relevance to my critique of the local turn, keeping the peace can lead to a trade-off between military and social spending, with the effect of adding to women's labor burdens.

Following Fishburne Collier (1988) and Meillassoux (1975), I also employ my structural feminist political economy framework to define the dual role of kinship in gender relations and class formation. It is essential to include kinship in the Timorese context because of its enduring role in class formation and brideprice. An examination of kinship relations thus reveals the interdependent nature of gender relations and class.

Finally, neoliberal globalization has been most apparent in second-generation regulation of economic life in Timor-Leste. Some interveners have favored access to markets as a solution to poverty, while others have advocated conditional cash transfers. Microfinance sets up a debt relation between poor women and international financial markets, while conditional cash can relegate caring work to the sole responsibility of women. Nonetheless, these contemporary relations of debt and power are grounded in older processes of class formation and accumulation. I now turn to the development of historically specific class and gender relations in Timor.

2
Class Formation, Slavery, and Militarization

Portuguese trade, taxes, and institutions played an integral role in the formation and consolidation of the Timorese liurai-dato class from the mid-nineteenth to the mid-twentieth centuries. In particular, as governance shifted from a patchwork of Portuguese–Timorese alliances and enmities to centralized bureaucratic rule that incorporated liurai and dato, vertical inequality among Timorese grew. Under the Indonesian regime from 1975 to 1999, this pattern of elite incorporation continued. Its corollary has been the subordination of other groups of Timorese as slaves, serfs, or bonded laborers, a process that remains relevant because of the kinship-mediated class system. The liurai-dato came to depend on the military for its well-being under first Portuguese and then Indonesian rule. In the political economy of the Indonesian occupation, unequal gender relations and conflict-related sexual and gender-based violence occupied a continuum that was manifested in the use of rape as a weapon of war, sexual slavery, the exchange of women, and polygyny. Militarization and sexual and gender-based violence thus provided the context for the emergence of a Timorese women's movement in 1975 to the present, and ultimately of gender-responsive budgeting, as conflicts over "heroes" and "victims" produced a gendered distribution of state resources. Class is therefore intimately bound into the concerns of this study.

The dominant class of Timorese society comprises two overlapping groups that are demarcated by kinship and expressed in the Tetun language as *liurai* (king) and *dato* (noble).[1] Liurai lineages are "aristocratic," on the basis of their position as the first settling or autochthonous family of any given area. Hence, those with liurai lineages are the effective landowners, determining others' rights to land within the area. Members of liurai lineages usually marry endogamously; that is, they marry other liurai or dato. Dato lineages are "noble," a lower status than liurai. In sum, the liurai and dato are respectively first- and second-ranked kin groups, linked by intermarriage, which together comprise a dominant class.[2] In the contemporary period, as in the past, members of this class dominate subnational political and economic institutions. A smaller number control Dili-based institutions, forming a recognizable political elite. How did they reach that apex of power?

The Portuguese Period, 1850–1975

Between the sixteenth and late eighteenth centuries, Portuguese traders were just one of many groups of merchants and missionaries in the eastern part of the Southeast Asian archipelago, and Timor was part of the informal Portuguese Empire rather than the formal Portuguese state.[3] For this reason, the beneficiaries of the Timorese slave and sandalwood trades were maritime traders, corporations, and the Catholic Church in Goa and Macao, not Portugal. From the late eighteenth century, Portuguese state-sanctioned and militarily supported trade in slaves and sandalwood grew, producing a deepening mercantile connection with Portugal that had consequences for the social and political structures in Timor.

Timor-Leste's exclave of Oecusse is a good illustration of how trade and military alliances with the Portuguese were the catalyst for the formation of the liurai-dato class. The stepping-off point was the conversion to Catholicism of the liurai of Lifau in Oecusse in 1641 (Davidson 1994, 57). Subsequent conversion and intermarriage of local rulers—liurai and dato—resulted in the emergence of Portuguese-speaking people in Oecusse, Flores, and Solor, termed "Topasses."[4] The Topasses exacted tributes of slaves and sandalwood from their subjects, and captured slaves and goods from enemy groups (Hägerdal 2012, 62). They sometimes held Portuguese administrative and military posts in Oecusse, but they were outside formal Portuguese control. For instance, Topasses fought both the Portuguese and the Dutch for control over the lucrative sandalwood, slave, and coffee trades. Later on, the Topasses da Costa family blocked repeated attempts by the Portuguese to sell or trade the nominally Portuguese-owned Oecusse exclave to the Dutch by making themselves indispensable, collecting taxes and supplying troops to the Portuguese during trade wars with the Dutch (Hägerdal 2012; Hicks 1983; Yoder 2016). These patterns of incorporation, allegiance, and enmity occurred across Timor and helped shape the districts seen today (Figure 2.1).

From the 1850s, a plantation economy based on coffee began to replace sandalwood and slaves, bringing socioeconomic change as the nascent liurai-dato class gained access to new resources. Coffee wealth

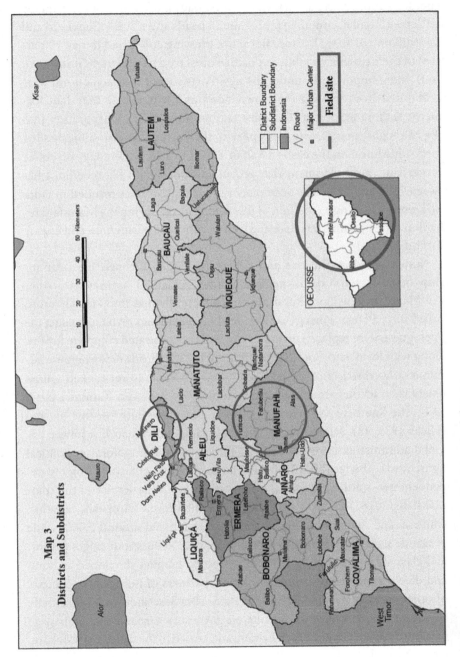

Figure 2.1 Timor-Leste, by district and subdistrict

allowed liurai to buy "more weapons and gunpowder, to raise more buffalo, stage more feasts, marry more wives, wage more wars, plunder enemy settlements and accumulate more human heads and slaves" (Shepherd and McWilliam 2013, 331). Those liurai not growing coffee had to pay 10 percent of their rice harvest, but in practice most paid irregularly (Gunn 1999, 160). More importantly, under the new Portuguese tax system, liurai were prohibited from levying their own taxes and tributes, as they had formerly, leading to violent resistance and marking their incorporation into the colonial system. During this period, the Portuguese also subjected the forty-nine liurai on the eastern half of Timor to a 20 percent levy on coffee production, a development that provoked seven major tax rebellions between 1860 and 1915. For example, in 1911, tax increases resulted in Dom Boaventura leading a rebellion of disaffected liurai during the Manufahi rebellion. The uprising was defeated by a coalition of Portuguese and enemy Timorese liurai.

Notwithstanding the rise and fall of individual fortunes, the relationship between liurai-dato and commoners remained asymmetric. After the Manufahi rebellion, liurai kingdoms were divided into smaller units, called *suco*, all over Portuguese Timor.[5] Liurai who had revolted against the Portuguese were replaced by those who had demonstrated complete loyalty, along with loyal dato. Some steadfast liurai became heads of Portuguese administrative districts or *regulo*, while others became lower-ranked village chiefs back in their home villages (Gunn 1999, 246–247; Kammen 2017, 135). The line between aristocratic liurai and noble dato became blurred (Hicks 1983, 23). More broadly, although some individuals lost power, colonial administrators realized the usefulness of retaining liurai as political figureheads. The result, as Douglas Kammen points out, was "a highly dependent neo-traditional revival of dynastic rule" in the service of the colonial state (2016, 102. See also Araujo 1975). Privileged Europeans, mestiço, Chinese, and "assimilated" liurai and dato numbered around 7,000, while peasants, slaves, and serfs numbered around 435,000, producing a pyramidal class structure (Jolliffe 1978, 42). Mestiço families developed as liurai and dato married or became the intimate partners of Europeans, Chinese, or other outsider peoples. Kammen (2016, 104) describes what I take to be a typical example: one of the Portuguese governor's sons was sent to manage his father's coffee plantations in Ermera and settled in the district of Maubara, where he took Madalena Lo Bete, a daughter of a local dato family, as his mistress.

Most crucially, after 1912, commoners were forced to provide goods and labor to liurai and dato who passed the taxes on to the Portuguese in a system of indirect rule. Taxes were thus fundamental to the formation and dominance of the liurai-dato class. Although it was the Portuguese who imposed levies, the administration and control of who paid taxes was crucial to developing liurai and dato wealth and power within the Portuguese colonial state. During their reorganization of the state after the end of the Manufahi wars in 1912, the Portuguese introduced a head tax. The *capitacão* was a direct and monetized taxation system to replace the 20 percent levy on coffee production and was equivalent to around four months' labor. Those who evaded payment in either cash or labor were jailed (Gunn 1999, 211–212). Liurai and *xefe suku* (village chiefs) were not only exempt from the head tax but also entitled to a twelfth of the corvée (road construction) labor extracted through the tax. The labor burdens were considerable and inescapable. Some of those unable to pay were forced to work as *auxiliar* (help), becoming domestic servants to civil servants and traditional chiefs, while others were compelled to labor on plantations and roads (Kammen 2003, 76). Brutal physical punishments during this corvée labor were the norm, meted out by higher-ranked Timorese (Jolliffe 1978, 48).

In the same period of reorganization after the Manufahi war, the Portuguese incorporated liurai and dato into the bureaucracy, systematizing vertical inequality between Timorese, as shown in Table 2.1. Of note, the Portuguese appointed new administrators for the head tax: village chiefs who were from either liurai or dato lineage. The position of village chief was inherited, but the individual was elected by the "consensus" of a quarter of the population of one village: the *male* members of aristocratic and noble lineages (Hicks 1983, 23). Candidates had to be male, from the right family, moderately fluent in Portuguese, and Christian. In the middle levels of the racialized colonial bureaucracy to which the Timorese had access, the liurai and dato dominated all available paid employment, such as the new subnational administration role, *xefe postu*, or chief of the post. Likewise, in the military, liurai were automatically commissioned, whereas the lower-ranked dato did not automatically gain officer status (Hicks 1983; Kammen 2016).

These class structures were mapped onto the parameters of a new Timorese political elite in Dili. Those in the capital city had more wealth and power than liurai and dato outside of Dili. In the early 1970s, educated youth from mestiço and liurai families working in the civil service, the military, and the press formed a recognizable intelligentsia in Dili, but events in Portugal

Table 2.1 Social rank during the Portuguese period, c. 1850–1975

	Plantation period, c. 1850–1910		Post-pacification, c. 1910–1950		Portuguese overseas province, c. 1950–1975	
Aristocrat	Dom Liurai boot	King Great king	Regulo	Petty king	Administrador	Administrator
	Liurai	King	Liurai	King	Xefe posto	Chief of the post
Noble	Dato	Noble	Xefe suku	Village chief	Xefe suku	Village chief
Peasant/ commoner	Ema reino**	Person of the kingdom, peasant	Ema reino	Peasant	Ema reino Toos nain	Peasant Farmer
Slave/serf	Atan Lutu-hum Ulun-houris Servi	Slave Retainer Chattel slave Serf	Atan Lutu-hum	Slave Retainer	Atan Lutu-hum	Slave Retainer

soon overtook them.[6] In 1974 a military coup against the fascist regime in Lisbon precipitated the decolonization of Timor. The Timorese intelligentsia responded by forming political parties—unsurprisingly, led by liurai—to prepare for independence (Hicks 1983, 8; Guterres 2006).[7] FRETILIN, formed in 1974, was the leftist party of independence that went on to lead the resistance against the Indonesian military for decades. Founding members Xavier do Amaral, Nicolau Lobato, Rosa Bonaparte, Justino Mota, and Xanana Gusmão were from liurai families, while Mari Alkatiri and José Ramos-Horta were from liurai/mestiço families.[8] Similarly, in the rival Timorese Democratic Union (UDT), founding member Francisco Lopes da Cruz was the son of a liurai, while members Domingos de Oliveira, Mario Carrascalão, and João Carrascalão were from a mestiço family.[9] Other prominent UDT members came from the Catholic Church, the Portuguese administration, or the Hakka-Chinese business community (Gunn 2011). Likewise, José Abilio Osorio Soares, who founded the pro-Indonesian integration party APODETI, was from a liurai family (Bovensiepen 2014a).

The Indonesian Occupation, 1975–1998

Fearing that the left-leaning FRETILIN would seize power and proclaim independence on its own terms, the conservative UDT staged a coup on August 11, 1974, with the backing of the police. The UDT advocated a slow process of decolonization, continued links with Portugal, and the retention of liurai power. Its members feared the social changes promised by FRETILIN's revolutionary program and called for the imprisonment of all members of the rival party following the coup. The subsequent civil war between FRETILIN and the UDT was marked by atrocities committed on both sides (CAVR 2006).[10] Backed by the army, FRETILIN defeated the UDT and declared independence on November 28, 1975. At the same time, Indonesian and Timorese troops skirmished on the border.

Using the UDT-FRETILIN fighting as a pretext, and with the backing of the United States and Australia, the Indonesian Armed Forces (ABRI) invaded Timor a few days later, on December 7. Indonesia and its allies justified the move by citing FRETILIN's socialism. Left-wing politics had been brutally suppressed during Suharto's 1965 takeover, and hatred of the leftist party propelled and vindicated the invasion of Timor-Leste. It was a brutal affair, with tens of thousands of Timorese killed (CAVR 2006; Jolliffe 1978, 277–279). Many Timorese fled Dili for the mountains, where they held out against the invasion. In districts close to Indonesian West Timor, the resistance was largely defeated by 1977. In contrast, the central mountains and eastern part of the island remained under FRETILIN control until the ABRI offensive of December 1978 crushed the last open resistance.[11] During this period, many liurai and dato who had previously been suspicious of the ostensibly Marxist FRETILIN lent their support to the anti-Indonesian forces under the party, despite its commitment to ending social hierarchies.

The twenty-four-year Indonesian occupation of East Timor was violent and coercive, but incorporation of the liurai-dato class was part of its political strategy of ruling with and through local populations to legitimate their rule (Jones 2010, 556).[12] Administratively, the *suku* or villages of the Portuguese period became *desa*.[13] In terms of personnel, Indonesian military men initially filled high-level bureaucratic positions such as *bupati* and *camat* but were later replaced with Timorese men (CAVR 2006; Hill 2001). As the former Timorese district administrator of the eastern district Lautem recalled, "Public servants from the Portuguese era were immediately appointed. Those of us who came down [from the hills] early and had been public servants were immediately appointed, whether FRETILIN, APODETI or UDT . . . just appoint him" (CAVR 2006, 46). His remark reveals the continuity of institutional personnel (see Table 2.2). Individuals from the old noble families were chosen to fill positions in a pattern of deliberate elite integration throughout Timor (Kammen 2016, 136). A significant number of liurai and dato were thus able to retain their privilege by becoming part of the Indonesian bureaucracy.

Like the Portuguese colonial government before it, the Indonesian government distributed material benefits to Timorese who cooperated. In Dili, high-level bureaucrats were rewarded for supporting Indonesian rule. The former manager of the Portuguese Banco Nacional Ultramarino (BNU), for example, grew wealthy managing coffee plantations for the Indonesian military-backed logistics firm PT Denok. Similarly, the wealthy Carrascalão family won back its plantations in the 1980s, and individuals from that family often held prominent positions within the Indonesian government.[14] Away from Dili, district and subdistrict administrators and village chiefs gained material benefits such as wages and access to resources through petty corruption and extortion or exploitation of other Timorese. The Indonesian military rewarded supporters with government jobs and material perks, creating a state-dependent elite and putting several thousand Timorese on the payroll.[15]

Despite these efforts at incorporation, Indonesian military rule alienated some members of the liurai-dato class, propelling them to join the resistance. In Maubara, for instance, the military and its associates took coffee plantations from some elite families and sidelined them from political office, while non-liurai families who had backed the pro-Indonesian APODETI were given posts in the administration (Kammen 2016, 136). An Indonesian intelligence report from 1982 suggests that some elites thought their social inferiors had usurped their positions: "Some of the GPK leaders [FALINTIL/FRETILIN leaders] are Liurai or the offspring of Liurai. Some traditional leaders were replaced as leaders of tribes because of the upheavals, and new leaders were appointed by Operation commanders. Some of these traditional leaders feel very resentful because they have lost their wealth and now find themselves in positions of disadvantage and moreover being led by people who are not the descendants of Liurai."[16]

The document reveals that the occupying forces considered control over disenfranchised elites to be crucial. Timorese elites in the administration were constantly under watch by intelligence operatives who monitored their loyalty (Budiardjo and Liong 1984, 102). The Indonesian military territorial command structure had counterparts to the administration at every level (Table 2.2), and these parallel military positions exerted authority over all Timorese, whether liurai, dato, or commoner.[17]

Table 2.2 Social rank continuity during the Indonesian occupation, 1975–1998

Aristocrat	Portuguese period, c. 1950–1975		Indonesian period, 1975–1998		Indonesian military territorial command structure[c]	
	Administrador	Administrator	Bupati	District administrator	Kodim	District military command
Noble	Xefe posto	Chief of the post	Camat	Subdistrict administrator	Koramil	Subdistrict military command
	Xefe suku	Village chief	Kepala desa Temukung	Head of the village Head of the lineage	Babinsa	Noncommissioned guidance officer or team
	Xefe aldeia	Hamlet chief[a]	Rukun tetangga (RT) Rukun warga (RW)	Neighbourhood association Administrative unit	–	–
Peasant/ commoner	Ema reino	Peasant	Toos nain Petani Wanra (Perlawanan Rakyat) Ratih (Rakyat Terlatih) Tenaga bantuan operasi (TBO)	Farmer Farmer People's Resistance[b] Militia-trained civilians Operations assistants	Indonesian regular soldiers	–
Slave/serf	Atan Lutu-hum Ultun-houris	Slave Retainer Chattel slave	Atan ba ema Budak	Slave to people, domestic servant Sex slave or in a servile marriage	–	–

[a] The headman of a lineage can be a commoner or of noble lineage.
[b] These are civil defense forces, within which militia leaders and pro-Integration officials were still largely drawn from the Liurai-Dato class.
[c] Based on Kammen (1999).

A struggle emerged within the FRETILIN-led resistance over whether to reform, relinquish, or reject the superior status of the liurai. In one camp was a center nationalist group that supported liurai leadership. This group dominated the party before the Indonesian invasion. In a revealing example from July 1975, in the first and only district-level elections organized by FRETILIN, Timorese were forced to vote members of the liurai class into the constituent assembly on the grounds that they were "competent" (Gunn 2011, 93). After the invasion, some liurai and dato members reimposed "feudal relations" in areas under FRETILIN control, "demanding that the masses give them the respect they had experienced when they were Portuguese civil servants" (Budiardjo and Liong 1984, 58). Tensions between liurai-dato and commoners manifested itself in criticism of the party's centrist president, Xavier do Amaral. His allegedly feudalistic attitudes and insistence on a comfortable lifestyle while living in FALINTIL's mountain bases provoked discord, and he was deposed in 1977 over his view that civilians should return to their villages instead of keeping up the fight.[18]

In the other camp within FRETILIN were radicals who campaigned against "tribalism, regionalism, arranged marriages and feudal servitude" (Budiardjo and Liong 1984, 59). Their view was represented in a 1974 manifesto that held Portuguese colonialism responsible for the "obsolete and anachronistic political and administrative structure" and aspired to be free of colonization and "other forms of domination and exploitation" (published in Jolliffe 1978, 328–330). This camp regarded raising awareness of class divisions through "conscientization" as crucial to social reform.[19] Ular Rihi, a commander of the party's military wing FALINTIL, describes how he came to recognize the presence and meaning of Timorese class hierarchy during the Indonesian occupation: "During the Portuguese times, I had been of the Liurai class; there was always the possibility of getting *ordinença* [ordnance; Tetun: military logistic support].... While we were going to school, they [the ordinença] were carrying our provisions while we were riding the horses. During the war, we found ourselves in their position, carrying everything, performing manual labour so that we could put ourselves in their shoes. I began to learn what it was to be oppressed and to understand how wrong class oppression was" (Rihi 2009).[20] The clash between the UDT and FRETILIN and infighting in the latter thus reveal that the superordination of the liurai-dato class generated conflict both within Timorese groups and among Timorese people (CAVR 2006).

Even though radical members challenged the position of the liurai, FRETILIN's commitment to social reform diminished in the 1980s. Many radical leaders had been killed during the war, while numerous Timorese elites had fled to Mozambique, Angola, Portugal, and Australia (Wise 2011). Some of those living in exile were social conservative members of the liurai-dato class. For example, 90 percent of Catholic nuns and priests, many of them from the liurai-dato class, left for Portugal during the civil war between the UDT and FRETILIN (Budiardjo and Liong 1984, 117).[21] More concretely, in 1984, commitment to reforming the Timorese class system was sidelined when Xanana Gusmão led the FALINTIL guerrilla army in a split from the political party FRETILIN to become a nonpartisan armed force. In the process, Gusmão established an umbrella nationalist organization, Council Nacional Resistance Maubere (CNRM), which included FRETILIN's rivals from the UDT.[22] The reorganization resulted in a softening of the radicals' position (Kammen 2012; Niner 2001), and by the 1990s FRETILIN had shifted to a reformist and nationalist ideology. After independence, many Timorese from elite families returned to the country, taking up positions of authority and influence in business, politics, and development work (Hughes 2011; Wise 2011).

The political views, actions, and allegiances of Timorese leaders during the Indonesian occupation were inconsistent, and they remain difficult to document. The presence of Timorese elites in Indonesian state and military institutions, the lack of records, and the defection and rehabilitation of guerrillas made it difficult for participants and observers alike to keep track of individual involvement in the independence movement (Hughes 2009, 44). To this day, the issue of those who sacrificed themselves and those who collaborated is highly contested (Kent 2016; Kent and Kinsella 2015; Rothschild 2017). Likewise, who is a liurai *loos* (a true liurai), rather than merely installed as a Portuguese or Indonesian collaborator, is a matter of debate. These disputes are particularly fraught because liurai lineages can claim a right to own land and to rule over others. Over time, a recognizable dominant class has formed, and despite contestation, occupation, and incorporation, that dominance continues.

The Legacy of Slavery

Important to the formation of the liurai-dato class was the historical development of slavery in Timor. Commercialized chattel slavery was an essential part of European trade in Timor, as it was in much of Southeast Asia. Slaves were the second-most valuable export from the island after sandalwood, and unlike the seasonal wood could be procured year-round. Timorese could be enslaved either directly by European traders or, more usually, by liurai and dato as a result of war or debt and then sold to European and Southeast Asian maritime traders. Demand could be high. After their genocide of the Bandanese in 1621, the Dutch needed new workers for nutmeg and mace plantations on Banda, which fueled the call for Timorese slaves. Later on, in the nineteenth century, demand for Timorese and other non-Javanese slaves intensified again because of a Dutch prohibition on selling Javanese slaves in Dutch-controlled ports (Andaya 2010, 406; Gunn 1999, 46; Kammen 2003).

Within Timor there existed various forms of unfree labor—termed "traditional slavery" by scholars—although conceptually distinct, these forms often blurred in practice (see Table 2.3).[23] Hans Hägerdal (2010, 33) identifies two terms that Timorese historically used for slaves: *lutu-hum* were personal retainers who were bound to a master because of debts (and were thus in bonded labor), and *ulun-houris* were chattel slaves who were usually prisoners of war, taken along their families, and could be sold. No specific term existed for women in domestic slavery. Liurai could simply declare someone a slave for any number of crimes and take their property (Hägerdal 2010, 25). Moreover, if commoners failed to pay taxes or corvée labor to their social superiors, they could face death or enslavement. The line between bonded labor and slavery was slippery and indistinct.

Although Portugal outlawed the practice in 1875, liurai, dato, and Portuguese colonists in Timor-Leste continued to use unfree laborers until the 1950s, long after the export of slaves had been outlawed (Kammen 2003, 78). Liurai and dato controlled and benefited from the bodies and work of retainers, war captives, and women in servile marriages well into the twentieth century. Hierarchies between master and slave could be extreme; one of Antero da Silva's interlocutors recalled seeing in the last years of Portuguese rule in the 1960s that when the "dead body of local Liurai was buried, his mattress was the human body of his human slave" (da Silva 2012, 115).[24] Thus, slaves were at the bottom of the four-tier hierarchy of lineages: first the liurai, then dato, then commoners, and finally slaves and serfs (see Tables 2.2 and 2.3). More than half the Timorese population were commoners, subordinate to the liurai-dato class. A much smaller number were bound in servitude to the liurai-dato or to colonial masters. To be clear, traditional slavery of either serfs or chattel slaves no longer exists in Timor-Leste. Nonetheless, many people descended from subordinate classes still live in debt bondage to their social superiors, and servile marriages are not uncommon (Khan and Hyati 2012).[25] Hence, the legacy of traditional slavery, which was part of the hierarchy establishing class formation, continues to shape social relations.

Widespread militia violence at the end of Indonesian occupation in 1998 was linked to social class. Militias had always been a crucial part of the Indonesian military's strategy of using Timorese to fight Timorese (Wandelt 2007). Kammen (2003, 82), discussing militia violence in the lead-up to independence, argues that militia members were recruited from what he refers to as the lumpenproletariat, meaning *preman* (gangsters), gamblers, and the unemployed. He documents a pattern of recruitment from among slave and peasant-commoner lineages in certain districts. For instance, in Lautem, militia members were from the *akanu*, or slave, lineages. Similarly, in coffee-growing areas of Ermera and Liquisa, militia members were the descendants of bonded and indentured plantation laborers. Kammen's two examples may indicate a wider pattern in which militia members were the sons and grandsons of slaves and unfree laborers, although Timorese militia and pro-Indonesian party leaders were from the liurai-dato class. This resembled the pattern throughout Indonesia, where preman were recruited from the underclass to do the violent work of the state (Wandelt 2007, 143).

Scholars of contemporary Timorese society and politics for the most part overlook the social ramifications of unfree labor taking the forms of slavery, debt bondage, and servile marriage. Instead, they tend to focus on institutions of political leadership that are dominated by the liurai-dato class. Studies drawing on the local turn in peacebuilding typically argue that layering "modern" state institutions on top of "traditional" village leadership is crucial to any analysis of contemporary Timorese politics and society (Brown 2012b; Cummins and Leach 2012; Hicks 2013; Fox 2008; Hohe 2002a; 2002b; Trindade 2008). In doing so, they ignore the influence of unfree labor and the power relations involved. "Traditional" social relations persist because liurai or dato status is almost a prerequisite for access to paid work, land, capital, welfare, education, political power, justice, marriage, and social position. These very power relations shape the outcomes of gender interventions.

Militarization and Timorese Social Forces

Militarization is an incremental process whereby an object or subject comes to depend on a military organization or militaristic ideas. In Timor, this process began after Portugal lost the colony of Brazil in the late nineteenth century. The Portuguese military sought new positions in other colonies—Timor, Angola, Mozambique—and increasing numbers of army and navy

Table 2.3 Types of unfree labor during the Portuguese period

	Portuguese	Timorese	Definition
Chattel slavery	Slaves exchanged for goods and money	*Ulun-houris,* usually prisoners of war and their families, are chattel slaves who can be sold. Now called *atan*.	The enslaver has right of ownership over the slave, with the intent to exploit through the use, management, profit, or transfer of that person.
Debt bondage	*Axuliar* (help) or *asuliar* (servant), laborer, farmhand, coolie	*Lutu-hum,* usually bonded as a result of debts, are retainers to *liurai* and cannot be sold.	Debtors pledge their labor, or the labor of a dependent, as security for a debt.
Serfdom	Generally an indentured laborer; bonded laborer, or corvée laborer working on plantations, roads, or in the home	Serfs are now called *atan* or *servo, servi,* or *servidori*.	By law, custom, or agreement, serfs are tenants who are bound to live and labor on land belonging to a landlord, to render a service to the landlord, and are not free to change their status.
Unfree labor affecting women only	Servile marriage or concubinage	Servile marriage, including polygynous marriage. *Serbi* was the term for Timorese women in sexual slavery in the Second World War.	Within servile marriage, a woman, without the right to refuse, is married on payment to her parents, guardian, or family of money or in kind.

Note: Definitions are based on Allain (2012, 277–279). Matsuno and Oliviera (2016) offer a useful discussion of Timorese female sexual slavery during the Second World War.

officers were appointed as colonial governors. Consequently, the political status of Portuguese Timor changed from a trading enclave to a permanent military outpost. Positions in the new colonial bureaucracy brought Portuguese military governors and their officers material benefits such as land, plantations, and access to unfree Timorese productive and reproductive labor.

Portuguese trade depended on fostering enmity among, and creating military and trade alliances with, different groups across Timor. Part of this involved granting military titles to Timorese rulers to cement relationships with the liurai and dato, who came to associate themselves with and benefit from the Portuguese state's military power. These classes gave the Portuguese loyalty, access to trade, and a supply of labor for warfare and other colonial tasks (Yoder 2005). In return, the liurai-data class benefited from a military association that supported their authority. Military titles symbolized Timorese elites' expanding control over organized violence and their access to Portuguese arms, wealth, and trade.

Over the course of the nineteenth and twentieth centuries, as military ideas and institutions became viewed as valuable and normal, the notional well-being of members of the liurai-dato class increasingly depended on these ideas (Enloe 2000, 3). Repeating an earlier pattern, liurai who had fought for the Portuguese were made lieutenants and colonels. As noted earlier, in the early twentieth century the Portuguese reduced the size of kingdoms while shaping newly formed districts into military commands. In the 1960s the colonial wars in Angola and Mozambique caused Portuguese military officers stationed in Timor to be transferred to other posts abroad. Liurai and dato replaced them, resulting in a Timorization of all layers of the military and the bureaucracy.

During the Indonesian occupation, resources and power flowed to Timorese who supported the occupiers. Again, this distribution of material benefits to armed men and military leaders contributed to militarization. On the one hand, Timorese men began to earn wages in the regular military and police forces, and by 1998 more than six thousand Timorese were serving in the Indonesian Army and police in the province of East Timor. On the other hand, many Timorese fought alongside the military but were not included as regular security forces. They became part of a civilian defense force called HANSIP, in line with the core military strategy and structure of a "total people's defense" that applied to all of Indonesia. After a time, they received salaries from the Indonesian Army (CAVR 2006, ch. 4).

After the 1980s the strategy of using Timorese to fight Timorese grew more pronounced. Large numbers of HANSIP members, Tenaga Bantuan Operasi (TBO) auxiliaries, and unpaid militia troops were deployed in an Indonesian counterinsurgency strategy of simultaneous civil repression and social welfare, as boys as young as twelve were recruited into the TBO. East Timorese militia who fought for integration with Indonesia, although not on the official military payroll, were rewarded with regular cash payments and other material benefits including rice, vehicles, transport, fuel, office space, communications equipment, medical supplies, and weapons (CAVR 2006, Annex 1; Wandelt 2007).

Militia leaders had overlapping roles in the military and civilian government and used their military associations to gain wealth and power in both contexts. High-ranking militia leaders made money from corruption and extortion. Crucially, the majority of Timorese militia leaders also held positions as government officials, village heads, and university vice chancellors. At the end of the occupation, in 1998–1999, the real fear of losing benefits was a factor in driving a significant minority of Timorese civil servants to support the violent pro-Indonesian militia (Tanter, Ball, and Van Klinken 2006).

Militarization in Timor also had ideological facets, as both Indonesian and Portuguese occupiers promoted armed masculinity, encouraging and justifying the use of violence by state and nonstate actors (Scambary 2009b; Wilson 2006). Henri Myrttinen (2005, 238) argues that the dominant form of Timorese masculinity has been characterized by readiness to use violence. The Indonesian military fostered this trait through martial institutions and rituals that embedded military values in society while at the same time creating auxiliary state forces (Scambary 2009b; Streicher 2011). Specifically, the Indonesian government militarized Timorese youth in the 1980s and 1990s by fostering martial institutions such the scout movement Pramuka, martial arts groups, and military-style ceremonies and events to celebrate national days (CAVR 2006, ch. 4; Wandelt 2007). Martial institutions encouraged young boys to mimic the work of soldiers, and many boys worked for soldiers by providing formal operational support in the TBO. Most viscerally, in the lead-up to militia violence in 1998–1999, the Indonesian military designed strange blood rituals for Timorese militias (Tanter, Ball, and Van Klinken 2006). Imitations of Timorese ceremonial animal sacrifices, these were intended to unify and strengthen militia members and inspire them to violence. Thus, through rewards, institutions, and rituals, occupiers perpetuated an ideology that celebrated violence and armed masculinity.

Historically, the Timorese resistance shared that ideology. Weapons were synonymous with resistance, as male membership in the FALINTIL almost always meant carrying and using arms (Myrttinen 2005, 240). The *clandestinos* and the exiled diplomatic front of FRETILIN, although neither group bore arms, also emphasized their association with weapons, treating FALINTIL as the vanguard of the liberation struggle (Aditjondro 2000). The celebration of armed masculinity also continued postindependence; the government, for example, chose to commemorate FRETILIN leader Nicolau Lobato with a ten-meter-tall monument of him carrying an assault rifle at the entrance to the Dili airport.

Significantly, armed masculinity is an ideal for elite Timorese men even when they are not necessarily armed. In other words, like all ideologies, its content, meaning, and representation do not reliably reflect the facts. At the end of Indonesian occupation, few men were still armed. Drawing on Indonesian intelligence reports, Kate Roll (2015, 71) notes that by 1995 just ninety-eight guns, in the possession of 210 fighters, remained. Unarmed members of clandestine networks and mass movements constituted the majority of the resistance, yet the strong association between armed men and victory in the independence struggle endured. Women earned praise as female comrades, support staff, and spies; as barefoot teachers doing FRETILIN's political work of conscientization in the guerrilla years; or as mothers, wives, girlfriends or sisters of guerillas (Cristalis and Scott 2005; Ingram, Kent, and McWilliam 2015; Kent and Kinsella 2015; da Silva 2012). Thus, Xanana Gusmão obfuscated when he argued that male soldiers were the "true heroes of the struggle." Neither he nor former president Taur Matan Ruak acknowledged that women bore arms, even though some did (Niner 2011, 424).[26]

The valorization of armed masculinity has had real material outcomes in East Timor. First, personal history as an armed warrior or least a high-ranking member of the resistance has become a prerequisite for political office. Thus, the ideal of armed masculinity has evolved in a civilian context to become a generalized notion of seniority, leadership, and entitlement associated with men in the liurai-dato class. Second, Timorese elites use this ideal to justify access to state resources in the form of pensions, construction projects, and so on, as I elaborate in Chapter 3. Because of the overlap between armed masculinity and the liurai-dato class, the power of men is not limited to their role as combatants. Instead, militarized masculinities intersect with other aspects of patriarchy.

Kimberley Hutching's (2008) insights are salutary here. She argues that the *relational position* of masculinity vis-à-vis femininity is most important to understanding gender ideologies. Although the ascribed qualities or content of what is masculine and feminine may vary, a fixed value hierarchy always exists between them. For this reason, she notes, it is necessary to look at the celebration of armed masculinity in relation to the construction, and denigration, of the excluded feminine. By arming vast numbers of men and marshaling them into military institutions, war "magnifies the distance between femininity and masculinity and enhances men's authority in a quantum leap" (Kronsell and Svedberg 2011, 23; Cockburn 2013). The valorization of armed masculinity is part of a value hierarchy that juxtaposes it with what is considered feminine (weak, dependent) and in need of (male) protection.

In Timor, militarization has had a significant impact on gender relations. In a feminist analysis, the logic of masculinist protection and its corollary of control was taken to an extreme during the war. One concrete way that Timorese and Indonesian armed men could control and denigrate women—as well as assert entitlement to sexual access to them—was through sexual and gender-based violence (SGBV). Thus, the celebration of armed masculinity and the denigration of victims of SGBV are two aspects of the same ideological hierarchy. Making this ideology explicit helps to explain the circumstances under which the Indonesian military and Timorese militia used SGBV to achieve political and military goals.

Conflict-Related Sexual and Gender-Based Violence

Historically, Timorese slaves, serfs, and bonded laborers were often low-ranked women. Women and girls were enslaved in large numbers, perhaps because they were useful in a greater variety of work roles than men, not only as agricultural workers but also as domestic workers, bearers of children, and sex workers., Timorese women and girls were also sexually exploited in the European-Timorese slave trade. Nineteenth-century French explorer Louis de Freycinet recorded in his diary that the physical appearance of Timorese female slaves determined their worth and that they and their families were sexually exploited (Gunn 1999, 46; Hägerdal 2012, 274; Patterson 2012, 335).

Other women and girls were kept purely as sexual slaves. At the turn of the nineteenth century, a Portuguese journalist accused Timor's governor da Suva of "maintaining, with the excuse of civilizing, harems [*serralhos*] in what he calls schools," indicating an early overlap between girls' educational institutions and institutionalized sexual violence on a large scale. This practice was repeated in turn by the Japanese and Indonesian militaries, both of which kept women as sex slaves in schools (Kammen 2003, 77; Matsuno and Oliviera 2016). The historical record thus points to the existence of institutionalized sexual exploitation and sexual violence linked to social hierarchies and the military.

In Timorese society, payment for female slaves overlapped with brideprice (a marriage payment from the groom's family to the bride's family). This is not unique. Globally, some 55 percent of societies that employ brideprice also hold slaves, and the use of brideprice more than triples the odds of finding institutional slavery (Patterson 2012, 337). In servile marriage—the relationship resembles slavery—a woman is given in marriage without her consent in exchange for payment to her kin. As a consequence of institutionalized slavery, the categories defining a woman as a war captive, a slave, or a bride become blurred because there is little to differentiate them in practice. Examining the comparable forms of slavery and brideprice, their co-occurrence, and the way they are mediated through kinship relations help to contextualize sexual slavery during the Indonesian occupation and reveal how conflict-related SGBV drew on existing unequal gender relations, including the gendered institution of slavery.

The Indonesian military used SGBV as a weapon of war variously to intimidate and dominate the broader Timorese population, as proxy violence against soldiers of the resistance, to control resources, and to break the guerrilla resistance (CAVR 2006, ch. 7). Early in the invasion, between 1975 and 1979, a pattern of gang rape during armed attacks emerged. Those who had initially fled to the mountains and then later surrendered or were captured were frequently raped, and women were often used as proxies for the intended target of violence. Gordon Peake and his colleagues describe a typical case in which Indonesian soldiers raped the wife of a pro-independence figure whom they had not managed to detain (Peake et al. 2014). The Indonesian military and the Timorese militia targeted the wives of resistance fighters in order to demoralize them. SGBV was also used to gain military intelligence. The Indonesian military kept the wives of guerrillas as sex slaves in order to communicate with their husbands in the bush and monitor their activities, and also employed sexual torture as a means to procure information (Aditjondro 1998, 206; CAVR 2006, 56–57). Conflict-related SGBV was about power and control: armed men's power over women's bodies and the Timorese population as a whole. One victim summed up the meaning of Indonesian military posts: "It is as if these posts, which were set up for security reasons, became in fact places where women were raped" (CAVR 2006, 18).

Following the practice of the Japanese troops who perpetrated sexual slavery in Timor during the Second World War—converting public buildings into military brothels known as *ianjo*—the Indonesian military also established institutions for sexual slavery. The detention of women for this purpose was done with the knowledge of the local military commander and supported logistically as part of standard military operations. Some women were imprisoned for extended periods in publicly visible institutions, such as schools or military bases, where Indonesian soldiers and Timorese militia repeatedly raped them (CAVR 2006, ch. 7).

Indonesian soldiers and Timorese militia men also forced women into relationships that mimicked marriages. During the occupation, a woman might "belong" to one man or several, or a soldier might live in her home and use her as a sexual slave. Women who were being held in either institutionalized or domestic sexual slavery were often compelled to perform household labor (Peake et al. 2014, 7). Some domestic sexual slavery was couched in terms of the existing practice of polygynous marriage, whereby sex slaves were second or third wives. One victim, fifteen at the time, described how a Timorese militia member had put a necklace around her neck and declared, "This is my war prize. As of now, she is my third wife" (CAVR 2006, 41). The perpetrator was thus echoing the practice of taking war captives as chattel slaves and secondary wives. Placing a necklace around her neck was an imitation of engagement and marriage ceremonies in which a groom puts necklaces on his bride (*tau korenti / tau morteen*) to signify their betrothal.

Thus, extant practices of slavery and polygyny shaped the form, institutionalization, and frequency of conflict-related sexual slavery in Timor. Conflict-related SGBV was an ongoing and unexceptional aspect of unequal gender relations (Davies and True 2015; True 2012). Likewise, armed men used the existing conventions of compensation and brideprice to enable and justify sexual slavery and sexual violence. Under the Japanese occupation, perpetrators are known to have paid a woman's family a "price" for her sexual slavery, imitating the exchange of women using brideprice.[27] During the later conflict, following a practice documented since the 1930s, victims of sexual violence or their families could obtain compensation in the rare case when a perpetrator of rape was called to account (CAVR 2006, 25; Nixon 2008, 316–320). For example, a Timorese militia member raped one woman repeatedly between 1998 and 1999. Eventually, his wife reported her husband to his commander, and the perpetrator was ordered to pay a fine to the family of the victim and to his own wife (CAVR 2006, 73). Compensation remains the usual form of punishment for SGBV in the courts and traditional dispute resolution today, as I explain in Chapter 4.[28] In cases of wartime domestic sexual slavery, parents had little choice but to allow their daughters to "marry" Indonesian military officers, and women were frequently exchanged to obtain security for the village or family (CAVR 2006, ch. 7, 69–70; Peake et al. 2014, 6–7). Again, the exchange of women as domestic sex slaves to prevent intergroup violence had historical precedents and was part of established patterns of gender inequality.

As is true of conflict-related SGBV generally, perpetrators could act with impunity because of the severe stigmatization of victims. Moreover, the weakest and most vulnerable—refugees, starving women, those who had lost their husbands and families, victims of other men's violence—were targeted, amplifying women's marginalization. Rape victims were seen as soiled, dishonorable, traitorous, or amoral, and perpetrators relied on their victims' feelings of shame to protect their identity. To the broader Timorese community, women who were sexually enslaved were considered to be taking goods and money for sex (Aditjondro 1998, 206).[29] Victims of SGBV could be blamed, shamed, revictimized, or rejected by their male partners, family members, and the wider community, and women who had been raped by soldiers were more likely to become "fair game" for sexual abuse by other men. In one case, a Timorese FALINTIL soldier raped a woman who was bringing food to the guerrillas, and one month later she was raped by the Indonesian armed forces for having helped the enemy (CAVR 2006, ch. 7). The social stigma attaching to victims, and the real socioeconomic effects of exclusion, abandonment, or spinsterhood, results in low levels of reporting in conflict zones (Ban 2012; Davies and True 2015). In Timor, it is not surprising that perpetrators could commit SGBV with impunity.

Perpetrating SGBV could in fact be a way to increase a man's rank or power. For instance, militia members, operation assistants (TBOs), or low-ranking civilian officials would "forcibly take women and pass them on to the military commanders in return for increased status and rewards with access to military power" (CAVR 2006, ch. 7). Further, armed men were often rewarded by being given free rein to commit sexual violence as compensation. As an illustration, FALINTIL commander Ular Rihi recalled how the Indonesian military directed him and fellow captors to watch pornographic films and invited them to rape girls with them, "as though this would win our hearts, as though we would think 'Wow, this is a really good life with the *Bapak* [Indonesian men]'" (Rihi 2009).

Occupation and Resistance

The Indonesian occupation also opened social and gender relations to transformation, but this represented an opportunity predominantly for elite women. The effects of the occupation on gender relations in Timor-Leste have been powerful and complex, as a number of authors have argued (Cristalis and Scott 2005; Joshi 2005; Niner 2016; Ospina 2006). In the first instance, the formation of FRETILIN and its women's wing, the Organização Popular da Mulher Timorense (OPMT), was a watershed. OPMT was crucial not only to the work of the armed and clandestine fronts but also to women's liberation. Female members of FRETILIN and OPMT saw themselves in a dual struggle against oppression, first as Timorese anticolonial nationalists and second as women seeking to end patriarchal practices, whether committed by Portuguese or by Timorese men in their homes and communities. Rosa "Muki" Bonaparte, who founded the Timorese women's movement, used the term *double exploitation* to describe the dual nature of patriarchal and colonial oppression (Loney 2015). Members of OPMT challenged gender relations by taking on roles previously reserved for male members of liurai families, such as teachers, health workers, and political educators. After these experiences, women in independent Timor-Leste were no longer prepared to subordinate themselves—and from their shared suffering, goals, and desire to transform gender relations, the women's movement was born.

In the early years of the resistance, however, women in the OPMT also took on established female roles, such as caring for orphans and the health and welfare of families in FRETILIN areas (Wigglesworth 2010). OPMT members offered "guidance" to village women and challenged prostitution (Budiardjo and Liong 1984, 204). Nonetheless, political representation of women in FRETILIN was initially very limited. In 1975 FRETILINs Central Committee had three female members out of fifty.[30] Further, these women were part of the Timorese elite, among the few with higher education (Wigglesworth 2010, 133). All were from liurai lineages and related to male members of the committee. Thus, although the struggle for Timorese women's liberation was both anticolonial and antitraditional, gender and class relations shaped FRETILIN—just as they continued to shape Timorese society as a whole in the postindependence period.

3
Class, Gender, and the Distribution of State Resources

A gulf exists in the Timorese economy, and income inequality is extraordinarily high (Sepulveda 2011). Driven by government spending, significant state resources from the petroleum revenues pool in Dili in the form of infrastructure and transfers to the wealthy, while the majority get by on subsistence and unpaid work. In times of acute crisis, such as the three-month-long annual hungry season, most households must survive on stored food before the first crops come in and families rely on the labor of women. Thus, the way in which state resources are shared matters for gender justice in Timor-Leste.

Inequitable distribution comes at the expense of budget areas that most benefit poor women and girls, such as water infrastructure, health, education, and food security. The impact on women is particularly significant because the burden of caring for others falls primarily on them. As Diane Elson showed early on, the extent of the care burden is directly related to macroeconomic policies, because state spending on areas such as health, education, and welfare reduces the onus on women to perform these key services (1993, 239). In times of crisis, the burden on women increases along with instances of domestic violence if state spending is reduced (Hozić and True 2016, 9). With one of the highest rates of poverty and deprivation in Asia and a rigidly gendered division of labor, in Timor the burden of care on non-elite women and girls is onerous (Asian Development Bank and UNIFEM 2005; Inder, Cornwell, and Datt 2015).

The nature of the independent Timorese state thus sets the context for attempts to introduce various gender interventions. The state itself—comprising and shaped by dominant classes in the Timor case—determines the types of institutions that emerge from it and how they are used, including institutions that implement gender interventions (Jones 2013, 70). Additionally, a very significant area of state resource distribution in Timor-Leste, and one that affects citizens directly, is cash transfers. Their origin holds a key to understanding the Timorese political economy.

The Politics of Cash Transfers

From 2007 to 2017 demobilization programs, including veterans' pensions, were heavily politicized and provided essential support for Xanana Gusmão's coalition. A statement in the program that was outlined by the incoming government in 2015 highlighted the obligation of the state to provide (certain) veterans with cash, indicating that they "rightfully" deserved the benefit and should be treated with "greater cordialness, deference and professionalism than ordinary citizens" (Democratic Republic of Timor-Leste 2015a). Veterans' pensions are a crucial, material part of statebuilding in a postconflict society, facilitating the reconstitution of military-era patrimonial networks. As Lia Kent and Naomi Kinsella (2015, 473) argue, the valorization of veterans uses a politics of memory for political gain and "promotes a culture of 'militarized masculinity' that elevates and rewards men who show the capacity to use violence." All told, cash transfers have been the single most significant political tool at the government's disposal to create alliances, reduce dissent, and gain legitimacy (Roll 2015, 121).

In Timor, cash transfers constitute 10 to 15 percent of the state budget. They include the veterans' pension (Pensaun Veteranu), the conditional cash transfer to mothers (Bolsa da Mãe), a disability pension, an ex-officeholders' pension (Pensaun Vitalisa), and "other personal benefits" paid by state agency employers to individual civil servants. Other than the Bolsa da Mãe, they are not means tested and do not come with any conditions. In 2016, $210 million, or about 13 percent of the budget, was paid out to individuals. Veterans alone took 5 percent of the budget, absorbing $104 million, compared to $47.1 million in other personal benefits, and $4 million in former officeholders' pensions (Lao Hamutuk 2016; Democratic Republic of Timor-Leste 2015b).

Cash transfers developed in response to the first decade of peacebuilding in Timor-Leste, which featured a number of security crises. Following the deployment of the International Force for East Timor, a multinational military intervention, the UN Transitional Administration in East Timor (UNTAET) acquired formal authority over Timor-Leste between October 1999 and May 2002. UNTAET was conceived as a maximalist form of statebuilding, with supreme authority over security and administration and a mandate to build new state institutions in line with international liberal standards. In other words, UNTAET used the model of liberal peace: establishing liberal democratic institutions, enforcing the rule of law, and creating liberal markets.

However, as a number of authors point out, in Timor-Leste UNTAET faced not a tabula rasa but a field of social conflict. Moreover, although UN missions positioned statebuilding rhetorically as starting from a blank slate, in fact institution building, development programs, and security employed Timorese people and had to use existing institutions and practices to achieve their goals (Hughes 2009; Jones 2010; Lemay-Hébert 2011; 2017; Richmond and Franks 2009).

After the first election, in August 2001 FRETILIN secured a fifty-five-seat majority among the eighty-eight Timorese members of the Second Transitional Government, and ruled with UNTAET in a co-governance model. FRETILIN secretary general Mari bim Amude Alkatiri was elected chief minister and his contemporary and rival, Alexandre Ray Kala "Xanana" Gusmão, was elected president. The division of positions between Alkatiri and Gusmão reflected long-standing factions in the Timorese resistance. Gusmão had led a majority of the FALINTIL guerrilla army in rejecting FRETILIN allegiance in the 1980s, an inter-elite rivalry that has been a decisive feature of Timorese politics in the four decades since. The restoration of Timorese independence was declared on May 20, 2002, and FRETILIN continued to lead the country.

In order to demobilize and reintegrate potential spoilers of peace in the new state, the first cash transfers for veterans were made during the UNTAET period under the internationally designed 2001–2002 FALINTIL Reinsertion Assistance Program (Roll 2015, 78). The program was designed and run by the International Organization for Migration (IOM) with support from Canadian and US aid agencies, and consisted of lump-sum payments of $1,060 each to 1,308 FALINTIL veterans. At the same time, then president Gusmão established special commissions to authenticate and verify veteran identity (Kent and Kinsella 2015, 480). The most involved donor was the World Bank, which contributed half a million dollars to the projects and received regular updates on progress (Kent 2006, 17). After the end of UNTAET's administrative control in 2002, however, the Timorese government changed its approach to veterans to focus on valorization, rather than demobilization and reintegration. Valorization rewarded individual veterans with money, government contracts, and jobs, based on the perceived worth of their service (Roll 2015, 89). Significantly, the four veterans' commissions from 2004 to 2006 were managed by the two former comrades-in-arms, Gusmão and Taur Matan Ruak. The commissions registered veterans who were considered most deserving of money, respect, and honor. Donor support for Gusmão to oversee both the veterans' commissions and security forces recruitment was instrumental in shaping who received money by way of valorization.

As Caroline Hughes has argued (2009, 134), in the early days of independence FRETILIN elites were squeezed between the conditionality of donor aid, which required market-driven development, and easily mobilized Timorese social forces that demanded redistributive policies. As the first government of independence, FRETILIN ran on a very tight, aid-dependent budget of a few hundred million dollars, while interveners spent conspicuously on salaries and accommodation. Donors mandated the creation of a Petroleum Fund to manage and save funds from the joint Timor/Australian gas development just south of Timor. Concurrently with Timorese independence, UNTAET was wound down and replaced with the much smaller, development-oriented Mission of Support (UNMISET). As UNTAET troops and staff withdrew, the economy contracted almost 40 percent, just as a famine hit the central highlands. While Dili underwent reconstruction, electricity and water supplies to most remote rural areas remained nonexistent (Chopra 2002; Goldstone 2013, 214; McWilliam 2011). In the context of these deficiencies and challenges, the relationship between the FRETILIN government and the United Nations deteriorated (Jones 2010, 559).

Although peacebuilders sought to demilitarize Timor and defuse FALINTIL claims on the state, many of those demobilized from FALINTIL expected to serve in the security forces (Hughes 2009, 104). In exchange for brokering the tense UN–Timorese government relationship, Gusmão was allowed to handle recruitment for the new defense forces, the Forças Defeza de Timor-Leste (F-FDTL), which he promptly staffed with allies from FALINTIL.[1] FRETILIN member Rogerio Lobato handled recruitment to the Poliçia Naçional de Timor-Leste (PNTL), however, and integrated three hundred members of the Indonesian-era police force into the new force. As these men were associated with the suppression of independence, tensions flared (International Crisis Group 2006, 22). Recruiting for both the army and the police excluded many who called themselves FALINTIL veterans, causing complaints (Scambary 2009b). The division of roles between the army and the police was also unclear, and since the interests of international groups in demobilization did not align with the interests of former guerrillas and others seeking employment in the security forces, demobilization was both partial and unsatisfactory (Hughes 2009, 104).

The strain between older ex-FALINTIL members, police officers, and F-FDTL recruits increased as UNMISET wound up in 2005–2006. As intra-elite rivalries intensified, competing politicians used the grievances over demobilization and security force "jobs for the boys" to their own advantage (Grindle 2012; Hughes 2009, 119). The tipping point came in 2006, when 156 F-FDTL members were sacked after unsuccessfully petitioning the government for changes to promotions and privileges. Police shot five demonstrators in the ensuing protests, causing violence to escalate. In fear of militia and gang violence, thousands of citizens again fled to the central mountains or over the border to West Timor. As a result, an expansive new military intervention, the Integrated Mission in East Timor (UNMIT), was launched in May 2006. Timor-Leste had gone from being a so-called UN peacebuilding success story to a "failed state" (Arnold 2009; Scambary 2009a). Although veterans had received some financial support for five years, disaffected veterans' factions and allied groups engaged in violent protests, clashes, and house burnings, culminating in what became known as the 2006–2007 crisis, a state of chaos fueled by disaffected politicians as well as veterans themselves. FRETILIN won the 2007 election by a slim majority but was unable to form a stable government in the face of political violence.

Eventually, President José Ramos-Horta nominated Gusmão to form the new government, and the latter's alliance took power. Still, violence undermined the stability of the government, and—with assassination attempts on both Ramos-Horta and Gusmão in 2008—veterans threatened the lives of key power brokers. The Timorese government sought to buy the peace and preserve itself by a variety of means.

The CNRT and the Reconstruction of Timor

Following the 2006–2007 crisis, Gusmão formed a coalition led by his new party, the Conselho Nacional de Reconstrução de Timor (CNRT; National Council for the Reconstruction of Timor). The CNRT began by remedying the years of austerity under peacebuilders and FRETILIN by using cash transfers and other state resources to gain the support of key constituencies—a pattern that continued throughout CNRT's three successive governments from 2007 to 2017. CNRT's tactic for obtaining political support was enabled by a massive increase in state revenues from gas fields in the Timor Sea, which began to be held in the Petroleum Fund from 2005 to 2006. Timorese citizens had seen their living standards decline, and their awareness of the new oil wealth increased public pressure on the Gusmão government to distribute it. Rather than offering a broad-based welfare program, however, the government chose to focus its largesse on veterans (Porter and Rab 2011, 5). The registers of veterans that various commissions had compiled were codified in a series of laws following the 2006–2007 crisis.[2] Under these laws the group of demobilized army veterans and gang members who fomented and participated in the crisis received individual grants of eight thousand dollars, and veterans' pensions were made much more generous. Veterans were also given expanded roles in the civil service, better health care, and infrastructure-building contracts averaging between five hundred thousand and one million dollars, as the National Program for Village Development (PNDS) was launched (International Crisis Group 2013, 3; Lao Hamutuk 2013).

During this period, international donors also supported aspects of payments for veterans, though they were wary of institutionalizing long-term claims on the state (Hughes 2009, 105; World Bank 2013). In addition to initiating small payments to demobilize FALINTIL before 2005, the IOM underwrote cash payments in programs to resettle internally displaced persons following the crisis, and donors also continued to provide funding for the veterans' commissions. From 2006, the United Nations Development Programme administered donor support. Allowing the Gusmão government to control cash transfers to veterans was one of the manifestations of a pragmatic local turn in peacebuilding. This approach received support from donors, underlined by the approval expressed by some peacebuilders and academics for the "charismatic," "unifying" hero Gusmão (Bexley and Nygaard-Christensen 2014; Kingsbury 2008).

Equally important to winning over key constituencies, in the 2012 legislative election the incumbent CNRT used state resources to win votes. To illustrate, on the second day of campaigning the CNRT coalition announced the expansion of veterans' payments to tens of thousands of voters, most of them men. The government then made payments totaling forty-seven million dollars, backdated to two weeks before the election (European Union Election Observation Mission 2012, 17). CNRT won with a convincing majority.

Overall, CNRT justified cash payments as necessary for peace, referring to the goal, articulated through numerous development plans, of ensuring stability by improving the economic position of "vulnerable" and "deserving" veterans (Democratic Republic of Timor-Leste 2011b, 8; 2015a; 2015b). At the same time, the government announced expansive infrastructure spending as part of a New Deal outlined in its 2011 Strategic Development Plan. The New Deal, also designed to consolidate political support, involved spending much of the budget on physical infrastructure such as roads, electricity, ports, and airports (Democratic Republic of Timor-Leste 2011b). The government and its supporters justified the big spending push by arguing that the state's role was to set the conditions for market-led development.[3] In 2016, for example, cash transfers and infrastructure spending on the free trade Special Zone of Social Market Economy (ZEESM) in Oecusse and the South Coast oil development project reached $475.775 million, just under a third of total government expenditure (Lao Hamutuk 2016; Democratic Republic of Timor-Leste 2015b).

Yet infrastructure projects have rarely been well executed in Timor-Leste, and observers increasingly consider them to be more about political patronage than development. Many projects have been awarded to influential veterans and their networks (Kingsbury 2017; Scambary 2015). Kate Roll describes the contract award process in a rural electrification project under the PNDS: "Contracts are awarded to a shell company registered in the names of former resistance members and tender processes are not required" (2015, 117). I documented similar cases of veterans receiving contracts for electrification in the Oecusse ZEESMs. Not only did prodigal spending on physical infrastructure benefit a relatively small number of people but corruption was particularly acute in these projects. According to data collected by the Timorese NGO Luta Hamutuk, only 30 percent of the money allocated was used to build infrastructure because of what is known as "KKN": corruption, collusion, and nepotism (Scambary 2015; *Timor Post* 2015f). Timor-Leste ranked 123 out of 175 countries in Transparency International's Corruption Perceptions Index for 2015, and the majority of the Timorese citizenry perceive their government to be corrupt.

As in other postconflict societies, giving spending priority to security, demobilization, and military restructuring as part of keeping or buying the peace has exacerbated gendered resource distribution in Timor-Leste. The valorization of armed masculinity—via preferential treatment for veterans—has helped elites to resolve ideological contradictions between a narrative of unified national liberation and the distribution of state resources to those same elites. It has also helped to consolidate the sociopolitical order.

Before describing the overlap of veteran status and the liurai-dato class, a note here on fieldwork methods for looking at social status and power in Timor is useful. Stark social hierarchy and control influenced how I conducted interviews. As I detail in the Methodological Notes, one of the key methodological issues in the field was trying to move beyond the patrimonial networks of influence to hear other voices. Over months of fieldwork, I developed strategies, including walking around with younger people (not older, elite men) so that people would not associate me and the team with the power brokers. I also tried to triangulate elite interviews with interviews with people who had no links to the village chiefs, or to our own patrons and gatekeepers. Another strategy was to note whether interviewees had relatives in the government and whether their families were Liurai or Dato. However, escaping patrimonial networks without someone to vouch for me seemed next to impossible. One reason was that I think interlocuters wanted to locate me in relation to someone, to some network, or better, to some family. And the authorities did too. On one field trip to the districts in Timor-Leste, my male research assistant was unwell and I decided to walk down to our field site on my own. *What was the harm?* I thought. *I had been walking around for over two weeks already.* Within half a day, the local police officer had come to ask me what I was doing and interrogated me informally on why I was asking about women's rights. In the end, our conversation turned into an interview on his work on domestic violence, but only after I had let him know that I was under the protection of a local member of parliament and he was vouching for me. A similar, but much scarier event happened in Indonesian West Timor when my male research assistant had to travel back to the capital unexpectedly. I had been interviewing former militia members from the war in East Timor when someone must have informed on us. At 9 p.m. several intelligence officers and police from the local command came to speak to me unexpectedly. The dogs barked like crazy and my host—a local village official and his wife—were genuinely worried. Only after the village official assured the officers that the local authorities were vouching for me did they leave.

These quite understandable constraints have implications for studying social status. As a result of my inability to move effectively beyond patrimonial networks, there is no real "view from outside" the system. Despite being an outsider to the Timorese social system, much of the critical perspective in the fieldwork data on social hierarchy comes from my observations and discussions, while positioned inside patrimonial networks.

Veteran Status and the Liurai-Dato

In the case of postconflict Timor, the distribution of state resources cannot be analyzed in terms of veteran identity alone. It is also shaped by class bias, and the overlap between liurai-dato status, veteran status, and position within the political/economic elite is complex. At the national level, high-ranking veteran identity overlaps with liurai or dato rank.[4] In other words, most leaders of the resistance belonged the liurai-dato class, and numerous prominent military and political figures are recorded as having liurai or liurai/mestiço family backgrounds (Guterres 2006;; Kammen 2016).[5] Earlier, throughout the Indonesian occupation, liurai and dato were military leaders for both pro-integration and pro-independence sides (Gunn 1999; Kammen 2016).

This association of militarized identity with political leadership has continued in the postindependence period, and most Timorese parliamentarians identify as members of the armed front (FALINTIL), the diplomatic front (FRETILIN, or the first CNRT), or the clandestine front (including, among other groups, the National Resistance of the Students of Timor-Leste, RENETIL). Francisco da Costa Guterres, who headed the secretariat of state for security under Gusmão from 2007 to 2015, claimed that FALINTIL veterans did not seek any political position or power due to their commitment to the group's principles of nonalignment (Guterres 2006, 235–236). In fact, veterans held a number of positions inside the government and in the diplomatic corps. For instance, former president Taur Matan Ruak was the last military commander of FALINTIL, until 1999, and commander of F-FDTL from 2002 to 2011. Former prime minster Rui Aráujo is from RENETIL, and former prime minister Xanana Gusmão was a FALINTIL commander. President Lú-Olo (2017–) belongs to FRETILIN and is also a former FALINTIL commander. Leaders of Dili-based militia and gangs during 2006–2007– who received substantial payouts and veterans' contracts—were from elite families, enjoying high levels of education as well as government and civil jobs (Scambary 2015, 290). The preeminence of military men, or those claiming veteran identity, thus had important implications for the distribution of state resources.

Pension Eligibility and Implementation

There are two aspects to class bias in veterans' pensions: in the design of eligibility criteria, and in the implementation of the scheme. With respect to the first, because pension rates are determined by seniority, rank (*grau*), and length of service, those able to claim the most money are elite. Historically, military rank (as well as political leadership) was determined by liurai and dato status, which determined access to resources, language proficiency, and literacy, and gave such men the hereditary right to rule. Thus, many top resistance leaders and those able to serve exclusively were men of the liurai-dato class. Lieutenants, captains, and other high-ranked members of the resistance therefore receive larger pensions than ordinary-ranked guerrillas and support staff. As one member of the parliament explained, "*Grau* 1, 2, 3 . . . signifies the person's work in the liberation, work in the resistance, which determines the amount of money."[6] Only a handful of men receive $345 to #575 per month (BELUN 2013; Roll 2015; World Bank 2013), and just fifteen prominent male figures receive the most generous lifetime pension of $750 per month (International Crisis Group 2013).

The elite-focused criteria for pensions contradicts the widespread view of Timorese that they contributed—indeed determined—the outcome of independence through their vote (Timor Post 2015d). The distribution of state resources to former guerrillas is seen as unfair for a number of reasons. In the first place, the war was idealized as a nationalist struggle in which Indonesian invaders were resisted by a united Timorese nation (Carey 2003). Because of the broad-based nature of the clandestine movement, all Timorese believe they contributed in some way to the resistance, and citizens see themselves as veterans of the struggle. Over one hundred thousand people registered for a veterans' pension, yet only a relatively small number have received one, around eleven thousand people in 2014 (Dale, Lepuschuetz, and Umapathi 2014; World Bank 2013, 3). The distribution of infrastructure spending and pensions to politically well-connected elites has met with widespread discontent, coming in for criticism from activists, media commentators, and academics (BELUN 2013; International Crisis Group 2013; Kent and Wallis 2013; Lao Hamutuk 2013; 2016; Roll 2015; Scambary 2015; *Timor Post* 2015a; 2015c; 2015e; 2015g). The nongovernmental organization (NGO) Lao Hamutuk has been especially critical of government spending that benefits only a few.

A second form of class bias is evident in the implementation of veterans' pensions. Being awarded veteran status—and thus a pension—does not depend on the key legal criterion of actual years of service, or "exclusive service," but in most cases on the claimant's position within patronage networks. For example, most high-level commissioners added their family members to the list of combatants, even when those relatives were not in the resistance (Roll 2015, 198).[7]

This pattern of elite capture exists not just within the Dili-based political elite but also in rural areas. Rural bureaucrats assigned to register veterans' pension are also members of the liurai-dato class, because veteran status overlaps with the role of village chief, which overlaps with membership in higher-ranked lineages (Cummins and Leach 2012, 99; Gusmão 2012, 184–185; Roll 2015, 135–136). During the war, leaders of the village-based network Nucleos de Resistencia Popular (NUREP) were elected, under a FALINTIL commander's supervision, by hamlet leaders. These male village leaders were often from liurai or dato families (Cummins and Leach 2012, 99). In rural districts in the postindependence era, FALINTIL-linked bureaucrats in charge of pensions often misrepresented an applicant's length of service. Doing such favors—"from the verandah," as Roll calls it—allows local military-linked bureaucrats to build their networks. Determining who is counted as a veteran therefore marks what she refers to as "the continuation of patronage politics along resistance-era lines and the conservation of these power networks in the post-conflict period" (Roll 2015, 194).

Thus, rather than entrenching a perception of veterans (and their families) as a privileged social group by virtue of their veteran status, pensions were allocated to an *already* privileged social group (Wallis 2015, 244). In other words, cash transfers distribute wealth to the already wealthy. Altogether the transfers—in the form of veteran, disability, and old age pensions—reach 23 percent of the population in the richest quintile. More than half of those below the poverty line do not receive any payment at all; the 61 percent who occupy the bottom two quintiles—and 56 percent of the poorest 20 percent of the population—receive no assistance from the main cash transfer programs (World Bank 2013, 50). In sum, the pattern of control over resources at the subnational level reflects historical patterns of accumulation.

Class bias in favor of the liurai-dato is most apparent in the distribution of pensions to members of the unarmed clandestine movement, some of whom receive the benefit while many others do not (Kent and Wallis 2013). Senior bureaucrat Eugenio, who works in the Oecusse ZEESMs, gives an example: "My father is a member of the so-called veterans. It means he participated. I don't want to say he's a veteran, because in different countries this has a different meaning. My father didn't get a gun and go into the wild to fight the Indonesians. He was a key member of the clandestine movement."[8] According to Eugenio's mother, his father receives a pension because he was a member of the political resistance.[9] In addition, he is also a member of a historically influential liurai family, which I suggest is the decisive factor in his veteran status.

Thus, some liurai-dato men gain access to a pension without having physically fought, but many other members of the resistance, especially women, have never received one. The valorization approach to pensions is biased in favor of a few men of the liurai-dato class, making status the crucial factor in determining eligibility.

Enforcing the Political Order

The distribution of resources to veterans also plays a significant role in holding together coalitions of urban and rural liurai-dato and in enforcing the political order. Two examples illustrate this: the village chief elections in 2009, and the government's use of veterans to resolve disputes over development.

Elections at the village level after 2005 were not supposed to involve political parties, but direct observation reveals that the village remains an arena of political mobilization along party lines. In 2009, payments to veterans helped them to campaign for local village leadership or to support candidates of their choice and organize the rank and file. Shortly before the village chief elections that year, Gusmão's government altered the veterans' pension law to make one-off payments of $1,380 to over 15,500 individuals who had been classified as ineligible for ongoing pensions. The payments demonstrated the willingness of Gusmão's government to offer support to veterans and help them mobilize resources (Roll 2015, 103, 138). Veterans' campaigning was also aided by the politicization of militarized hierarchies that inhibited members from opposing the policies of their commanders (Guterres 2006, 235). Thus, payments to veterans constitute an important material link between the Dili-based and rural members of the liurai-dato class.

In social conflicts over land use and rapidly expanding infrastructure development projects, veterans are often called in to resolve problems and thus to enforce the political order. Traditional dispute resolution favors male power holders of the liurai-dato class. It is commonplace for the government to enlist liurai-dato veterans to ameliorate conflicts between infrastructure project developers and ordinary Timorese citizens using so-called traditional dispute resolution. A female village secretary in Oecusse described the process arising when the community resisted the regional government's attempts to develop land for ZEESMs: "Village chiefs and hamlet chiefs use *adat* [tradition]. For example, in ZEESMs, when they meet with people who don't like ZEESMs, they take the *katua adat* [elder] with them. When you are going to do something, to implement ZEESMs, to build roads, *adat* helps with the development. They have done this many times to implement development. It helps a lot with the socialization of the ZEESMs program."[10]

A clear example arises again from the case of Eugenio's father, a ZEESM bureaucrat and a *naizuf* who also received a veterans' pension.[11] ZEESMs employed him as a traditional mediator on the government side in land disputes. Numerous disputes have arisen during the construction of roads, ports, and airports in the ZEESMs. People have been removed from their homes and had their gardens and agricultural lands seized to make way for new roads. In response to my casual questions about such conflicts, Eugenio's father stated that *ema kiik* (little people, i.e., ordinary citizens) were not knowledgeable. He reported that during dispute negotiations, citizens had told him keeping their land was a human right, but in his view human rights were different from cultural rights. He further argued that if people wanted development, they must expect to sacrifice their land.[12] His case illustrates the role of members of the liurai-dato class in suppressing dissent and mediating complaints, in turn allowing the government to proceed with road building and land clearing for the free trade zones, sometimes without compensating landowners (*Journal Independente* 2017).

Anecdotally, people in Oecusse have rarely been compensated for land taken for development projects.[13] In a similar example, Roll also observed the mobilization of veteran authority for political ends in rural areas in 2011. Gusmão met with veterans regarding the government's rural electrification program under the National Program for Village Development (PNDS), which at the time consumed a controversially large proportion of the budget. One of Roll's interviewees said that veterans drew on their status and used intimidation to ensure communities that lost land would not make claims for compensation. In return for their role as enforcers, veterans were rewarded with contracts to install the infrastructure on the electrification projects (International Crisis Group 2006, 14; Roll 2015, 120; Scambary 2015). The overlaps and links between veteran status, liurai-dato heritage, and government employment and contracting reveal the concentration of power in the hands of certain elite families.

These families dominate government jobs, which are the primary source of cash in rural districts. To look again at the typical case of Eugenio, many members of his family are employed in the Oecusse public service. Eugenio's cousin, for example, is a program director at the Secretariat of State for Vocational Training and Employment (SEFOPE) and earns a seventy-eight-hundred-dollar annual salary, around twenty times the average annual income (Democratic Republic of Timor-Leste 2016). In response to a question about his family's work in the civil service, Eugenio suggested, "Are you asking me if I am from a dynasty? My family here is in the government or the private sector or politicians—but is it because of their exposure to education?"[14] Like many members of his class, Eugenio is uncomfortable speaking about class hierarchy, preferring to ascribe his family's preeminent position in the state and access to its resources to educational achievement.

Gender and Cash Transfers

While class bias is a significant factor, the veterans' pension—indeed the entire cash transfer system—also has a well-documented and inbuilt gender bias. The length-of-service criterion eliminates both non-elites and women from claims to veteran status, because they worked as subsistence farmers or cared for dependents during the war. As women were largely excluded from military leadership roles, their lack of rank also disqualifies them from generous pensions. Even female leaders were initially excluded from the veterans' commission, on the grounds that they had held political rather than military positions (Kent and Kinsella 2015, 480). The valorization of armed masculinity is a lens through which women's work in war becomes invisible (Kent and Wallis 2013). Roll heard a succinct description of the pension criteria: "'If you didn't carry a gun, you don't get money'" (2015, 94).

Members of Timorese women's organizations lobbied against the narrow definition of "veteran," and the law was amended in 2009 to allow women to receive pensions. Still, only 13.5 percent of veterans' pensions go to women, and most receive it on behalf of a deceased male relative. They also receive the lowest level of pension, around $230 a month (Kent and Kinsella 2015, 481; Roll 2015, 104).

The Devaluation of Suffering and Labor

The desire to prevent further claims on the state is particularly apparent in the avoidance of reparation payments to those who were victims of SGBV during the Indonesian occupation. Most significantly, reparation recommendations made by the Commission for Truth and Reconciliation and Reception (CAVR) in 2006 have not been acted upon, despite ongoing lobbying (Asia Justice and Rights 2017). In independent Timor-Leste, veteran status is privileged whereas victim status is marginalized, as numerous scholars have noted, echoing the question that Timorese women leaders like Maria Domingues-Alves posed: why is it that men who are tortured by military forces are seen as the heroes, while women who are tortured (and raped) are seen as traitors (Harris-Rimmer 2010, 125; Kent 2016; Rothschild 2017)? Again, what we find is a deliberate strategy of associating men with heroism and armed masculinity and women with victimhood and—because of the stigma attached to widespread sexual violence—treachery (Kent 2016). When I was in the field in 2015, some of those I interviewed voiced this kind of sentiment, as Serafina, a village secretary, articulates: "Veterans get more money than women or victims of violence because the government thinks more of the heroes because they fought in the war."[15] A masculinist lens is blind to the fact that SGBV was used as a weapon of war: an explicit war strategy with material costs and benefits. Many of the women subjected to SGBV were targeted precisely because of their involvement with the resistance.

An unequal and gendered division of labor provides another avenue to devalue women's wartime contributions and justify their exclusion from a share of state resources. Therefore, gender relations are a key ideological aspect of how the dominant class secures its position in independent Timor-Leste. Former president and current prime minister Taur Matan Ruak has stated that women "just sat there" during the war (Kent and Wallis 2013). This perspective renders invisible women's crucial role in feeding, clothing, protecting, and working in the scattered guerrilla resistance and the clandestine movement. Overlooking and diminishing the value of women's work is part and parcel of the commonplace gender order. Again, village secretary Serafina questioned the government's plans for "veterans getting even more money because women are on the receiving end of violence and they have the children. I don't understand the government."[16] As she suggests, determining who deserves state resources by dividing victims from veterans is incomprehensible to women who watch their labors and suffering go unacknowledged.

The Bolsa da Mãe

Another cash transfer, the Bolsa da Mãe, was introduced in 2008 as a part of the New Deal targeted at women. For policymakers, the program's focus on vulnerable women defined it as an intervention to increase gender equality and reduce poverty (da Cruz 2014, 19). This claim ignores that although the recipients were mothers, the targeted beneficiaries were their children. As such, how the cash transfer was supposed to increase gender equality—here equated with "better" mothering outcomes— is not clear.

Unlike the veterans' pension, Bolsa da Mãe is means-tested and conditional. It is given only to single and widowed mothers with children up to age seventeen (UN Women 2015a). Like the Pensaun Veteranu, the program was run by the Ministry of Social Solidarity under the National Directorate for Social Reinsertion (DNRS). The aim was to reduce intergenerational poverty and improve education outcomes by giving a small amount of cash to vulnerable households. Similar conditional cash transfers have been rolled out by donors and governments in many countries, with the broad logic that making transfers conditional on school attendance would reduce poverty because "higher levels of education will ultimately translate into higher salaries and better jobs and thus break the intergenerational transmission of poverty" (Ulrichs and Roelen 2012).[17]

A comparison of state spending on the Bolsa da Mãe and Pensaun Veteranu highlights the significant and ongoing gender injustice embedded in the allocation of state resources. In 2011, veterans received between $2,760 and $9,000 per year (World Bank 2013, 3). Bolsa da Mãe, in contrast, paid between $60 and $180 annually. In 2015, the *minimum* pension for a living veteran was $3,312 a year, over forty times the average Bolsa da Mãe payment of $80 per year, and the top pension is more than ten times the per capita monthly non-oil gross domestic product (GDP) (Fernandes 2015, n26, 116). Even measured in terms of the very modest Timorese national poverty line of less than $0.88 per capita per day, the Bolsa da Mãe payment didn't put a household above the line and therefore cannot be regarded as having effectively reduced poverty. Moreover, the program paid $5 per child up to a maximum $15 per month, although most families have more than three children.[18] In rural areas, interviewees suggested that the high price of goods meant the program did not help the most vulnerable.[19] At the individual level, receiving a veteran's pension puts a household far above the poverty line, while Bolsa da Mãe barely helps a family to survive.

In terms of the national budget, a vast gulf exists between the two programs, as Figure 3.1 shows. The budget for Bolsa da Mãe was $9 million in 2014, compared to $90 million for Pensaun Veteranu, and in 2016 veterans' payments were again tenfold the spending for vulnerable mothers.[20]

Veterans' pensions have accounted for an average 5 percent of the total state budget since 2008. Moreover, they consumed 60 percent of the Ministry of Social Solidarity 2015–2016 budget.[21]

Bolsa da Mãe ought to have been strongly associated with the enactment of gender justice through the distribution of state resources to the most vulnerable. Yet its inadequacy and small size relative to the veterans' pension reflect deep-seated social and gender inequalities. Illustrating dissatisfaction with cash transfers, a 2015 Timorese NGO shadow report to the Convention on the Elimination of all Forms of Discrimination Against Women (CEDAW) complained, "In the current 2015 State Budget, US$130.4 million has been allocated to cash payments to veterans, out of a total US$176.4 million allocated to the entire social welfare program. Women are marginalised from the veterans' pension scheme and the very low investment in other social welfare programs for the poorest households has a disproportionate impact on women. This is only one example of the cumulative failure to address inequalities between women and men through Government policy" (JSMP, PRADET, and ALFeLa 2015, iii).

Although the program was aimed at vulnerable women (single mothers, widows and mothers with low incomes), the same problems of elite capture seen in veterans' pensions befell Bolsa da Mãe. Over the duration of the program, about 40 percent of recipients did not meet the qualitative criteria stipulated by the law: public servants, wives of village chiefs, and veterans' families who were not eligible were given the monthly stipend(da Cruz 2014, 21; Fernandes 2015).[22]

One reason is that the public servants and village chiefs responsible for disseminating information about Bolsa da Mãe and choosing beneficiaries co-opted the program, as commissioners have done with respect to veterans' pensions (da Cruz 2014, 21; World Bank 2013). Information failed to reach the community level, especially in remote areas, and very few poor women I interviewed in rural communities had even heard of the program. Even fewer had received payment, despite meeting the criteria. Deep social inequalities are thus reflected in the targeting, outcome, and susceptibility to corruption of Bolsa da Mãe, just as they are in veterans' pensions.

Extensive elite capture of all the cash transfer programs points to the centrality of state resources in securing the political order. Across all the programs, there has been significant leakage of monies to nonveterans and the nonpoor. While often portrayed as a technical problem of implementation, Roll argues that the state plays a key role in deciding who has access (see

Dale, Lepuschuetz, and Umapathi 2014 and World Bank 2013, *contra* Roll 2015, 17). I go further, suggesting that the state itself comprises members of the liurai-dato class who shape the implementation of these programs to their benefit. Gender and class thus intersect over the distribution of state resources. In response, gender-responsive budgeting was introduced in Timor-Leste in an effort to tackle gender bias in the distribution of state resources.

The Case of Gender-Responsive Budgeting

Gender-responsive budgeting (GRB) has two goals: to remedy the distribution of state resources and to make gender a mainstream aspect of budgetary policy. GRB is a tool of analysis and planning for budgetary policy, based on the idea that policies that contribute to women's well-being and increase women's empowerment ought to be well funded by the state, while policies that detract from women's well-being, or amplify men's power or gender inequality, ought not to be funded. This approach results in a budget that is responsive to areas requiring more gender equality. GRB can include the creation of new, costed policies; funding commitments to national action plans on gender and women's empowerment; and accountability mechanisms to ensure that money is spent where it has been committed. Another aim of GRB is to create gender-disaggregated data and time-use statistics in order to improve the quality of information on the gendered nature of the economy (UNIFEM 2009).

As feminist economic analysts have long argued, the gendered distribution of state resources sustains generalized impoverishment and gender inequality (Elson 1993). GRB has been promoted by international donors since the 1990s because the highly gendered nature and impact of decision-making regarding taxation policies and the distribution of public financial resources are increasingly recognized (Costa 2018; UNIFEM 2009, 17). Overall, then, GRB seeks to make governments accountable for ensuring that their budgets promote gender equality and women's rights, especially among the poor. Many countries have piloted GRB initiatives, but few have proceeded to implementation (Costa 2018, 16).

Timor-Leste has implemented a few GRB-related initiatives with the overall goal of making the national budget more responsive to gender inequality (Democratic Republic of Timor-Leste 2010c). Their introduction was linked to two other gender interventions: increasing women's national political participation, including via gender quotas for parliament; and, subsequently, creating the Group of Women Parliamentarians in Timor-Leste (henceforth referred to as the Women's Cross-Party Caucus). The first effort to mainstream gender in budgetary decision-making, as a precursor to GRB, took the form of an attempt to establish a standing parliamentary commission for gender affairs, equality, and children. The enabling legislation went before parliament in 2004 and was defeated, reportedly because some parliamentarians considered the proposal to be discriminatory against men (Soetjipto 2014, 34). The defeat showed that introduction of GRB would be difficult. Subsequently, the Timorese parliament did pass a resolution to include gender equality, but as one of several areas presided over by Parliamentary Commissions E (2007–2012) and F (2012–2017).[23]

Next, UN Women held workshops on GRB with the national parliament and the United Nations Development Programme in 2008. Following the workshops, Gusmão's government included gender budget statements in the 2008 and 2009 budgets (Costa 2018, 3). Such statements are documents or sections of documents that highlight how budget spending or revenue promotes gender equality (Budlender 2015). The 2009–2010 Gender and Culture Statement urged consideration of gender in formulating departmental annual action plans. The aim of GRB in this case was to mainstream gender across the policies and programs of government departments.

In 2010, parliament next instituted a gender-sensitive budget, issuing Resolution No. 12/2010 to support the move. In the same year, then-president José Ramos-Horta issued Presidential Decree No. 13/2010, urging the Timorese government, through the Ministry of Finance, to implement budgetary policy rules that took gender equality into account. Again, male parliamentarians initially resisted, arguing that it could be construed as giving special treatment to women and thus in fact be contrary to gender equality (Costa 2015, 107). The resolution text justified the measure by noting that gender equality considerations contribute to "growth and prosperity" and therefore help Timor-Leste to reach its social and economic objectives. Nevertheless, Resolutions 12/2010 and 13/2010 interpreted gender as an essentialized sex difference; in other words, it assumed that women and men had different concerns and needs (Democratic Republic of Timor-Leste 2010a; Democratic Republic of Timor-Leste 2010c). These resolutions did not see gender as involving power relations and therefore did not address this issue. Further, the resolution explicitly *precluded* creating separate budget lines (*rubrica orçamental separada*), which limited the ability to conduct gender-disaggregated spending. Consequently, the line budget did not match programs, and linking budgets to particular gender-related activities involved a great deal of follow-up.[24] Likewise, the process of translating gender equality into detailed policy and budget allocations encountered resistance (Costa, Sharp, and Austen 2009).

Throughout the 2007–2017 period, gender mainstreaming of budgets—ensuring that spending policy addressed gender equality—was conducted primarily by parliamentary institutions such as the Women's Cross-Party Caucus, Commissions E and F, and the government's gender equality office, the Secretariat of State for the Support and Socio-Economic Promotion for Women (SEM). The Women's Cross-Party Caucus introduced, implemented, and monitored gender mainstreaming in national institutions (see Table 1.2). One of the main roles of the caucus was to advocate for gender-sensitive policies in parliament and parliamentary commissions, and for proper implementation of already introduced policies.[25] Currently, SEM, not the more powerful finance ministry, reviewed the action plans accompanying each ministry's budget, making GRB of ministries' budgets a limited and internal process (Democratic Republic of Timor-Leste 2014, 77).

The gender budget statements accompanying each budget did not continue. Instead, the Timorese parliament established the Gender Working Group (distinct from the earlier UN-created Gender and the Law Working Group) in 2011 to use GRB tools to monitor budget spending and implementation, in cooperation with the Women's Cross-Party Caucus. The group comprised Timorese women's organizations and received technical assistance from UN Women to examine the drafting and execution of the national budget.[26] At this point, then, the involvement of civil society organizations meant that GRB became a "social accountability" tool to hold public officials answerable for their behavior (Rodan and Hughes 2012, 367). On the parliamentary side, the Women's Cross-Party Caucus was established by parliament in 2007 to introduce, implement, and monitor gender mainstreaming in national institutions (see Table 1.2). One of the main roles of the Women's Cross-Party Caucus was advocacy in parliament and parliamentary commissions for gender-sensitive policies, and for proper implementation of already introduced policies.[27] In tandem, the Gender Working Group and UN Women used GRB to monitor government departmental action plans on gender-sensitive spending. The working group evaluated budgets and spending with reference to an existing system under which departmental director generals had responsibility as "gender focal points";

that is, the director would report to SEM regarding the implementation of gender-sensitive budgets.[28] Since gender budget statements to parliament stopped in 2010, however, GRB has become more internal, technocratic, and ineffective, mirroring reductions in budget transparency across the board (Lao Hamutuk 2016, 3).

Civil society–based monitoring separate from parliamentary procedure has not able to achieve concrete gender-sensitive budgeting. As one member of the Gender Working Group put it in 2015, civil society involvement is in fact just a process of rubber-stamping the budget: "They just ask us to come and give input at the end. It is just a formality. They do not implement it."[29] This recalls other examples of the limitations of participatory budgeting in Southeast Asia, where civil society energies have been directed largely toward demanding technical and administrative measures to improve governance (Rodan and Hughes 2012, 372). Equally, the 2015 NGO report to CEDAW complains that government gender-equality measures have not been concerned with effecting real change. Chiefly, "While the Government expresses its commitment to gender mainstreaming through various gender-working groups and gender-responsive budgeting, successive budgets since 2009 have not included any gender equality impact assessments" (JSMP, PRADET, and ALFeLa 2015). Thus, despite rhetorical support, for the most part there has been little real accountability with respect to the outcomes of GRB.

Why Does Gender Responsive Budgeting Disappoint?

An oft-cited shortcoming of GRB is lack of "capacity." Institutions or analsysts are said to lack the technical skills to be able to perform gender responsive budgeting. However, but this is frequently "accompanied by and can be a screen for—political resistance" (Budlender 2015, 41). The orthodox view among economists working on postconflict states is that a complex policy tool like GRB is incompatible with postconflict states' characteristic lack of capacity, and should be postponed until a state is more stable and prosperous (Costa 2018). Although technical and informational barriers exist, I believe other factors are more crucial. Poor outcomes in Timor-Leste have stemmed from an unwillingness to introduce and implement GRB, or the necessary strategic compromises and prioritization, and from the outright capture of state resources by the liurai-dato class.

Male Resistance

Advocates for progressive gender reform in Timor-Leste have regularly faced opposition to lobbying for more resources for women, even from within the ministries that women's organizations consider to be receptive to gender equality. One gender advocate recalls a conversation about what she saw as disproportionate spending on veterans compared to victims of violence. This advocate's opinion was that many male legislators and ministers alike ignored or sidelined the plight of women, especially victims of violence.[30] The former vice minister of Social Solidarity, one of the ministries most friendly to gender perspectives, responded to her regarding the issue of reparations to female victims of violence: "I do not agree with these points about gender equality."

Knowing that their agenda is contentious and that male decision-makers are likely to oppose them if they take an explicitly feminist approach, Timorese women's organizations must moderate or reframe their argument. For instance, one gender advocate reported telling male parliamentarians and bureaucrats that gender is "simply" about women making their own decisions because women's and men's experiences are not the same, explaining, "But we do not say feminist, because if this enters into the conversation, they say we are against men. They say we want women to be able to do anything they want. Sometimes in Timor, they see the word *feminist* as too extreme.... That is why you still have to have the NGOs who understand these problems. The view is that feminism is something bad."[31]

Legal anthropologist Sally Merry explains it in the following terms. When local women's organizations take up international norms on women's human rights, they need to "translate" them for a domestic context, a process whereby "new ideas are framed and presented regarding existing cultural norms, values, and practices" (Merry 2006, 39). In this view, translation from global to local contexts results in a hybrid feminist discourse, which, by drawing on authentic local tradition, is more legitimate and thus makes feminist actions more effective. While this accords with ideas embodied in the local turn, I interpret it as a political strategy rather than a translational act. When Timorese women's groups avoid using the term "feminist," they are entering political compromises with male decision-makers to avoid being branded anti-men. Reframing the argument downplays challenges to male power, but it may also secure some victories. As an illustration, in the face of disappointing GRB outcomes, the Gender Working Group and the Women's

Cross-Party Caucus have made a strategic decision since 2011 to focus only on the budget for the implementation of the 2010 LADV (Costa 2018).

Technical Constraints

Technical constraints stemming from a lack of data also come up frequently in discussions of GRB in Timor-Leste. A member of the Gender Working Group confirms the lack of data and line responsibility that obstructed efforts to monitor spending on the LADV. Only two out of seven responsible line ministries (the Secretariat of State for Security and the Ministry of Social Solidarity) could show her how they had spent money allocated to the LADV. This is significant because the working group has focused on this type of monitoring since 2011. Spending by the Secretariat of State for Security, which has a budget allocated to the Vulnerable Persons' Unit (VPU; a special police unit for GBV victims), is easily traceable, but in the ministries of Education and Health, and Justice,

> They simply said this money is for the implementation of the LADV, and there was no line budgeting. . . . After a year of implementation, we asked Justice, for example, how much is allocated for training on anger management for the prisoners? And they said they did not know how much they allocated. They told us to ask Finance, but they did not know. Then we asked the Director General, who led the gender working group in each ministry, but sometimes they are very busy. And then we asked for their spending data, which is a difficult thing for them. We [the Gender Working Group] also don't have time to look at that.[32]

Thus, there was a disconnect between budget allocation, planning, and expenditure in some ministries, even though departmental directors general, as gender focal points, were responsible for implementing GRB.[33]

More problematically, spending earmarked for measures to improve women's access to security under the LADV, for instance, was used for other items on an ad hoc basis. The Gender Working Group member continued, "Then, there is a conflict between areas of spending in the budget. The departments prioritize other things. They might have marked it for the LADV, but then they put it into other things. There's a new priority."[34] Reallocation of funds suggests not merely an inability to track item expenditures but a more general problem of commitment to gender-related funding, even in departments that notionally prioritize gender.

Corruption and Transparency

Another and related reason for poor GRB outcomes is that tracking spending is not merely a technical issue. Lack of transparency and state capacity merge with corruption, social hierarchy, and gender ideology. Coupled with political competition for state resources, lack of transparency leads to limited implementation of GRB. Spending is the real issue, as the budget for the Vulnerable Persons' Unit (VPU), the frontline police unit in implementation of the LADV, clearly illustrates. In a review of the national police (PNTL) budget, the Gender Working Group recommended that the VPU receive a new vehicle to serve GBV victims in a particular rural district. The government granted the request. When the vehicle was delivered, however, the male police commander of the district simply took the car. When the group complained to the line ministry, the Secretariat of State for Security, the minister told the group that his department could not order the commander to return the car because his action was part of "the hierarchy, the structure" of the PNTL.[35]

It is undeniably the spending, not just the budgeting, of state resources that makes their distribution so uneven. Spending is accomplished according to the interests of dominant members of social and gender hierarchies.

Class Factors

Further, because GRB advocates are largely from the liurai-dato class, any radical redistribution of state resources to poor women is constrained.[36] As during the Portuguese and Indonesian periods, membership in the liurai-dato class can be used as leverage to gain jobs and resources at the national level in government and political parties—and in NGOs. Because the liurai-dato class dominates paid employment in the public and NGO sectors in Dili, that elite also tends to dominate the Timorese women's movement. For example, Maria Maia dos Reis e Costa, a member of parliament (MP) from 2007 to 2012, was the daughter of a liurai in Baucau (Loney 2015). Ilda Maria da Conceição, a FRETILIN MP from 2001 to 2007 and reelected in 2017, was the daughter of a liurai in Viqueque. Female liurai-dato also fill better-paid jobs in Timorese women's organizations and NGOs, paralleling male liurai-dato dominance of military and government jobs. Notably, a meaningful number of women's NGO leaders are direct descendants of liurai. For example, a president of the Rede Feto umbrella organization for women's NGOs is the granddaughter of a liurai of Baucau. And Laura Pina Menzes Lopes, of the liurai of Maubisse, led PATRIA, an organization that works with UN Women to raise women's political participation. After the 2017 election, Lopes entered parliament as a FRETILIN candidate and became secretary of state for gender equality and social inclusion. Another liurai descendant heads a prominent Timorese microfinance organization and is also a political party member. Significantly, like their male counterparts, most female members of parliament—about 70 percent, according to one source—were members of the resistance.[37]

As a result of their patriarchal bargain with men of their class, members of women's organizations and female parliamentarians have not always challenged the gender injustice embedded in cash transfers. As members of the liurai-dato class, which overlaps with resistance and political party leadership, women working on GRB can benefit from the current distribution of state resources. Quite often, women in both parliament and civil society either receive the veterans' pension on behalf of a family member or have a male family member who does so (Kent 2016). Members of the Timorese women's movement have at times adhered to an ideology that valorizes armed masculinity, even while they are sidelined within it.

Omissions from Gender-Responsive Budgeting

GRB has not yet been used to reduce the gender injustice inherent in cash transfer programs administered by the Ministry of Social Solidarity (see Figure 3.1). In that sense, the aim of GRB to mainstream gender in government policies and departmental programs has not worked, but a female member of parliament makes the case that different types of cash transfer cannot be linked or compared: "You cannot say, 'This person was a victim of Indonesia, nor was a victim of some other kind of violence.' For the veterans' pensions, we do not look at whether someone was a victim in the past." She suggests that the needs of vulnerable women were instead being met through the Bolsa da Mãe and, understandably, that progress on poverty reduction could not happen overnight.[38] The issue of prioritizing cash transfers to veterans over support for SGBV victims or other vulnerable women thus seems to find little traction within the Women's Cross-Party Caucus.

Another area of state spending with considerable gendered impacts has not been part of GRB. Physical infrastructure projects such as the ports, airports, roads, oil refineries, and hotels built in Timor-Leste since 2007 have been politicized and turned into an aspect of patrimonial networking. For example, Gusmão has been personally responsible for spending on a series of hundred-million-dollar projects, first under the National Program for Village Development (PNDS) (2012–2015) and then as infrastructure minister (2015–2017). Surprisingly to some, his rival from FRETILIN, Alkatiri, was given responsibility for the massive project to develop the physical infrastructure that would enable Oecusse to become a free trade zone.

The Women's Cross-Party Caucus has supported these high levels of physical infrastructure spending, despite criticism of its unequal gendered impacts by Timorese women's organizations and gender experts (Centre for Women and Gender Studies 2014; UN Women 2015a). For instance, a female

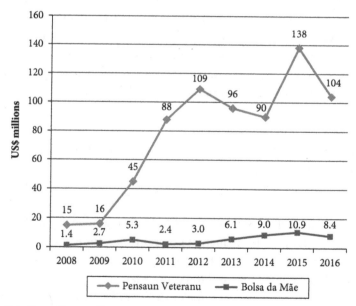

Figure 3.1 Spending on Pensaun Veteranu and Bolsa da Mãe, 2008–2016

Note: The 2015 Bolsa da Mãe figure is an taken from DNRS line budget estimates in 2013 and 2015 and may include nonprogram spending such as disability pensions.

Sources: Lao Hamutuk (2016); Democratic Republic of Timor-Leste (2015b); World Bank (2013).

FRETILIN member of the caucus described its support for ZEESMs as setting the conditions for market-led development: "The Women's Cross-Party Caucus also approved the money for ZEESMs.... The people in ZEESMs are not going to make the factories, they are not allowed. *This is about creating the conditions.* This means building basic infrastructure. This is to make a public-private partnership, to make an investment, ZEESMs has to start at the beginning—basic infrastructure—to create the conditions in order that investors come."[39]

At the individual level, state distribution in favor of men through jobs in infrastructure means that women have less control over resources and must access money through men (UN Women 2015a). At the national budget level, spending limited resources on physical infrastructure rather than health, water access, and girls' education takes money away from areas that improve women's material well-being. Indeed, spending on health (4.2 percent of the national budget) and education (8.7 percent) in Timor-Leste is low, even though the number of preprimary- and primary-school-age children has increased dramatically, according to Lao Hamutuk (2016, 6). There is also a severe lack of medical equipment and medicine, and disease is widespread.

Thus, although infrastructure spending would have benefitted from GRB, the Women's Cross-Party Caucus has not yet been publicly critical of the gendered distribution of resources in this area.

International Involvement

Finally, GRB is limited by the need for international staff involved in gender interventions to work with members of the Timorese elite, as all interveners must, rather than with a broader cross section of society. UN staff members in Timor-Leste are aware of class privilege within Timorese women's organizations.[40] One female UN manager observed that, similar to women's movements in Malaysia and Indonesia, Timorese women's organizing remains middle-class and city-centered, with some notable grassroots exceptions.[41] The implications for international gender experts have been a lack of information and a reliance on local women's organizations to implement their programs.[42] Further, as these women's organizations have long served as "conduits of information, preferences to governments, and suppliers of government or market services," they have shaped the focus of GRB in accordance with their own political compromises and interests, narrowing its scope (Rittich 2006, 223).

Overall, international interveners have been in no position to neutralize the role of class in shaping GRB outcomes. Because female members of the Timorese political elite (with overlapping identities as members of the liurai-dato and the resistance) control and carry out GRB, they do not challenge prevailing hierarchies that currently benefit them and their families in the distribution of state resources. It is possible that GRB, like other participatory budgeting measures, can inadvertently help to preserve power hierarchies and limit the scope for critical evaluation of the prevailing reform agenda, despite the goals of participants (Rodan and Hughes 2012, 368). Monica Costa (2015, 208) has similarly shown that traditional gender politics, along with accepted priorities for the allocation of resources, continue to undermine positive change in Timor-Leste, even following the codification of budgetary processes.

The nature of the state—made up of members of the liurai-dato and shaped by the historical monopolization of resources by armed men—establishes the context within which gender interventions take place. The greatest barrier to a just distribution of state resources has been a gendered class process that enables groups of elite men to monopolize them, justifying their dominance by valorizing armed masculinity. Limiting GRB's scope of to exclude the distribution of state resources thus limits its ability to effect gender justice.

GRB using a gender justice lens could entail a radical challenge to state distributional patterns in order to end material inequalities between women and men that result in women's subordination to men. However, such a redistribution would transfer state resources away from the control of men of the liurai-dato class. The lack of state resources has real consequences for women in all areas of daily life. It also sets the conditions for high levels of violence against women, a subject to which the subsequent chapters turn.

4
The Political Economy of Domestic Violence

Rates of domestic violence—violence committed against women by their male intimate partners—have remained high in Timor-Leste since independence. In 2013, three years after the promulgation of the Law Against Domestic Violence (LADV), the overwhelming majority of domestic violence cases in the courts were perpetrated against women by their husbands or intimate partners; only 6 percent involved female perpetrators. Thus, domestic violence in Timor-Leste can be defined as a case of male violence against women.

Around 30 percent of ever-partnered women globally have experienced domestic violence.[1] The Timorese rate is higher (García-Moreno et al. 2005). Around 60 percent of women experience domestic violence, and 50 percent have done so within the last twelve months.[2] Moreover, the violence has higher levels of recurrence; 81 percent of Timorese women who have experienced violence at the hands of their partners have done so many times.

Domestic violence had traditionally been handled at the family and village levels. Traditional dispute resolution, also called *adat* or *lisan*, is controlled entirely by male village leaders. It is a nonstate, noncriminal process for resolving lawbreaking in the community.[3] Traditional dispute resolution processes nearly always prohibit women from acting as mediators or even giving evidence (Myrttinen 2005). Women are instead represented by their fathers, brothers, or uncles, and in Timor men usually also hold formal political positions as the village head (*xefe suku*) or hamlet head (*xefe aldeia*).

The liurai-dato class has retained leadership in Timorese villages for generations. A general revival of tradition has been evident across Timor-Leste since independence—much as adat in Indonesia and *kastom* in Melanesia are experiencing renewed significance—and new laws (introduced in 2009 and rewritten in 2016) on local government have (re)formalized rule of the village by liurai or dato. Although the process is nominally democratic, villagers typically elect leaders who are also from the liurai-dato class, in what Cummins and Leach (2012) call a "co-incumbency" model.[4] Scholars report that the control of village male elites over dispute resolution is justified on the part of villagers and village chiefs alike by the longue durée of such authority and the belief that assigning leadership to a non-elite family would disrupt the cosmological order and bring ruin on the village (Brown 2012a; Cummins and Leach 2012).

Some anthropologists describe traditional dispute resolution as *nahe biti boot* (literally, spreading the mat), meaning to sit together and talk (Babo-Soares 2004). During fieldwork, I more commonly found that people referred to *uze adat atu resolva problema* (using tradition to solve the problem). The process of traditional dispute resolution requires deciding who is at fault and awarding compensation. The aim is a return to peace, harmony, and consensus—in other words, to preserve the order of things.

Significant barriers such as cost, distance, and lack of courts outside Dili prevent access to formal systems, with the result that the 40 percent of domestic violence victims who speak up and seek help usually go through a traditional dispute resolution process (Kniepe 2013). According to village chiefs, much of their job involves mediating violent domestic disputes even though this is prohibited under the LADV, which categorizes domestic violence as a public crime that requires formal intervention by the police and the courts.[5] Traditional dispute resolution has different aims: in cases of domestic violence, the role of village chief mediators is to preserve the marriage and prevent divorce. In the view of village chiefs, violence against women is not inherently disruptive to the community. Instead, conflicts over compensation and redress are disruptive because they cause family members to disagree (Khan and Hyati 2012). The LADV takes a very different approach.

Gender Interventions and Domestic Violence

The 2010 LADV was the most ambitious and controversial area of gender intervention attempted in Timor-Leste. Domestic and international coalitions articulated strong positions both for and against, and it took ten years of national and international advocacy to pass the legislation. Women's organizations are proud of the achievement, yet the outcomes have been uneven. Women's shelters have been established in districts run by women's organizations, supported by the government under the 2012 National Action Plan to fund and implement the LADV (Kniepe 2013; UN Women 2015b). Legal aid and evidence gathering have improved, and community awareness of domestic violence as a public crime rather than a private issue has grown.

On the other hand, funding for the LADV remains precarious, police and lawyers have not implemented its recommendations, few women have access to formal justice, and violence against women, including domestic violence, remains very high. None of this is surprising in the postconflict context, but it warrants explanation. Moving away from the level of the state to examine how rural women actually experience programs intended to promote women's empowerment—in this case, the LADV—gives insight into the governance of domestic violence, and with it some explanation of why the new law has had only qualified success.

Creating and implementing a law against domestic violence was a key aim of the Timorese women's movement and international staff working in various gender interventions. Timorese women's organizations, notably the Popular Organization of Timorese Women (OPMT), had struggled since 1975 on two fronts: for Timorese independence from colonial structures that also oppressed women, and against social structures that were traditionalist and patriarchal (Loney 2015). Even prior to international involvement, Timorese members of women's organizations lobbied for women's rights, both within FRETILIN and within Indonesian New Order state-sponsored women's organizations such as the Family Welfare Movement (embinaan Kesejahteraan Keluarga; PKK) and Dharma Wanita (Smith 2015a, 59–62).[6]

In 1998, amid the heady air of anti-Suharto and pro-independence rallies, the East Timorese Women's Communication Forum (FOKUPERS), an umbrella network of women's organizations, organized a demonstration to protest systemic violence against women (Hall 2009, 314). The forum wanted a law against domestic violence, and a national campaign of support emerged (Hall 2009, 316). In 2000 FOKUPERS then organized the first National East Timorese Women's Congress, paid for by UNTAET. Most of the over five hundred delegates were Timorese. After they presented findings from a series of subnational meetings that had been held prior to the congress with women's organization members and activists, a Platform for Action was formulated. The document made recommendations on giving priority to "poverty, law and order, reconciliation and justice, [the] culture of violence and decision making and institution-building" (Hunt 2008, 196–197). In the context of widespread conflict-related SGBV and increasing domestic violence in the postconflict era, a law on domestic violence was a central demand. Rede Feto, another network of women's organizations, was formed at the same time, and together with FOKUPERS became a key advocate for such a law.[7] Rede Feto aimed to train the members of its twenty-four constituent organizations to advocate for and help implement domestic violence prevention and awareness programs across the country (Hall 2009, 316).

At the same time, members of the Gender and the Law Working Group established under UNTAET campaigned from 2000 to 2002 for the protection of women's rights in the Timorese constitution. With technical and capacity support from UNIFEM, Timorese women's organizations drew attention to the need to deal constitutionally with key areas of gender inequality such as forced marriage, informal dispute resolution of domestic violence cases, and brideprice (Charlesworth and Wood 2002; UN Women 2015b). The working group reviewed the constitution in accordance with international women's human rights frameworks and then wrote a Charter on Women's Rights, with the aim of including it in the constitution.

Most importantly, the charter sought to reform traditional dispute resolution by inserting a constitutional guarantee of "women's participation in traditional decision-making processes." Their lobbying for this guarantee demonstrates that Timorese women's organizations had long viewed traditional dispute resolution as a key site of gender injustice. Their efforts went unheeded, however, as the constitution, which was finally promulgated in 2002, did not include regulation of such practices. Nonetheless, in 2003 the newly independent Timor-Leste acceded to the 1979 UN Convention on the Elimination of All Forms of Discrimination Against Women (CEDAW), which obliges state parties to protect and fulfill women's human rights (UN Women 2015b).

Although Timorese women's organizations had arisen out of the preindependence activist landscape, their national campaigns soon found donor support. A wide variety of international organizations (UNIFEM—now called UN Women as well as the UNFPA), international NGOs (Oxfam, the Asia Foundation), and bilateral donors (USAid, AusAid) provided Timorese women's organizations with funds and expertise. For example, UNIFEM paid for staff within women's NGOs and for gender experts in ministries, and also directly funded women's NGOs and programs. Transnational alliances of academics, gender experts, and practitioners were subsequently responsible for implementing gender interventions.

As FOKUPERS and other Timorese organizations drew on international human rights frameworks in their advocacy for women's rights, they came to focus on violence against women (VAW) (Allden 2007; Grenfell and Trembath 2007; Hall 2009). Nina Hall (2009, 316) also contends that the application of international human rights law and the presence of the United Nations in the postindependence landscape allowed Timorese women to broaden their campaign against VAW to include Timorese perpetrators, not just Indonesian ones. Within a nationalist framework, there had been little political space to campaign against domestic violence during the resistance, because the effort undermined male resistance figures and thus the independence struggle.

After 2004 UNIFEM received funding under the CEDAW Southeast Asia Programme to help Timor-Leste implement policies to comply with its commitments under CEDAW (UN Women 2015b). The goals of this program were to help the country to "develop new and revised legislative frameworks," such as laws criminalizing domestic violence (UN Women 2015b).

Resistance to the LADV

Domestic violence laws nearly always cause controversy in the countries that introduce them. In Ghana, for example, the government, claiming to be the voice of the people, deployed a discourse of cultural sovereignty during the introduction of a bill against domestic violence, asserting that both the legislation and Ghanaian women's rights activists represented the imposition of foreignness (Hodžić 2009, 331). In peacebuilding missions with large, visible military and other forces, the issue becomes particularly acute, and the introduction of women's rights legislation has regularly been framed by governments as entailing imposition of so-called Western feminist values (Chaudhary, Nemat, and Suhrke 2011). These sentiments were common among Timorese politicians and in the public sphere more generally, as those pushing gender-regressive positions sought to characterize Timorese women's organizations as centralist, Westernized, or top-down (Corcoran-Nantes 2009, 169; Niner 2011).

Unsurprisingly, then, when put before the Timorese government's Council of Ministers in 2003, the LADV was first rejected, but after an internationally supported campaign by Timorese anti-VAW advocates, the draft legislation passed in 2004. The law was not promulgated for another six years. Similar to the implementation of gender-responsive budgeting, opponents claimed that technical difficulties and limited capacities were an obstacle. Parliamentarians blamed the delay on the need to harmonize the legislation with the criminal and civil codes (Trembath, Grenfell, and Noronha 2010, 135).[8] Another technical screen was the use of the Portuguese language, which reflected deeper problems of exclusion and elite capture (Taylor-Leech 2007, 189, 219, 246; Ross 2016). The LADV was drafted, introduced, and promulgated in the official national language, Portuguese. In Timor-Leste in the early period of independence, male Portuguese speakers outnumbered female speakers five to one, and the language of the legislation thus presented a barrier to members of women's organizations who were not fluent in Portuguese (Corcoran-Nantes 2009, 168).

More significant than the delays justified on technical grounds, the LADV was painted as a foreign imposition of the peacebuilding intervention rather than a key demand of the Timorese women's movement and a response to the material threat of domestic violence in Timorese women's lives. Prominent female Timorese politician Milena Pires remarked on the frequent invocation of cultural discourse "to quash attempts to introduce discussions on women's rights into the East Timorese political equation" (Charlesworth and Wood 2002, 336). Parliament was also unable to reach a quorum during debates on the LADV, as male parliamentarians simply refused to discuss it. One senior NGO manager believed that the LADV was blocked deliberately because "policymakers' perspectives are still dominated by male authority. And, they thought, if this law on domestic violence is passed, then divorce cases will increase and women will have more courage; [the LADV] was threatening to them."[9] According to this interviewee, the LADV threatened male legislators' entitlement to use violence against their own wives and intimate partners.

Indeed, some prominent male Timorese parliamentarians have been accused of or arrested for crimes of domestic violence. A prominent early case was Health Minister Sérgio Lobo, who escaped prosecution for allegedly "beating his wife with a stick and injecting a sedative into her arm with a syringe he had brought for this purpose" (Rede Feto 2001). Another anonymous female source said it was widely known that the then-director of FOKUPERS "was beaten by her husband, a member of parliament, Maun Osório" , Osório Florindo da Costa in 2004. The interviewee added that this was part of a pattern of abuse by male members of government, policemen and civil servants: "sometimes the wives of these popular men, when they face violence, are ashamed to come to the court, because they are embarrassed or afraid of losing their position."[10] Thus, conflicts over the introduction of the LADV were not only between liberal interveners and Timorese but also within and across different groups of Timorese people, and between elite Timorese men and women.

International pressure was applied to the Timorese government to pass the law. In July 2009 CEDAW's "Concluding Observations" urged the government to "speedily enact the Law on Domestic Violence and to make it widely known to public officials and society at large and to monitor its effectiveness," as well as to criminalize marital rape, improve rural women's access to justice, and ensure that justice was enacted through the formal justice system (CEDAW 2009). Following the passage of the penal code in 2009, the LADV was passed the next year and was hailed as a great success for transnational mobilization (Hall 2009). The legislation criminalizes domestic violence and makes it prosecutable under the criminal code. It defines domestic violence as acts committed by a family member, or an intimate partner, that "resulted, or may result, in physical, sexual or psychological injuries or suffering, economic abuse, including threats such as intimidating acts, bodily harm, aggression, coercion, harassment, or deprivation of freedom" (Democratic Republic of Timor-Leste 2010b).

The LADV requires all cases to be reported to the police. Crucially acknowledging the economic conditions and structural inequalities that establish the conditions for domestic violence, the law sets out the legal obligation of the state to prosecute perpetrators and to support and protect victims of violence (Kniepe 2013). It lists the state's duty to provide specialized police services, women's shelters, and court processes, at no cost to the victim. The 2010 law was followed up by the 2012 National Action Plan (NAP) on implementing and funding the LADV (Kniepe 2013; Kovar 2012; UNDP 2013). In the LADV's introduction and promulgation, it is clear that coalitions for and against parts of the gender intervention often crossed the supposed local-international divide.

After 2010, however, several problems arose in the law's implementation. As was the case with gender-responsive budgeting, political compromises with social forces stymied implementation. Specifically, use of traditional dispute resolution continued—in direct conflict with the law. Moreover, peacebuilders were working at cross-purposes, as support for the local-turn approach by those who were focused outside the gender mainstreaming area challenged the gender intervention underpinning the LADV. The actions of these local and international coalitions significantly affected the LADV's implementation.

The Local Turn and Domestic Violence Programming

Scholars and practitioners of the local turn in peacebuilding argue that the explanation for ongoing conflict and violence lies in the disconnect between local and international institutions, cultures, and practices. Some scholars therefore take what sociologist Gearoid Millar (2014) terms a prescriptive view of hybridity, suggest that a hybrid justice system could reduce violence. In Timor, hybrid peacebuilding found the greatest purchase as a blend of formal processes for resolving community crime and traditional dispute resolution mediated by village leaders, chiefly for cases of domestic violence. Local-turn advocates justified this hybrid approach—which was supported by international peacebuilders and local elites—as pragmatic, cheaper, and more culturally legitimate. As a result, peacebuilding initiatives incorporated hybrid approaches into programs designed to support reconciliation and justice and into national laws.

In practice, however, the local turn in peacebuilding ideologically strengthened parliamentary coalitions that were keen to oppose the LADV, as well as programs that inadvertently helped to legitimize village elites' control of traditional dispute resolution in cases of domestic violence. As such, it negatively affected the LADV's introduction and implementation.

I have already noted that historically specific power and gender relations have hindered the success of gender interventions in Timor-Leste. Power relations are grounded in social relations of control over resources and, in gender relations, control over women. Feminist scholars have pointed out that traditional dispute resolution has been problematic for women's rights in postconflict Timor-Leste (Harris-Rimmer 2010; Myrttinen 2005; Swaine 2003). I suggest further that by promoting hybrid approaches to justice, advocates for hybrid peace reproduced the gender and class biases of Timorese elites and village leaders. Traditional dispute resolution in cases of domestic violence has been problematic for gender justice because perpetrators, village leaders, and the male relatives of victims benefit from a system in which male leaders and family members are compensated with cash and animals, and male perpetrators can buy impunity. In analytical terms, supporting local approaches to traditional dispute resolution inadvertently props up a political economy of domestic violence.

The local turn heavily influenced domestic violence programming, domestically and internationally. Like much mainstream work, academic descriptions of—and prescriptions for—hybrid peacebuilding rarely recognized or addressed VAW as a form of conflict. Moreover, such work tended not to pay attention to empirical research that drew a link between conflict-related SGBV and domestic violence and noted that these can increase after fighting ends (Cockburn 2013; True 2014a). This glaring lacuna has provoked two parallel debates on peacebuilding in Timor-Leste: one, regarding transitional justice peacebuilding and hybridity, ignores the other, regarding feminist approaches to VAW and legal pluralism.

Within the initial period of international administration under UNTAET, from 1999 to 2002, some groups of staff advocated for specific measures to protect women from violence, while others saw this as a less urgent problem. In accordance with the Women, Peace, and Security agenda put forward by United Nations Security Council Resolution 1325 (UNSCR 1325), UNTAET ought to have implemented gender mainstreaming in all aspects of its mission. However, as Vijaya Joshi (2005, 205) argues, UNTAET was only superficially supportive of the Timorese women's movement and did not prioritize domestic violence. VAW was in general seen both as a corollary of war, which peacebuilding would end, and as less disruptive than civil strife in the postconflict period. UNTAET carried on using laws from the era of Indonesian military occupation. These did not protect women's and children's rights, criminalizing adultery but not marital rape and failing to treat domestic violence as a distinct crime (Charlesworth and Wood 2002).[11] Moreover, UNTAET allowed alternative justice mechanisms to continue at the local level and postponed the development of a new criminal justice system (Nakaya 2010, 101). Its early decision to allow VAW cases to be dealt with by traditional dispute resolution did not accord with international human rights instruments such as CEDAW. In Sumie Nakaya's estimate, "UNTAET seemed content to accept the role of traditional justice forms for 'minor crimes' without defining what constituted a minor crime" (Nakaya 2010, 101).

In Timor-Leste, two reasons have been used to justify bringing together formal justice and traditional dispute resolution. First, hybrid justice was seen as pragmatic and cheaper because neither the United Nations nor the new government had the capacity to provide justice in rural areas. Second, hybrid courts were perceived as culturally legitimate because they avoided a clash between interveners' culture, ideas, and institutions and local ones. In particular, according to some scholars, the court system was "fundamentally Western" because it did not "resemble the population's understanding of justice" (Hohe 2003, 336). In this view, differences between liberal and local ideas, institutions, and cultures led to more violent conflict between Timorese.

Following this logic, some scholars asserted that a liberal-local hybrid system could balance international liberal practices with local ones and thus lead to better outcomes (see, e.g., Wallis 2012). Scholars of the local turn influenced international intervention in a number of peacebuilding programs:

- The World Bank's Community Empowerment Program (CEP) local governance program, 2001–2003
- The Commission for Reception, Truth, and Reconciliation (CAVR) community reconciliation program, 2002–2004
- Asia Foundation justice sector programs, 2002–present
- UNDP-UNCDF local governance programs, 2003–2012

The concept was also incorporated into the Timorese constitution (2002) and the Law Electing Community Leaders (2009 and 2016).

Community reconciliation events under the CAVR aimed to bring together victims and perpetrators of lesser crimes in villages in an alternative to the formal justice system (Kent 2004). As explained earlier, the CAVR was a UN-mandated commission to establish the truth regarding the nature, causes, and extent of human rights violations from 1974 to 1999. Under its community reconciliation program, over fourteen hundred events were held across all subdistricts in Timor-Leste from 2002 to 2004. They mixed criminal law, civil procedure, and traditional and spiritual practices to resolve lesser crimes more cheaply and quickly than the formal court system could, while remaining sensitive to human rights and women's rights. The aim was to ameliorate community anger and facilitate peace in the future. Under the program, perpetrators initiated the request to the CAVR, the reconciliation event would hear the case, and the victim—in many cases, a whole hamlet or village—would forgive the perpetrator, who was then immune from formal prosecution (Burgess 2006; Kent 2004, 10). The use of traditional dispute resolution excluded women from the process, and many female victims did not participate (Kent 2004, 37).

The Asia Foundation seminar held in Dili in 2003 advocated a hybrid approach to conflict resolution (Hicks 2013, 26; Trindade 2008). Hybridity advocates Tanya Hohe and Rod Nixon (2003) prepared a report that suggested giving village chiefs power to mediate in low-level disputes. In another report, this one on the World Bank's CEP, Hohe and Sofi Ospina recommended the (nondemocratic) inclusion of traditional male leaders from liurai and dato families on Village Development Councils, by way of formal appointment (Hohe and Ospina 2002, 118). These approaches did not connect the rule of elite men to the position of women in communities. Although gender power imbalances were mentioned, community cohesion and peace were considered more important than women's experience of violence. Hohe and Nixon assert, for example, that for the community, failing to adhere to prescribed marriage patterns between families endangers society more than a case of domestic violence (2003, 18).

Hybridity as a form of peacebuilding was subsequently incorporated into the national policy sphere, especially after 2007. For example, Dionísio Babo-Soares, an anthropologist and high-ranking minister in Xanana Gusmão's government from 2008 to 2017, published a paper arguing for the hybridization of traditional dispute resolution and state law. In it he asserted that "this village-level concept of achieving peace and stability could be fitted into the broad concept of state justice" (Babo-Soares 2004, 16).[12] Views such as his tended to emphasize the importance of consensus and unity, to prioritize general community peace over individual rights, and to view hybridity as culturally legitimate and practical (Hohe 2003; Hohe-Chopra, Pologruto, and de Deus 2009; Jackson et al. 2003; Kirk 2015; Kovar 2012; Simião 2007).

Timorese national policymakers also supported this approach. The constitution itself contains provisions for the institutionalization of nonjurisdictional resolution of disputes. This provision was further developed in the 2009 Law Electing Community Leaders, which empowered village leaders, 95 percent of whom are male, to create "grassroots structures" for the resolution and settlement of minor disputes (Democratic Republic of Timor-Leste 2009; Wallis 2012, 749).[13]

Gender Bias in the Local Turn

Some scholars writing from an anthropological perspective promoted the use of hybrid approaches to peacebuilding on the basis that gender interventions were inauthentic. David Hicks (2013, 26) urged the Timorese government and the United Nations to stop promoting "Western values of governance and jurisprudence," suggesting that accommodating local adat to create "a single political culture" would promote peace and give Timor-Leste more chance of evolving into "a unified nation-state." His rejection of Western values applies most strongly to the area of law and gender, where he sees an acute division between international and Timorese views on "hot-button issues such as 'domestic violence,' 'sexual abuse' and rape, which obsess the United Nations and their fellow agencies" (Hicks 2013, 31). Revealingly, Hicks notes that he encloses "domestic violence" and "sexual abuse" within quotation marks to signal that he finds them imprecise in the context of scholarly analysis.

Brazilian anthropologist Daniel Simião argues that the concept of domestic violence was "invented" by international interveners, because what Timorese victims may have understood as a normal "act of aggression" was then "*perceived* as an act of violation and violence" (Simião 2007, 2). In this view, and ignoring the long history of women's rights advocacy in Timor-Leste, by naming VAW as domestic violence, and thus as a part of a relation of power and inequality, the gender intervention invented it.

According to Tom Kirk, Timorese village leaders have rejected the state justice system's interventions on domestic violence because they impose "alien institutions onto a population that has historically fought to retain its identity" (Kirk 2015, 435). Likewise, Kirk suggests that the LADV can be interpreted as "a top-down imposition of norms and practices that are still struggling to find widespread acceptance in Timor-Leste," on the grounds that resistance to formal legal processes for domestic violence cases "continues a long tradition of Timorese resistance to top-down and alien governance arrangement" (Kirk 2015, 441, 455).

Some of those who were contracted as gender analysts in postindependence Timor-Leste advocated "flexible approaches" to traditional dispute resolution. Some contended that the concept of VAW came from Western feminism, again disregarding the history of Timorese women's activism and effectively dismissing VAW as an issue. For example, Annika Kovar, who worked for the UNDP as the access to justice adviser to the public defender general, argued in 2012, "Much of the previous research may have approached domestic violence issues from a Western perspective or a centralised one, coming from the capital city, Dili. This has in some instances *led to a coloured interpretation of the reality of domestic violence* in Timor-Leste" (2012, 210, emphasis added). Kovar's assertion of a binary difference between the Western and Timorese understanding and approaches to domestic violence, like much of the writing on traditional dispute resolution, is based on work by practitioners trained as anthropologists who advocated for hybrid justice, including Babo-Soares (2004) and Hohe (2002b; 2003). Subsequent research has not supported the assertion that reports of domestic violence are "coloured interpretations," that is, overstated or overestimated. Instead, given better prevalence data, early reports are said to have underestimated the extent, severity, and frequency of domestic violence (Asia Foundation 2016; Wigglesworth et al. 2015).

Hybridity was also used to advance the cause of "taking local agency seriously" in terms of further empowering traditional dispute resolution and families to deal with cases of domestic violence. Nixon makes two claims based on this school of thought. First, he argues that women should have a choice about whether to deal with crimes of violence through traditional dispute resolution or the courts. Second, he puts forward the notion that many so-called rapes are in fact consensual acts, agreed to on the basis that marriage will follow. The claim that an act of rape took place is then said to occur when the man subsequently reneges on the promise to marry (Nixon 2008, 333, 370). Indeed, there is confusion within communities over what constitutes a sexual crime, but Nixon's statements minimize the extent, prevalence, and seriousness of sexual violence, especially against girls, who are often in no position to reject men.

In the debate over traditional dispute resolution procedures, as in other areas of intervention, advocates of hybridity ignore the extent to which extant local law and practice had been combined with Indonesian modes of governance during the occupation.[14] For instance, the privileging of community welfare and unity over individual rights is a feature of New Order ideology. The New Order heavily promoted consensus-driven decision-making (*musyawarah-mufakat*), which aimed to maintain harmony in the material as well as the spiritual world (insofar as the prevailing order was sacralized). The promotion of consensus-style decision-making through the practice of adat "tried to freeze Indonesian society in the stasis of a mythic vision of the Indonesian past, which stressed consensus, harmony and tradition, but also obedience and passivity" (Aspinall and Fealy 2010, 5). Research has failed to recognize this strong legacy. In their evaluation of the World Bank's CEP, for example, Hohe and Ospina (2002, 68) describe Timorese village decision-making as characterized by discussion and agreement. In sum, advocates for the local turn have in effect reproduced ideological legacies of the New Order that emphasize the importance of preserving the social and political order, which subsequently supports power holders from the liurai-dato class.

The Political Economy of Traditional Dispute Resolution

Traditional dispute resolution has material outcomes that impair gender justice. As previously mentioned, the process involves deciding fault, reaching consensus, and paying compensation, rather than meting out punishment. Along with payments to mediators, compensation can run into hundreds of dollars and numerous animals. I understand this practice to represent the persistence of structural relations of which traditional dispute resolution processes are but a part. Unequal class relations intersect with gender relations and explain barriers to achieving gender justice through the gender intervention supporting the LADV.

Domestic violence cases progress up a ladder of resolution mechanisms from the family to the hamlet, and then to the village level. The material exchanges involved are essential to elites' control over resources and legitimacy. In the context of high rates of poverty, traditional dispute resolution takes much-needed resources from poorer villagers and women and transfers them to male family members and male village elites. The sums involved are significant, as tens or hundreds of dollars mean a great deal in a place where cash incomes, generously estimated, are around four hundred dollars a year (Inder, Cornwell, and Datt 2015). Three groups benefit: the female victim's family, the mediators, and the male perpetrator. Conversely, victims are marginalized and endangered at each step.

On the first rung of the ladder, the male heads of the perpetrator's and victim's families "sit together" to resolve the problem. Traditional dispute resolution can also begin if a victim has run away from her husband, or if her natal family has complained that she is being treated badly. The family heads then decide whether the violence is the husband's fault or the wife's.[15] Even though prevalence surveys show that domestic violence is overwhelmingly perpetrated by men against women, a woman can be found to have caused the violence (Khan and Hyati 2012, 18). Legitimate reasons for a husband using violence against a wife can include her burning food, neglecting the children, having affairs, or questioning him over his extramarital affairs or polygyny (Wigglesworth et al. 2015). During my fieldwork, some men, including a boy of fifteen, reported to me that they had assaulted their wife or girlfriend after she questioned him regarding sexual liaisons outside their relationship.[16]

If family-level male mediators decide the husband is at fault, he pays a fine, often a pig or other small animal, to the *umane* (the wife's family, or wife givers). Compensation varies from district to district but can include animals, palm wine or palm spirit, cash, or woven cloths (UNDP 2013). Thus, the victim's family benefits in the first step of traditional dispute resolution. The higher the status of the wife's family, the easier it is to compel the husband to pay the fine; a low-status family is in no position to do so (Graydon 2016, 130). Moreover, the gender division of labor holds women responsible for small animal husbandry, including of pigs, meaning that the victim has usually raised the pig that is then taken to pay compensation. Her husband thus pays a fine for violence toward his wife by using the proceeds of her work. The material implication for victims is that by bringing cases of domestic violence to their families and leaders, they risk being either blamed or in effect fined themselves. A woman therefore has no real material interest in pursuing traditional dispute resolution.

Resolution at the family level fails if the two families do not agree on who is to blame, or if the wife presses for separation or divorce. In such cases, dispute resolution progresses to the second step of the ladder. Mediators at this level are village chiefs, hamlet heads, and spiritual leaders (*lia nain*), and therefore typically of the liurai-dato class. As some young women reported, the authority vested in these all-male mediators is ultimate because Timorese elders can curse a person of lesser status, especially young people, with death.[17] Two young women explained that they feared their uncles because "if they talk (koalia), it won't go well for you... you can die. We Timorese are like that. There'll be a curse, you will face a disaster."[18]

Village leaders benefit materially from traditional dispute resolution at this level. In return for their mediation, they sometimes receive a small animal such as a pig, cigarettes, cash, or palm wine, and always the ritually important areca nut and betel leaf (*bua malus*).[19] Sometimes mediators received hundreds of dollars. Significantly, gifts offered by the perpetrator's family influence village leaders to favor him, reducing the compensation he will be required to pay to the victim's family (Alves and Alita 2009, 67). Dispute resolution at this level ends with a ritual meal. A *haan hamutuk* is a small-scale adat ceremony, to which only the mediators and male heads of the wife's and husband's respective families are invited.[20] Afterward, having received compensation and a meal, village leaders consider that balance is restored, and the victim returns to living with her husband (UNDP 2013). One hamlet chief reported to me that he preferred traditional dispute resolution because it made perpetrators stay with their wives: "If it goes to court, then he will leave his wife; they will separate."[21]

Because kinship links are integral to the organization of Timorese society, leaders' control over domestic violence also strengthens their control over village law and politics. Village leaders are the apex of separate but related kinship groups linked together through marriage. Because their source of authority lies in their role as heads of lineages, which depend on marriage, they require political control over marriages. Liurai and dato therefore have an interest in preserving or restoring the balance of kinship links. Their control over traditional dispute resolution does not represent the continuation of an authentic cultural tradition, but of structural superordination.

The third beneficiary of traditional dispute resolution is the perpetrator, as certain men can buy impunity: "This phenomenon empowers men to commit violence because when a man has money, horses and buffaloes, he is free to do violence against women" (Alves and Alita 2009, 18).

For some, the final rung of the ladder is a formal court of law. For instance, families sometimes turn to the courts if traditional dispute resolution has failed, especially if the families cannot agree on compensation amounts.[22]

Legal Pluralism, Accumulation, and Control

Very few women report violence through the formal processes prescribed under the LADV, even though domestic violence is the largest category of crime committed in Timor-Leste (JSMP, PRADET, and ALFeLa 2015). The LADV requires police to call specialist victims' services, such as a woman's shelter, when a victim does come forward. The LADV contains provisions to remove a perpetrator from the home instead of the victim, but these are rarely deployed. While the woman stays at a shelter, specialist staff arrange an examination to collect forensic evidence for the court. They then work with a legal aid agency to prepare the case.[23] It takes some time before cases reach one of the periodic mobile courts or the Dili court. Most often, the weakest charge under the LADV is brought—"simple physical assault characterised as domestic violence"—rather than the stronger charge of repeated assault or an aggravated charge of sexual assault or attempted manslaughter (Kniepe 2013, 2).

The implementation of the LADV under local-turn conditions has resulted in a widespread and well-documented practice of legal pluralism with respect to domestic violence cases (Charlesworth and Wood 2002; Grenfell 2013). Court decisions in these cases tend to reproduce the gender injustices present in dispute resolution, engaging in a fault-finding exercise that resembles traditional processes (Kniepe 2013, 3).[24] Judges often send cases back for traditional dispute resolution, and the court frequently orders the perpetrator to pay a fine, often around thirty dollars in cash over a period—again a similar outcome to traditional dispute resolution. As one hamlet chief said, although the LADV has brought some change, certain outcomes are similar: "Nowadays you have to go to the justice system. You can't just tell someone to go here or there to pay compensation. . . . But some things are the same. Both have their headaches. You have to take money to the *umane* [the wife's family]. With the state, it's the same."[25]

Most problematically, the court system has relied on fining perpetrators instead of making civil compensation. Provisions in the LADV for the state to provide compensation in the form of economic support for women victims, including alimony, welfare, and school payments, are very rarely used (JSMP, PRADET, and ALFeLa 2015; Kniepe 2013, 4). Thus, despite meeting program goals of socialization and training, the LADV is not being implemented as intended.

Another reason that traditional dispute resolution is still common despite the LADV is that police remain unwilling to treat domestic violence as a crime (Khan and Hyati 2012). Formal police and judicial processes have often deliberately turned to traditional dispute resolution or deferred to male family members in charging perpetrators (Kniepe 2013). By 2015, education programs about or "socialization" of the LADV had raised awareness that traditional dispute resolution was not permitted for domestic violence cases because it was a crime and required police involvement. To avoid the mandatory reporting, however, two levels of domestic violence have emerged: normal or everyday violence (*violensia bai-bain*) and serious violence, usually involving blood (*violensia boot*).[26] Male leaders maintain that only serious violence requires action by community members or police. Everyday violence can continue to be mediated between the families.

Another similarity between traditional dispute resolution and the current state of legal pluralism concerns the lack of posttrial protection for the victim. Global research on domestic violence has shown that the breakdown of a relationship is the most dangerous time for a female victim of violence (Morgan and Chadwick 2009). In Timorese courts, the most common punishment issued by courts is a suspended sentence. Thus, the perpetrator continues or returns to live in the family home, putting the victim at risk (Kniepe 2013, 2). The LADV provides for protection orders, but they have never been applied (JSMP, PRADET, and ALFeLa 2015).

Some scholars who back hybrid approaches do not see these risks to the victim as problematic. Nixon, who worked on justice issues for the Asia Foundation Timor-Leste, asserts that traditional dispute resolution of rape using compensation payments has been judged too harshly "under the powerful beam of the human rights spotlight" (Nixon 2008, 333). Kirk has advocated for "practical hybrids" to restore community balance in domestic violence cases, proposing the continuation of the practice whereby legal aid lawyers "assist clients to submit reconciliation letters to judges, which use them to justify a suspended sentence or a fine, allowing the offender to return to his family" (Kirk 2015).

I argue that seeing legal and traditional dispute resolution as either a clash between or a hybrid of international and local institutions, cultures, or processes is misplaced. First, this view ignores Timorese feminists' long struggles against gender inequality within their families and society (Loney 2015; Niner 2011). Second, the issue is not whether an institution has more legitimacy at the local level. We must ask what kind of power relations the justice system supports.

A feminist political economy analysis shows that it is in the interest of male members of the liurai-dato class as senior family members and village leaders (roles that overlap with those of perpetrators) to retain control of domestic violence dispute resolution. When we look at material outcomes, fines issued both by the courts and through traditional dispute resolution benefit those in authority and disadvantage female victims of domestic violence. Crucially, a feminist political economy approach highlights the underlying power relations of traditional dispute resolution.

This analysis reveals traditional dispute resolution to be a process of control over both material resources and women. Some researchers have taken women's continued use of traditional dispute resolution as evidence of its effectiveness and legitimacy (Graydon 2016). An equally reasonable assumption is that because 60 percent of women never tell anyone about abuse by their partner, the evidence suggests that female victims of violence do not trust either formal or informal systems since both are dangerous and neither supports victims' interests (Asia Foundation 2016; Kniepe 2013).

Over a decade of research on domestic violence in Timor-Leste clearly shows that women facing domestic violence have few protections, while perpetrators can expect only limited punishment. Further, domestic violence is driven by social and gender relations entailed in kinship systems that are based on the exchange of women through brideprice. An analysis of the distribution of money and goods using brideprice reveals another compelling set of explanations for the uneven outcomes of gender interventions in Timor-Leste, and chiefly for the qualified results of the LADV.

5
Brideprice and the Exchange of Women

Brideprice is a controversial and common topic in Timor-Leste, and one with significant effects on outcomes of the gender intervention on domestic violence. It is a longstanding practice, having been recorded during the colonial period in both Portuguese East Timor and Dutch West Timor, in particular among liurai lineages. And the majority of Timorese still practice brideprice. Only around 12 percent of Timorese are matrilineal; in these cases, the groom's family still makes a payment to the bride's family, but the much smaller amount is effectively a bride token (see Table 5.1). Brideprice comprises high-value "male" gifts: buffalo and cash. The bride's family counters with fewer and less valuable assets: pigs, necklaces, and traditional woven cloth, or *tais*.

In the western exclave of Oecusse, a liurai village chief explained to me that he would charge a high brideprice for his daughter because, "Now adat is stronger. For example, my children have attended school. If a man comes to marry her, then I will charge twenty thousand dollars. She's young and will look after her family well. Then you get a price of twenty thousand dollars or fifty thousand dollars."[1] This chief lives in quite a simple house with a basic garden, but his daughter's education will allow him to charge a high price for her, many times his yearly income. Given the low average rural income, brideprices are the some of the most substantial sums that ordinary Timorese citizens ever deal with. Brideprice can vary from a bride token of two hundred dollars in matrilineal families to around seventy thousand dollars, but the common range is ten thousand to twenty thousand dollars (see Table 5.2). By way of comparison, the average annual income in rural Timor-Leste is around $384 (Democratic Republic of Timor-Leste 2011a).[2]

Anthropologists and gender practitioners in Timor-Leste have hotly debated the definition, meaning, and significance of brideprice, along with the terminology used to describe it. The common term in the anthropological literature is *barlake* (or *barlaque*), but different dictionaries variously

Table 5.1 Types of marriage payment

	Direction and volume of valuables
Brideprice (bridewealth)	Net assets move from groom's family to the bride's family.
Dowry (marriage portion)	Net assets move from bride's parents to the groom or his family. Sometimes the assets are considered the bride's property, but they most often pass into the practical control of the groom or his family.
Dower (bride gift)	Net assets move from the groom and his kin to the bride. The payment is to insure her against divorce or the death or incapacity of her husband. Dower payments made to, or controlled by, the bride's family are referred to as brideprice.
Brideservice	A groom labors for a given period for the bride's family in exchange for his wife.
Bride token	Marriage payments are relatively small, but still move from the groom's family to the bride's family.
Gift exchange / Sister exchange	Marriage payments are reciprocal or involve the exchange of sisters and valuables.

define it as "common law marriage" or "brideprice."[3] The word *folin*, the Tetun noun for "price," has wide currency in the society itself, along with the verb *hafolin* and the phrase *feto nia folin*, which is Tetun for "woman's price."[4] Thus, brideprice is the closest translation to the Tetun terms, although the blended Indonesian-Portuguese term *barlake* is also widely understood to mean assets passed from the groom's family to the bride's. The term "adat" also stands in for brideprice, and indeed when I asked interviewees to define "adat," most responded by discussing brideprice. To many Timorese, adat is all about marriage and sexual rights, as a hamlet chief in Oecusse explains: "Adat is barlake. . . . If you have paid the barlake, that means that person is mine, not everyone's. This is adat. Adat is important everywhere in Timor. There is just one adat. The barlake is then like a tara bandu [an official prohibition]. If someone else tries to tama [interfere with or enter], they'll be scared because that person has a husband already. You can't interfere with her because there's a bandu."[5]

The scholarly debate over terminology is linked to a fundamental divide on the issue of gifts versus commodities. Anthropologists in the tradition of Émile Durkheim emphasize the cultural aspects of the practice and tend to use the term "bridewealth," framing it as an exchange of gifts rather than a

Table 5.2 Brideprice costs

Publication	Date of data	District	Descent	Minimum payment	Maximum payment	2017 US$
Hessing and Timo (1923)	1918–1923	Dutch West Timor (Atoni group)	Patrilineal	ƒ150 ($720 $Purchasing Power Parity)	ƒ1,000 ($4,800 $PPP) for a royal marriage	720–4,800
Gunn (1999, 38)	1880s	–	–	30 buffalo	100 buffalo	36,000–120,000
Forman (1980, 342)	1970s	Baucau	Patrilineal	6–9 buffalo	50 buffalo + 50 Makassar swords + *belak* (jewelry)	7,200–60,000
Mearns (2002, 50)	2002	Viqueque	Patrilineal	–	30 buffalo	36,000
Field (2004, 184–188)	2000–2003	Dili	Patrilineal	–	A$400 + A$100 *bee manas* (bride token) + A$400 for birth certificate	670
McWilliam (2011, 751)	2004–2011	Lautem (Fataluku)	Patrilineal	–	77 buffalo	92,400
Wigglesworth (2010)	2007	Lautem	Patrilineal	–	80 buffalo	96,000
Silva (2011, 156)	2008	Ainaro	–	–	$2,000	2,000
Silva (2011, 157)	2008	–	–	–	$2,000	2,000
Silva (2011, 154)	2008	Dili	–	$500	$3,000	500–3,000
Khan and Hyati (2012)	2009	Manatuto	Matrilineal	$500	$1,000	500–1,000
Khan and Hyati (2012, 27)	2009	Suai	Patrilineal	–	$5,100 + 6 *belak*, 5 buffalo	11,100
Khan and Hyati (2012, 27)	2009	Betano, Manufahi	Patrilineal	$2,500 + 10 *belak*, 10 buffalo	More than $2,500 + 10 *belak*, 10 buffalo	14,500+

Table 5.2 Continued

Publication	Date of data	District	Descent	Minimum payment	Maximum payment	2017 US$
Silva and Simião (2012, 368)	2010	–	–	–	$10,000	10,000
Niner (2012, 145)	2010	Dili	–	–	77 buffalo	92,400
Wigglesworth et al. (2015, 25)	2014	–	–	–	$10,000	10,000
Field research	2015	Oecusse	Patrilineal	$1,000 (for matrilateral cousin marriage)	$50,000	1,000–50,000
Field research	2015	Manufahi	Matrilineal	$100	$200	100–200

Note: Currency is in US dollars unless otherwise indicated. All buffalo/US$ calculations are estimates, using 2017 prices in which one 200-kg live weight buffalo is worth around US$1,200. Traditional events may require buffalo with special markings, which can cost $2,000 to $7,000. These calculations do not include estimates of the dollar value of jewelry (Tetun: *belak*), which contributed to the brideprice.

transaction. French sociologist Marcel Mauss, drawing on Durkheim, said in 1925 that a bride is a gift resulting in a debt so valuable and irreducible that it can be repaid only with the further gift of a bride, such as a sister or daughter (Strathern 1988). In other words, bride giving sets up interdependent family relations, and brides themselves are gifts that are "embedded in relations of reciprocity and mutual dependence" (Jolly 2015). Anthropologists using this approach have made important points regarding the political and economic functions of brideprice. First, brideprice sets up relations of group interdependence, which supports welfare. Second, brideprice sets up alliances for peaceful relations to enable groups to exchange goods and thus have the means to live and grow. Third, societies that exchange women for brideprice have often taken careful steps to try and decommodify brides, such as by exchanging special kinds of marriage gifts rather than money, or reckoning the amount of brideprice in buffaloes and then paying in cash (Hoskins 2004). As such, scholars in the Durkheimian tradition believe that changing practices like brideprice disrupts the sociocultural fabric. Given their emphasis on cohesion and solidarity, such scholars tend to view such change negatively.

Marxist-feminist scholars approach the issue differently, emphasizing production and hierarchy. Brideprice is viewed as an aspect of the structuring of power relations and the social order (Fishburne Collier 1988; Meillassoux 1975). This has a material basis. Because brides are paid for using items with exchange values outside the marriage market—that is, cash or cows or cowries can be used to buy items other than brides—women themselves become items with an exchange value (Meillassoux 1975). In other words, brides become a commodity in the circuits of material power. Using a gendered lens, my fieldwork suggests that a woman's participation in brideprice is as one of the objects exchanged, not as agent and beneficiary.[6] In this I concur with Gayle Rubin. In her critique of social anthropologist Claude Lévi-Strauss's analysis of the exchange of women, Rubin argues that the woman is the "conduit to the relationship rather than the partner to it." Importantly, she notes that as a linking mechanism, brideprice benefits men: "The result of the gift of women is more profound than the result of other gift transactions because the relationship thus established is not just one of reciprocity but of kinship. The exchange partners have become affines [relatives by marriage] and their descendants will be related by blood" (Rubin 1975, 174).

The second point of difference between cultural anthropology and Marxist-feminist approaches concerns justifications for brideprice. Brideprice societies revere women and reproduction. This emphasis should be seen as ideological. That is, reverence for reproduction has to be understood as the justification for a social and political order, "with reference not to biological constraints but instead to local and specific forms of social relationship and, in particular, of social inequality" (Rosaldo 1980, 400). From this understanding of gender ideology, Jane Fishburne Collier and Michelle Rosaldo conclude that societies using brideprice tend "in their rituals and cosmology to display a preoccupation with female reproductive capacities; women are valued as mothers but feared for their polluting blood" (1981, 278–279).

The Extent, Form, and Visibility of Brideprice

Payments for marriage are practiced in around 75 percent of human societies today and take six different forms (see Table 5.1; see also Hudson 2016; Hudson and Matfess 2017). The most widely practiced of these is brideprice. Siwan Anderson estimates the global average brideprice at around four times the annual income of a family, and dowries at around six times the family's annual income.[7] Brideprices in Asia vary greatly. Some families don't pay them at all, but for the many who do, brideprice ranges between four thousand and eighteen thousand dollars in Myanmar; fourteen thousand and twenty-eight thousand dollars in Cambodia; four thousand and forty-five thousand dollars in Thailand; six thousand and seventeen thousand dollars among Malays in Malaysia; twelve thousand dollars among the Batak in Indonesia and twenty-eight thousand dollars in Sumba, Eastern Indonesia; and averaging twenty-nine thousand dollars in parts of China (Blomberg 2019; Human Rights Watch 2019; Martinus 2020; Pinghui 2019; Su-Lyn 2013; Thongyoojaroen 2017). All things considered, brideprices involve the transmission of significant volumes of property and labor and thus have economic functions as well as symbolic ones (Anderson 2007; Goody and Tambiah 1973, 1).

Internationally, there is substantial overlap between brideprice and women's subordinate status in law, women's ill-being, and GBV (Hudson 2016; Jolly, Stewart, and Brewer 2012). Unsurprisingly, perhaps, governments have nonetheless generally been reluctant to challenge male dominance in areas of personal law such as brideprice. A few have tried to regulate or ban marriage payments, including India (1961), Pakistan (1976), and Bangladesh (1980), but these efforts have been relatively unsuccessful.

Academics have largely overlooked the importance of brideprice in social and political life. Taking up this theme, Valerie Hudson and Hilary Matfess (2017) argue that brideprice has been hiding in plain sight as a decisive factor in violent conflict. As they point out, the links between brideprice, conflict, and war are in need of further research, but the link between brideprice, kinship, hierarchy, and community-level conflicts has been established, notably by feminist anthropologist Fishburne Collier (1988).

One of the economic processes arising from brideprice is social stratification that occurs in two related processes: it establishes rank, and it transfers wealth from lower-ranked lineages to higher ones. Societies with ranked lineages using brideprice are class-based, but class domination is expressed in the language of kinship and partially obscured by age and gender hierarchies within ranks, confusing ethnographers (Meillassoux 1975, 86–87). Brideprice societies usually have four ranks: three hereditary ones and a slave or outcast rank (Fishburne Collier 1988, 147).

Brideprice establishes and confirms a person's rank. In turn, rank determines access to, and control over, food, goods, land, education, labor, and choice of marriage partner. When brideprice comprises goods with market values, such as ivory and gold (or, in Timor-Leste, buffalo, metal breast disks, and cash), groups with greater access to valuables can use them to pay higher brideprices, confirming their high status. Men with more assets can also pay to marry more than one wife, another marker of high social status. At the same time, women for whom high brideprices are paid are seen as higher status and bring honor to themselves and their families.

Brideprice is also a kin-based means of accumulation and transfer of wealth: higher-ranked men gain materially from brideprice, chiefly because their daughters "cost more" but also because they are able to pay less or delay payments for wives (Goody and Tambiah 1973, 13; Fishburne Collier 1988, 144). As a result, higher-ranked men can afford to be polygynous, and higher-ranked women become first wives. Lower-ranked women and slave women are second and third wives, and so on. Crucially, polygyny provides high-ranked men with daughters from their liaisons with wives of lower ranks (or slaves), whom they can exchange to lower-ranked men in return for brideprice, further increasing their wealth. In contrast, a low-ranked man who is unable to pay any brideprice at all must labor for his father-in-law or wife's uncles as a debt bondsman (Fishburne Collier 1988, 146–148).

The role of brideprice in the creation of rank, or social stratification, is not well recognized either by its practitioners or by scholars, because the focus is usually on a bride's economic function or value. Societies engaging in brideprice see the practice as reflecting a woman's value, a view that is often replicated in ethnographic reporting. In this interpretation, brideprice is paid for the bride's productive and reproductive labor (Alanamu 2015; Boserup 1989; Goody and Tambiah 1973; Jolly 2015, 68, 71). Anthropological nomenclature describing the groom's family as "wife takers" and the bride's family as "wife givers" supports this perspective: brideprice compensates wife givers for the loss of a daughter's labor and fertility, and wife givers are valorized as the givers of life. Relatedly, brideprice is seen to vary according to the marriage market; scarcity of brides leads to higher brideprices (Anderson 2007).

Nevertheless, the economic functions of marriage need social and political contextualization, in part in order to recognize how brideprice and social inequality are related. Brideprice and polygyny overlap all over the world, and where they do so, slavery is likely to occur. High brideprices mean that a small number of men monopolize marriageable women. Orlando Patterson (2012, 337) suggests that this shortage of women prompts men of limited means to take low-status, low-cost, or enslaved women as sexual partners until they can afford to marry. Polygyny reinforces a view of women as domestic laborers and reproducers, and even when it is a rarely practiced option, it weakens women's status within the household and society because her husband's power to take a second wife can pressure a woman into conforming to his wishes. Finally, polygynous relationships are more hierarchical, competitive, and violent, and women in such relationships are likely to be poorer and less educated (Gaffney-Rhys 2011; Rees et al. 2016; Thomas et al. 2011, 372).

Advocacy against Brideprice

Timorese women's organizations have campaigned against brideprice for years, but despite its links to domestic violence, there has been no explicit, long-term, or well-funded gender intervention to challenge the practice. Indeed, although women's organizations have long argued that brideprice is a problem for women's rights, there is no mention of it in the LADV. The enduring centrality of brideprice explains the limited effectiveness of the law, in part because of the key role it plays in structuring class. Brideprice links gender relations to class relations in a material way.[8]

Unsurprisingly, perhaps, governments all over the world have generally been reluctant to challenge male dominance in areas of personal law, such as brideprice, except where it suits their interests. The earliest regulations were colonial and self-interested. The British and Dutch colonial governments sought to regulate it in nineteenth-century Indonesia, although the British entrenched dowry in India (Boomgaard 2003; Ranjana 1997). Later, various postcolonial governments instituted bans and reforms: India in 1961, Vietnam in 1970, Pakistan in 1976, and Bangladesh in 1980 (Anderson 2007; Boomgaard 2003; Teerawichitchainan and Knodel 2012). Zimbabwe's law explicitly allows marriage without brideprice, and the 2014 Kenyan Marriage Act requires only a "token payment" to legalize customary marriage, with agitation to standardize marriage payments (Republic of Kenya 2014). The Taliban and the Afghani and Saudi Arabian governments have tried to regulate brideprice markets to reduce costs (Hudson and Matfess 2017). Legislation in India, Pakistan, and Bangladesh has not reduced the frequency or volume of marriage payments, although they were successfully curbed in North Vietnam (1945–1976) (Anderson 2007, 161; Teerawichitchainan and Knodel 2012).

Many scholars working on Timor have demonstrated that kinship networks in Timor are constituted through complex exchanges, and that these networks are structured to cope with poverty in the absence of state welfare. They are not relations of equals, however, but of ranked families, and the payment of brideprice creates and reproduces these hierarchies. Members of the liurai-dato class use the practice to extract more valuables from lower-ranked lineages by marrying their daughters into families in these lower ranks and charging significantly high brideprices. Timorese leaders, including national, village, and hamlet chiefs, are at the apex of concatenated lineages and form a recognizable liurai-dato class. The exchange of women therefore has distributive outcomes, and it is of particular importance to liurai and dato families in rural areas because they do not have the same access to other material resources as urban-based members of the same class.

Brideprice contributes to the continuation of domestic violence because of the differential power that it gives to men, and because brideprice undergirds the social order and has distributive effects. First, women themselves do not have access to brideprice paid to their male kin. Second, when a marriage is violent, it is not in the interest of parents to aid their daughter to obtain a divorce if her husband has already paid her brideprice in full, as they will have to return the payment to his family. Conversely, if parents encourage their daughter to return to her violent husband they will receive compensation through traditional dispute resolution, as described in the previous chapter. Third, paying brideprice allows men to justify control over their wives. Dowry and brideprice negatively affect violence against women around the globe (UN Women 2013; Hudson 2016).

In the 1970s, before the invasion, Timorese women intellectuals living in Portugal analyzed the role of brideprice in the social and economic status of women in Timorese society. Early on, women in FRETILIN and then in the diaspora debated and criticized the practice (Loney 2015; Wigglesworth 2010). And after independence, a report by FOKUPERS described brideprice as "oppressive" because it caused women to be treated like chattels and *atan* (slaves) (Charlesworth and Wood 2002, 336).

In 2001 the Gender Affairs Unit (GAU) of UNTAET supported an unsuccessful campaign to regulate brideprice. GAU provided monetary support and technical assistance to the Gender and Law Working Group to draft the Charter for Women's Rights, containing ten articles that Timorese women's organizations wished to include in the new constitution. Among them was a call for the government to "regulate the dowry system to prevent violence against women" (Gender and Constitution Subcommittee 2001). Only Article 3, on nondiscrimination in access to political rights, was included in the constitution.

Subsequently, in 2008–2009, a widespread consultation was conducted with over eighty-three urban and regional women's organizations in order to produce a shadow report to CEDAW. Some 90 percent of participants thought that cultural practices regarding marriage payments reflected extreme discrimination against women: "When a man pays dowry [brideprice] to a woman's family, the man's family gains a full right to control the women. Because of the [brideprice] system, men often consider women as their property rather than their partners. Women must serve the men's families; vote according to men's choices; work in the kitchen all day during traditional ceremonies and have their meal at midnight after all the people have eaten. Women have no right to civil or cultural privileges and benefits related to their families and social life family life" (Alves and Alita 2009, 17).

The report concluded that brideprice damaged women's power within the household and kinship group and constrained their claims to their own children. It bound them more tightly to the gender division of labor and gave them less access to food.

The women's organizations involved took a material view of brideprice, seeing it as a form of commodification. For example, they argued that the use of cash and buffalo as brideprice equates women with livestock, to be disposed of freely (Alves and Alita 2009; Meillassoux 1975, 72–74). For that reason, the report saw brideprice as a significant obstacle to women's rights and a contributing factor to violence against women. The report concluded that an anti-brideprice law was needed to regularize the practice in Timor-Leste (Alves and Alita 2009, 17).

The Anthropological Argument

The lack of action on brideprice has stemmed in large part from anthropological arguments over whether it represents a gift or a commodity, a question that has influenced national and international policymakers because of the prominence of anthropology in the local turn. Disagreements about the meaning of brideprice can be partially explained by a long history of what Margaret Jolly (2015, 73) terms "anthropological queasiness" about the commodification of women. In the Timor case, this has resulted in the preference for the term "barlake" instead of brideprice, although, as I explained at the outset, brideprice is the more accurate translation of the Tetun term *folin*. People practicing brideprice also generally deny that they sell their daughters, even though they charge a price. A village chief I spoke to firmly declared, "Your children are not things to sell."[9]

Many anthropologists have taken a culture-based view of brideprice in Timor-Leste as a symbolic act of gift giving rather than a commodity exchange. Anthropologist Kelly Silva, for example, asserts that an authentic Timorese view considers brideprice as a gift or noncommodified exchange. She states, "Criticisms of *barlake* are often grounded on the view that it amounts to the selling of women. As such, it is judged to be illegitimate following the (Western) ideology that persons and things are incommensurable" (Silva and Simião 2012, 366). David Hicks similarly uses a Durkheim-influenced model to reject both Timorese and international feminist criticism of brideprice. First, he argues that Timorese people themselves do not consider brideprice to involve buying or selling a woman. Second, he suggests that a bride has a nonmaterial value because her ability to work and reproduce means she cannot be substituted for a set of material objects. Third, he contends that the exchange of a bride for valuables cannot be a sale because brideprice sets up a kinship relation (Hicks 2012, 129–130).

Timorese practices and beliefs about women, childbirth, and marriage are depicted in great detail in anthropological works (Forman 1980; Fox 1980; Francillion 1980; Hicks 2004; Therik 2004; Traube 1980). Yet despite many studies of gender, gender dualisms, kinship, and marriage, anthropological work on Timorese kinship has been inattentive to the power relations embedded in gender relations. This literature is characterized by a focus on dualisms (of male/female, cooked/raw, inside/outside) as the organizing principle of Timorese society, without concomitant analysis of the implications.[10] In essence, such scholars have not adequately explored the political or economic implications of unequal *gendered* dualisms such as male/female, wife giver / wife taker. Namely, these always privilege one term (male, right hand, outside, cooked, purity) over the other (female, left hand, inside, raw, pollution), although both are seen as necessary and complementary. The link between marriage and rank is thus naturalized as the expected order of things, and gender relations are taken for granted.

Concurrent with the local turn in peacebuilding, peacebuilders relied on these anthropological works to frame their understanding of Timor-Leste.

An example of anthropologists shaping practice can be found in a 2002 report by Australian anthropologist David Mearns. He describes the discussion of brideprice during a training session about domestic violence in the district of Viqueque: "Some of the women involved were well educated and very articulate but they remained committed to a worldview that the western women found incomprehensible. This extended to the desire to keep a brideprice system "because this shows how our parents value us." However, they were prepared to concede that current rates (around 30 buffalo [about thirty-six thousand dollars] and other payments) were probably too high. Clearly, the value systems inherent in village people's understandings and their systems of justice remain significantly at odds with those of the western educated social transformers employed by the UN" (Mearns 2002, 50).

As I showed in the previous chapter, support among some interveners for traditional dispute resolution was apparent in the justice system intervention. This approach also extended to brideprice.[11] Silva (2011) argued against government regulation of brideprice, claiming that the controversy demonstrated the divergence of local views and Westernized, government, or educated views. As such, she considered the brideprice issue to be a matter of *foho* (mountains) versus Dili.

More recently, some have suggested that matrifocality and respect for women can function as a starting point from which to improve women's rights, specifically by leveraging reverence for reproduction to reform traditional dispute resolution processes (Graydon 2016, 144). Academic and practitioner discussions on how best to rebuild Timorese society have begun with the assumption that Timorese institutions, laws, and culture are definable, distinct, authentic, and therefore more legitimate than anything imposed by international peacebuilders. Thus, the local turn in peacebuilding supported the retention and even reinvigoration of brideprice.

In the literature on brideprice in Timor, scholars have rarely asked, "Where are the women?" (Rosaldo 1980; Tickner 2006). For instance, Andrew McWilliam describes negotiations during a *kore metan* (death ceremony or end-of-mourning ceremony), in which male kin hammer out the final settlement of brideprice owed to the late woman's natal family. The process involves "lengthy and often theatrical negotiations over payment of outstanding debt obligations usually fuelled by liberal quantities of palm liquor and tobacco as *others prepare baskets of steamed rice and boiled meat for feeding guests*" (McWilliam 2011, 751, emphasis added). The "others" are women: invisible workers and also the objects of discussion. In other words, women's labor and men's agency in controlling women's roles in production and reproduction go unnoticed as McWilliam focuses on the public theatricality of men.

Similarly, women in Timor-Leste are not the primary decision-makers regarding brideprice; they do not decide the nature of the exchange, who will be exchanged, for what price, or who will supply the goods. Although women may participate in the discussions, it is mostly senior men—uncles and *katuas* (male elders)—who negotiate the sums involved. A preferred marriage takes place between a bride from a higher-ranked lineage and a groom from a lower-ranked lineage. The large brideprice involved demonstrates the high status of the bride's lineage. The prestige and honor of brideprice thus accrues to wife-giving lineages (patrilineages) in recognition of their higher status. Prestige also accrues to wife-taking lineages in recognition of their ability to afford such a high-status and costly bride for their male relative and because of the new marital connection forged with their social superiors.

In Timor-Leste brideprice systems, women do not directly benefit from brideprice as they are the objects of, not parties to, the exchange. As Gayle Rubin lays out, when women are exchanged as gifts between lineages, the link established between families also implies a distinction between gift and giver: "If women are the gifts, then it is men who are the exchange partners. . . . The relations of such a system are such that women are in no position to realise the benefits of their own circulation" (Rubin 1975, 174).

In Timor, the cash and goods constituting brideprice are given to the wife's father, who then distributes them among his kinsmen (Hicks 2012, 128).[12] Women do not control access to or redistribution of the money, buffalo, pigs, *belak* (jewelry), swords, or tais (woven cloths). The brideprice is distributed to male relatives according to whether they contributed cash or goods to the upbringing of the girl-child, their importance in the family, age, and status as a katuas (male elder). As Silva recounts about a ceremony she witnessed, brideprice was "distributed among all the men of his house/family. The elder would get more than the younger, but they would all receive their share for having contributed, one way or another, to the upbringing of the bride" (Silva 2011, 156).

Women's lack of access to money or valuables from brideprice reflects the tendency for men to have ownership or control of capital. Similarly, within a patrilineal clan system, women do not inherit land, although they may feel they have ownership rights (McWilliam 2011, 750). Even among groups with matrilineal descent and often matrilocal residence, although women consider land to be held jointly with their husband, registration is in the husband's name only. When asked about upcoming registration in the new land cadaster, one woman replied as follows:

Brigida: The land, it is far away—my husband and I own it together.
Melissa: If the state finally comes to give you a certificate, whose name will be on it?
Brigida: Just one. My husband's.[13]

Ambivalent Attitudes toward Brideprice

Brideprice is often presented as "pan-Timorese" and "iconic" (Hicks 2012), or as "cosmologically vital" (Hohe-Chopra, Pologruto, and de Deus 2009) and enjoying the support of all Timorese. But not all Timorese people experience brideprice as a positive practice. The existence of a wide variety of negative and ambiguous attitudes across the country challenges any easy characterization of views on brideprice as "rural versus urban" (cf. Hicks 2012; Silva and Simião 2012).

Rural Impoverishment

Brideprice is fairly commonly seen as damaging for rural communities' economic development, including by rural residents themselves. Despite expectations that people without education are more likely to support brideprice, an illiterate elderly hamlet chief in Oecusse viewed a perceived decrease[14] in brideprice positively, given the difficulty of making a living: "Before adat [brideprice] was strong; now it is not as strong because now we have an enlightened life—*moris naroman*—the kids go to school, people care for each other. But adat has decreased because people also have to look for food and drink [sustenance]. If you are just hunting for brideprice, what are you going to eat and drink?"[15] In his view, high brideprice impoverished families, and their extended families were no longer so eager to help. Thus, he thought that a reduction in the cost of brideprice would be beneficial, "because children also have rights, mothers and fathers have rights, families have rights. If they are going to pay brideprice and suffer, who is going to help them? Their parents can help them, but this is the new kind of life now, and it's not the same as mine, or their parents."

Some Timorese, even rural residents with low levels of education, express serious reservations about brideprice. Consider this statement from a young mother in Oecusse: "We heard about the government's programs to try to reduce the amount of money people spend on festivities. Before, when a man goes to ask the woman's parents for her hand in marriage, you had to pay money or give an animal. Now there is a tara bandu [a ban]; you are only allowed to bring coffee or cake or *sirih pina* [areca nut and betel leaf]. This is better. It reduces the problems for *ema susar* [poor people with difficulties]."[16]

Finally, a member of a Timorese women's organization told me that despite having access to employment, many residents of Dili had stopped paying brideprice: "Some people still use it, but not many. They start to feel embarrassed about paying it. But in the rural areas, it is strong, very strong. Not stronger, just the same as before."[17]

Female Status and Value

Nonetheless, some Timorese women from elite families view brideprice as part of a woman's honor. Serafina, a young woman employed by the local government as a village secretary, told me, "Adat is very important. If you do not have adat, women do not have honor. It is the idea of dignity."[18]

The support that some educated women evince for brideprice suggests that neither education nor a traditional worldview alone informs understanding of the practice (Graydon 2016, 57; Niner 2012). Based on my fieldwork, I argue instead that class interests shape individual views. Serafina, for example, was related to the district administrator of Passabe, a subdistrict of Oecusse. Brideprice signaled her family's high rank, and she was therefore in favor of it. Because the brideprice system benefits high-ranking families, women from these families tend to support the practice as part of their patriarchal bargain and in the belief that it values them.

Perhaps unsurprisingly, some members of matrilineal groups in Manufahi do not share this view. Their families do not practice brideprice, and their perceptions of it tend to be negative. Lucia, wife of the village chief, argued that brideprice was used to justify domestic violence, because if a woman's husband beat her, "then the man will just say, 'Oh that's my money; that's like one of my cattle.'"[19] Lucia asserted that because her lineage does not pay brideprice, the risk of violence against women was reduced, a point that evidence supports.

She also argued that brideprice forced women to remain in violent marriages, and that her matrilineal system was superior: "Here there is no *folin* [brideprice]. Here they just pay one hundred or two hundred dollars. In the future, if the price is ten thousand or twenty thousand dollars, if the woman returns to her family [after divorce], you have to pay it back."[20] Vanda Narciso, Pedro Henriques, and Mário Tilman (2012) suggest as well that matrilocal residence also strengthens a woman's position in this regard because she has access to a support network.

The impetus to regulate brideprice practice has come not only from women's organizations but also from within communities, but in the latter case it is not necessarily based on concern for women's rights. In one interesting case a village eliminated brideprice, and the village chief explained why: "In the past, in my grandmother's time, *barlake* could be $500 to $1,000, and only when this was fully paid would the wife be released to the husband's family. But this left the parents without someone to care for them in their old age because the husband would not allow her to come [back to her natal family after paying so much brideprice]. So we changed the system" (Khan and Hyati 2012, 28). Of its own accord, this community now accepts no brideprice when daughters get married, because women's labor is too crucial to be allocated entirely to a husband's patrilineage, given the need to care for the elderly in an environment with little infrastructure or broad-based welfare support.

The Effect of Monetization

Scholars differ over the effect that (partial) monetization has had on brideprice. McWilliam (2011) contends that a change from buffalo to cash payments has been simply a matter of convenience and does not represent the commodification of brideprice because it remains a symbolic gesture. He suggests that because the system features token reciprocity—the gift of pigs and cloth from the bride's family to the groom's—brideprice should still be considered a gift even when it is paid in cash.

Yet some scholars believe that monetization—as development and modernization take hold—will diminish brideprices: "Social expectations that the 'generic' bridewealth should amount to a substantial proportion of a family's wealth will be supplanted by a desire to invest resources in the individual's own family rather than redistribute it to affines [in-laws] with whom, in any case, reciprocal ties will have become increasingly tenuous" (Hicks 2012, 133).

Others say the monetization has led to inflation: "The shift to a cash economy has meant that in contemporary times, brideprice is commonly paid in monetary currency, a transition associated with a rapid inflation in the cost to the husband and his family" (Rees et al. 2016, 2). Likewise, according to the majority of my interlocutors, with one or two exceptions, the monetization of brideprice has not decreased its size, frequency, or importance. Their assessment is confirmed by a survey of brideprice costs reported in the literature (see Table 5.2).

As others note, societies using brideprice usually try to decommodify the payment by calculating it in terms of special items (cf. Hoskins 2004; Strathern 1988). In contemporary Timor, brideprice is usually reckoned in buffalo and jewelry, although it is often paid in cash. Because of this careful semantic decommodification, it is necessary to look at the accumulation of labor, debts, animals, and cash in more general terms. That is, I propose that brideprice is a consistent feature of the Timorese political economy that facilitates accumulation by the liurai-dato class. Nowadays, these already powerful lineages look for other material bases on which to build wealth, such as elected office or patrimonial networks. Nonetheless, they still benefit from brideprice materially, as they have historically.

Social Forces and Brideprice

Brideprice is less about the value of a woman, or about market factors, than it is about rank and class. Like other brideprice societies, Timor has ranked, named, hereditary status groups consisting of several families (Fishburne Collier 1988, 143). Societies using brideprice typically have four ranks, and Timor-Leste conforms to this pattern (Table 5.3). Many individuals can nonetheless claim the high rank of king/noble. In any given Timorese village, around half the inhabitants are ranked as high status and half as peasants. Thus, around half the Timorese population is from the liurai-dato class. Although nearly everyone in these villages faces poverty and deprivation, the difference in wealth between high- and low-ranked people is starkly defined and regulated through marriage.

Table 5.3 Rank in Timor-Leste, by district

	Oecusse	Manufahi	Lautem
Language	Meto/Baikeno	Tetun	Fataluku
King	Naizuf	Liurai	Ratu
Noble	Tobe Meo (warrior class)	Dato/Baino	Paca
Peasant	Tob	Ema reino Toos nain	Akan
Slave	Ata	Atan	Acar

Note: Lautem's ranks are castes, not classes, which favors caste endogenous marriage.

Timorese society is also a gerontocracy, with elders outranking youth. Age hierarchy is referred to as a *maun-alin* (older brother–younger brother) relationship. Wife-giving lineages outrank wife-taking lineages. The most rigidly stratified groups in Timor have castes, not ranks, and, at least in theory, little social mobility. The district of Lautem has the most rigidly stratified groups in the country, with a caste system rather than ranks: "If a couple were not of the same caste, then there would be no marriage. In recent times, young men and women are able to choose their partners but they are still expected to marry from within their own caste. Inter-caste marriage is still frowned upon; women are not permitted to marry men of a lower caste but in some circumstances men may do so" (Corcoran-Nantes 2009, 177). Taken to an extreme in Lautem, brideprice and the exchange of women are crucially bound up with social status across all of Timor-Leste.

The ranked kinship system is based on patrilineage, defined by patrilineal descent (kin groups are related through males) and patrilocal residence (newly married couples live near the husband's family); it affects land and property inheritance, rights to labor, and access to material resources. Most Timorese practice patrilineal descent and patrilocal residence. Less than 12 percent of the population is organized by matrilineal descent, and many matrilineal groups incorporate patrilineal features (Narciso, Henriques, and Tilman 2012; Thu, Scott, and Van Niel 2007). Within patrilineal groups, males are counted as part of the father's descent group, and females marry into the husband's descent group. Male children remain part of the father's house, while female children move to another family upon marriage. Because of the preference for patrilocal residence, a groom's family pays a brideprice for the bride to enter its lineage group and for control over her labor and children. A woman is thus obliged to perform labor (cooking, childcare, washing, cleaning, gardening, and farming) for her husband's family.

For Timorese patrilineal groups, a matrilateral cross-cousin marriage is ideal because it limits the amount of brideprice due (Hicks 2015, 23). In other words, a man marries his mother's brother's daughter. In Lautem, Fataluku society follows this pattern of alliances, and I documented the same preference in Oecusse. Here, a village chief told me, "Years ago, I married [my wife] and I paid her price. Now, if my boy marries my wife's niece, there is no price. It wouldn't be right to charge. That's culture: the right path or the wrong path. There is not a contract."[21]

For the chief, following the "right path" means that his son will follow the same marriage pattern as his father, marrying his maternal cousin or an equivalent relative from the chief's sister's family. It is important to understand how this sets up relationships between patrilineal clans over generations. As depicted in Figure 5.1, it establishes a pattern of marriage between families, which is why it is metaphorically a well-traveled road—the "right path," as the village chief puts it. Timorese favor matrilateral cousin marriages because everybody knows everyone already, they live close to one another, and the two lineages are of a similar status (McWilliam 2011, 750). They are also favored because the brideprice is much lower.

As autochthonous inhabitants—those who settled first—members of liurai lineages are accorded the right to rule, also partially justified through marriage (Bovensiepen 2014b; Yoder 2016, 116). It is also justified through myths, wherein the first-settling high-ranking lineages give wives and land to the in-migrating group, which must pay a brideprice for brides from the liurai lineages. Accordingly, the highest rank, liurai, intermarries with dato lineages but not with the commoner or slave lineages. James Fox (1996, 144) notes that "a settlement lord [liurai] establishes his position as progenitor by giving a woman to the first, and possibly the second, in-coming member" of a different lineage. The second incoming group in turn gives wives to other incoming groups, in theory producing an ordered hierarchy of lineages in which the wife-giving house is described as the male house and the wife-taking house as the female house. Even today, deliberation among noble and aristocratic lineages claiming to be the autochthonous group is a common method for determining land ownership, although competing claims can lead to intra-elite conflicts, such as in Oecusse.[22] Marriage and rank thus determine access to land and therefore to wealth.

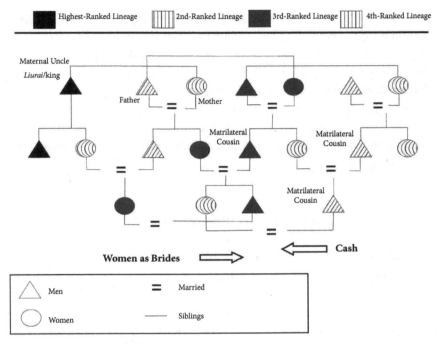

Figure 5.1 Matrilateral cross cousin marriage

In Timor-Leste, higher-ranked, first-settling lineages continued to control political and economic power during Indonesian rule and do so into the present. Antonio, for example, a member of a high-ranking, first-settling lineage in Manufahi, explained a problem with incoming settlers: "Fehuk hamlet in the village of Mota is my land, and people from Fetokiik hamlet have settled here. I command them to go, but they refuse. They want to stay here permanently. There has been no solution as yet. They live in Mota but give allegiance to another village! That's what we don't want [them to live here]. They don't want to register to vote here because they don't like the leaders of our village."[23] After prompting, Antonio expanded on the issue: villagers from Fetokiik were reluctant to give allegiance to Mota because of the brutality of the village chief under the Indonesian occupation. The chief had had two men from the lower-ranked lineage in Fetokiik strung up a tree and beaten, leaving one dead.

Importantly, this violence was structural. It was committed by a high-ranked village chief against the members of a lower-ranked lineage who live nearest near a flooding river, close to malaria-prone lowlands, and farthest from the sacred mountain area. After the assault, the low-ranked villagers sought refuge in another village. Following Timorese independence in 2001, they returned to the lowlands in the Mota area but refused to participate in an election for the high-ranked Mota chief because he was a relative of the former chief, the one who had beaten them. Because of their refusal to acknowledge higher-status lineages, those living in Fetokiik now have no access to roads, electricity, or services. Antonio saw the Fetokiik villagers as interlopers who had been granted land and should thus pay allegiance to the Mota village chief.

Accumulation through Brideprice

In brideprice societies, marriage organizes social inequality (Fishburne Collier 1988). For this reason, a change in the practice would challenge the preeminence of higher-ranked lineages as well as their ability to accumulate cash. Higher-ranked lineages always receive more valuable gifts, and brideprice transfers wealth up the ranks (Figure 5.2). Lower-ranked wife takers will continue to give more expensive gifts of buffalo and cash, while wife givers always give pigs and cloth (McWilliam 2011, 749–752). The gift giving is symmetric, but the volume and value of gifts are asymmetric, as is typical in brideprice systems.

Marriages between high- and low-ranked people ensure a generations-long, unequal exchange of money and goods between families, which intensifies during periods of economic stagnation and crisis. Silva (2011) has described debt as "idiomatic" in Timorese society, but it is in fact a material relation with real material effects.[24] Brideprice debts can be quantified and are not reciprocal and egalitarian, as some scholars argue (Silva and Simião 2012). They are in fact "calculative forms of mutual appropriation or expectations of engagement" (McWilliam 2011, 757).

When brideprices are sky high, the husband's family remains indebted to the wife's family for years or even generations, as sons are obliged to pay their parents' brideprice debts (Corcoran-Nantes 2009, 91; Wigglesworth 2010, 127).[25] As a result, brideprice has been a means of kin-based accumulation for the liurai-dato lineages, where brides marry down ranks (hypogamously) and buffalo and cash are redistributed upward (Figure 5.2).

This process has intensified in the postconflict economy. In the stagnant Timorese postindependence economy, marriage-mediated exchanges

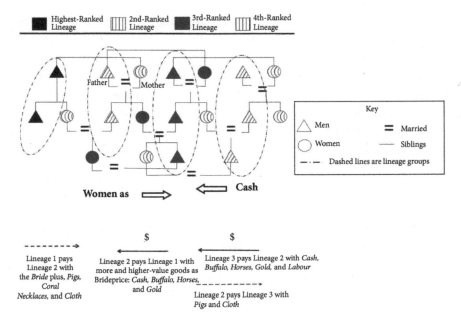

Figure 5.2 Brideprice wealth transfer

created opportunities for "the reassertion of ascribed social hierarchies and the public expression of personal prestige" (McWilliam 2011, 747). That is, the socioeconomic context provided an additional driver of brideprice as a means to accumulate and solidify class relations between the liurai-dato and their debtors. This reinvigoration made changes to brideprice through a gender intervention unlikely, given the power and interests of this class.

Labor and Rank

It is important to realize that in brideprice societies, labor is divided by rank, and access to laborers is also often organized by marriage (Fishburne Collier 1988, 143). To illustrate, at all cultural events, higher lineages do not work to prepare the food, drink, and festival areas; they merely arrive after preparations, as one female farmer in Oecusse explained: "Rich people just come on the night. We ordinary folk do the cooking. Those people are not used to cooking. At their homes, they never cook, right? They always need a *pembantu* [maid]. There's always someone who helps *bapak sira* [misters/higher-status men] to cook. They go to work and come home and just eat."[26]

As the highest-ranking group, men from liurai-dato lineages do not perform the labor necessary to produce valuables for brideprice and other ceremonies; they rely on low-ranking men and women to do it for them. As Fishburne Collier points out, "High-ranking families are free to pursue culturally valuable activities [like war or politics] because they have slaves, outcasts and debt-bondsmen" to labor for them (1988, 143).

Consider one of Mateus Tilman's interlocutors, a spiritual leader (*lia nain*) justifying the extraction of valuables by a liurai in Viqueque:

> If the *Liurai's* child wants to get married . . . the people give buffalo as the brideprice. The [*liurai*] parents cannot give buffalo as a brideprice otherwise the marriage won't endure, they could all die, from the children up to the mother. Their [the people's] role is to work in the vegetable garden and rice fields to give food to the *Liurai*. . . . During traditional celebrations with dancing if the Liurai wants to take a *Tais*, sword or *Belak* from one of his subjects then the person will give it to him. When playing cards for money, if the *Liurai* wants to take everything then he will. (Tilman 2012, 198)

The passage makes it clear not only that liurai charge more for their daughters but also that when their sons marry, lower-ranked people sometimes pay the brideprice for them. When they pay it themselves, access to paid work adds to the ability of the liurai-dato men to operate at the high end of the brideprice market because many have paid jobs.

Labor and Debt

Further, marriage and brideprice play a role in organizing labor through debt bondage. For example, if a lower-ranked man marries the daughter of liurai, he takes on an enormous debt and becomes his father-in-law's debt-bondsman (Nixon 2008, 316). Gunn reports that in 1880s Timor, a husband could become enslaved to his wife's family (1999, 47). Brideprice causing debt bondage is common in the closely related cultures of eastern Indonesia (Hoskins 2004, 97). Again, a difference in rank causes a high brideprice, leading to debts, and ultimately to control of labor by higher-ranked lineages.

It is important to note that debt and social inequality are strongly interlinked through brideprice in Timor-Leste. In other words, kinship organizes social inequality, and the mechanism that reproduces this inequality is debt between lineages. Brideprice initiates complex networks of exchange and obligation in which social and material debts are repaid using animals, goods, belongings, land, labor, favors, promissory notes, or even sons and daughters, such as by selling (the labor of) a child. Social relations—like kinship relations—are shaped by and constituted of debt. Sons owe debts to fathers and uncles, children to parents, citizens to war veterans. Describing these relationships as a form of debt expresses a more significant and more important association than one created by debt that can be repaid simply in time or money. Drawing on the concept of moral economy, some argue that social debts create a notion of reciprocity and cohesion in Timor-Leste (Scott 1976; Shepherd and McWilliam 2013).[27]

To illustrate the way in which brideprice permeates different parts of the economy, Figure 5.3 employs an iceberg model derived from Kabeer (2003, 28). The different modes of brideprice payment are located in various parts of the economy, some formal and recognized, some unrecognized and informal.

To start at the bottom tier, brideprice pays for the reproductive and care labor of the bride. The bride's labor is thus a part of the reproductive economy, which is unrecognized in the formal economy. In the tier above

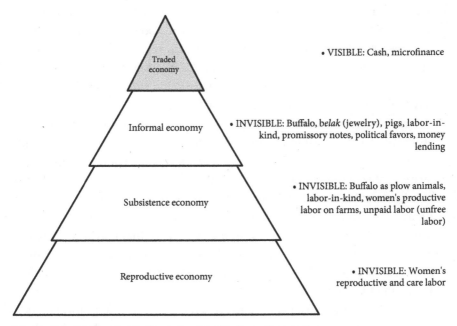

Figure 5.3 Brideprice in the formal and informal economy

that, brideprice is reckoned in buffalo, which farmers use as work animals. A woman's labor in her husband's fields is also part of this subsistence economy, as is (unfree) labor owed by a man to his father-in-law in partial payment of brideprice. Above that, barter in buffalo is part of the informal economy. Brideprice can also take the form of labor-in-kind owed by male relatives of the husband to the bride's house, and in this case is part of the informal economy as well. At the top of the iceberg, brideprice paid in cash or paid for in part by a microfinance loan becomes part of the formal, traded economy.

Only the top quartile of the economy, the traded economy, is visible. Because brideprice is thus largely invisible, and associated most concretely with the subsistence and reproductive parts of the economy, its role in class-based accumulation is obscured.

Brideprice and Domestic Violence

In general, brideprice can cause higher rates of domestic violence because it marks a woman as the property of her husband and his family. Paying a brideprice means that a husband, and his family, has access to and control over a woman's productive work in the fields, her domestic labor, and her children (Alves and Alita 2009; Boserup 1989; Meillassoux 1975). In the Timor case, research shows that men refer to brideprice as a way of reinforcing their rights over their wives (Khan and Hyati 2012, 37). Specifically, if a husband has paid the brideprice in full, he can justify being violent to his wife to ensure that she labors for him (UNHCR 2004, para. 53).[28]

Violence is not the only consequence. When women are considered the property of men, kinship groups come to dispute rights over them. Ruth Streicher's ethnography of masculinity in Dili provides a common contemporary example of this phenomenon, when she quotes a young man describing how fights arise: "So when the other groups [from other communities] have a party, and we go there, and there are a lot of girls, and we want to dance with them, but maybe they refuse to dance with us, that maybe also creates conflict" (2011, 64). Streicher concludes that the young men's behavior is based on the concept that women are the property of communities, and thus any conflict involving them becomes a competition about the honor of the men and the community. I witnessed the same dynamic—in the form of men controlling whom their young sisters and female cousins danced with or dated—at three cultural celebrations in 2015: at a wedding, after a traditional dispute resolution, and at a kore metan (end-of-mourning ceremony).

The connection between brideprice and traditional dispute resolution sets the conditions for high levels of GBV. Fishburne Collier's model of brideprice societies provides an explanatory model for this connection because it explains disputes (1988, 3). She argues that because kinship organizes inequality in brideprice societies, disputes over women are endemic. Common dispute topics include arranged marriage, rape, conception, inheritance, rights to labor, divorce, adultery, domestic violence, and brideprice payment. With respect to the last of these, the status of payment (in arrears, partially paid, or fully paid) can start or prevent common disputes. For example, when brideprice has not been not fully paid, domestic violence is considered principally a violation of the rights of the wife's natal family, entitling it to material compensation. Although the natal family may wish to protect a female relative, it thus has a material incentive to return her to her husband.

Moreover, in the case of divorce, across many countries brideprice must be returned (Goody and Tambiah 1973, 12). In Timor-Leste, more evidence is needed, but Carolyn Graydon describes two women who sought divorce following domestic violence but failed to receive sanctuary because their natal families feared having to return the brideprice (Graydon 2016, 57). Divorce also puts the alliance between the patrilineages at risk; any children—valued for their labor and brideprices—remain with their father's kin. Economic and political losses for a woman's natal family, especially under conditions of debilitating poverty, therefore make divorce very unlikely. In this way, brideprice sets the structural conditions for the continuation of high levels of domestic violence.

High brideprices also constrain the choice of marriage partner, which, according to some young male interlocutors, increases the rate of adultery and adultery-related violence. A marriage between lineages that are not of the same status requires higher brideprice because it represents a new path of alliance between families. Timorese parents then have to *tuur hamutuk* (sit together) to negotiate the payment. This can lead to intractable arguments when one person's lineage requires a very high brideprice and sometimes prevents a marriage altogether even when the parties desire it.[29] Interviewees in Manufahi suggested that the combination of high brideprice and the inability of lower-status men to afford to marry higher lineage women, who were also more desirable, led to grief, extramarital affairs, and domestic violence.[30] As described in the previous chapter, adultery and jealousy were often identified as a driving cause of domestic violence.

Crucially, brideprice can increase the rates of domestic violence because it puts financial pressure on households to give money to the wife's family. In the economically depressed postindependence period, many Timorese came to depend on the exchange economy, which is based in part on brideprice (McWilliam 2011, 748). As I mentioned earlier, the role that brideprice plays in accumulation may be increasing because of continued economic stagnation, which in turn leads to greater pressure on families to give gifts to the bride's family (wife givers). In my view, the return to these marriage-mediated exchanges stems from inequitable distribution of state resources rather than representing renewed kin ties and community spirit.

Obligations to wife givers are observed around once or twice a month, whenever there is a cultural ceremony—a birth, a death, a marriage, or a kore metan. These ongoing and smaller brideprice payments are the responsibility of the conjugal household, although couples will also call on other family members in the patrilineages for help. Under these circumstances, payment places a heavy burden on couples, sometimes leading to financial problems, and these debts are almost universally described as the primary trigger for violence (Khan and Hyati 2012, 37).[31] Wives are under pressure to make sure their conjugal household pays money to their natal household, and my interviewees most frequently gave economic reasons for the occurrence of domestic violence, as Antonio described: "The problem was because of economic problems in their house. Their household income is not enough. Insufficient. They did not have enough to take to the cultural ceremony. The women nags, *pipipipipip*.... Then the man [makes hitting gesture]. Now they are good. No, the household economy is not any better, but she does not nag any more, because she is scared."[32]

Pressure on the household to pay money to the lineage increases the economic burden, which affects women's labor (as they share the responsibility to pay) and their experience of domestic violence (that arises from the financial strain). Indeed, a recent quantitative study found that "women with the most severe problems with brideprice also reported a threefold increase in conflict with their spouse and a fivefold increase in conflict with family" (Rees et al. 2016, 1). Moreover, difficulty repaying brideprice has greater implications for poverty-affected households than wealthier households. In the same study, the women who reported the most severe problems with brideprice had twice the poverty scores as those who had no problems with the custom.

Brideprice is part of the foundation of the Timorese political economy. Scholars who advocate for cultural approaches to brideprice and traditional dispute resolution have inadvertently supported a system that relies on material expropriation from lower-ranked to higher-ranked lineages and violent control over women. Approaches that see brideprice as a cultural phenomenon overlook its connections to the political economy and to the material conditions of domestic violence and debt.

Ironically, a woman must pay for her brideprice through laboring to provide cash payments to her father's family over many years. Men and women in Timor-Leste cite indebtedness and poverty as the main reasons for domestic violence, and constant repayment of brideprice fuels this strain. Debt can lead households to marry off their daughters forcefully, one example of the connections between brideprice, debt, and sexual violence. Many lineages now pay brideprice in cash, and the practice has become more closely connected to the cash economy, financed using microfinance loans that are subject to high interest rates.

When viewed through the lens of gender justice, the centrality of brideprice marks a continuity between patriarchy in the private sphere and in government and market spheres. The use of brideprice strips many female citizens of legitimacy, marking them as exchange objects in a marriage market. Brideprice involves large sums, accumulation, and extraction. Because of its role in cementing and reproducing class relations, power holders have little incentive to reform these relations.

6
Microfinance Interventions

International finance institutions such as the UN Capital Development Fund (UNCDF), the Asian Development Bank (ADB), and the World Bank's International Finance Corporation (IFC), along with bilateral donors such as USAID and Australian Aid (AusAid), have promoted microfinance as an indispensable policy to reduce poverty at the individual and community levels and to empower women in Timor-Leste. By 2016 the country had a sizable formal microfinance sector, with three microfinance institutions (MFIs) holding loan portfolios worth at least $14.5 million.[1] These loans are held by fourteen thousand borrowers, most of them women. Yet promotion of microfinance has continued without robust evidence of its effectiveness in either poverty reduction or women's empowerment.

Microfinance did not arrive in Timor-Leste with UN peacekeepers, although the literature has tended to underhistoricize it as a creation of international interveners. In fact, Indonesian-era microfinance shaped the Timorese political economy under conditions of violence and coercive militarized conflict. The Indonesian military, its supporters, and village elites have all benefited. Despite the association between microfinance and the authoritarianism of the New Order, however, the practice received support from both major Timorese political blocs in the postindependence era, FRETILIN and the CRNT.

In using microfinance as a market-led development strategy in Timor, international interveners in fact found common cause with national elite policy. Instead of reducing poverty and empowering women, their support of microfinance has contributed to the financialization of the postconflict economy and society—with adverse outcomes for many of the poor, especially women, and at the expense of gender-just state resource distribution. Microfinance extracts capital from Timorese borrowers at high interest rates, which accumulate as profits. By encouraging the flowering of self-help group (SHG) and MFI microfinance, interveners have promoted class-based strategies of credit-led accumulation. That is, high interest rates transfer sums of money from poorer Timorese to richer ones. By placing microfinance in a global context first and then analyzing its history and development in Timor, we can better understand how class and gender dynamics have undermined the aims of interveners and deeply qualified the results of microfinance initiatives.

Forms and Aims of Microfinance Interventions

Microfinance encompasses financial services using small or micro amounts of money, and the processes involved are similar around the world.[2] Microfinance loans, savings, insurance programs, and remittances are designed for people with very low incomes, such as subsistence farmers and petty traders. Banks do not normally lend to these low-income earners, because they lack collateral or reside in remote areas where services are limited. Despite the broad use of the term "microfinance," micro*credit*—that is, loans—remains the predominant form (Haase 2013; Karim 2011; Mader 2015).[3] The loans are intended to allow investment in existing or new productive activities to generate income, employ family members, and smooth economic shocks.

At a basic level, microfinance is a gender intervention because it targets women clients. In early iterations, it drew on feminist thinking wherein a pivotal obstacle to women's rights was lack of access to and control over resources (Eyben, Kabeer, and Cornwall 2008; Garikipati 2010). Thus, making loans to women through microfinance ought to increase their access to income at the individual level and lead to economic empowerment vis-à-vis their position in the household. A source of livelihood separate to male relatives was said to give women more autonomy and a stronger voice in the household (Cameron and Ananga 2015; Kabeer 2003). Where women experienced strong patriarchal controls on their movements, microfinance allowed them capacity for income without necessarily disrupting domestic responsibilities or patriarchal norms as wage labor could (Kabeer 2000). Since microfinance was supposed to help redress gendered power relations in the household, it was hoped it would also reduce violence against women (VAW). In cases of domestic violence, or abandonment or divorce, microfinance allowed women to have an independent income and live separately from a male partner when no other social safety net existed.

Table 6.1 Types of microfinance in Timor-Leste

	Formal microfinance initiatives	Self-help groups (SHGs), also known as financial cooperatives and credit unions	Nonfinancial cooperatives (agricultural)	Informal credit markets (moneylenders)
Number	3: Banco Nacional Commerçio de Timor-Leste (BNCTL) and two microfinance instituitions (MFIs)	25 credit unions (2011); unknown number of SHGs	Unknown	Unknown
Origin of initial loan capital	MFI	Group savings or NGO supporter	Group savings or NGO supporter	MFI or SHG or lender's own capital
Connection to financial market	Through financial intermediaries (FIs)	Unconnected	Unconnected	Unconnected
Interest per annum	Approximately 35%	24–120%	n/a	240–360%
Profit sharing	Loans repaid to MFI	Loans repaid to group and profit split between members, in principle	Loans repaid to group and profit split between members, in principle	Moneylenders make loans at higher interest rates to people outside SHG of MFI, profits to individuals or split between SHG members
Regulation	Regulated and supervised	Some registered, some not, generally unsupervised except by NGO supporters	Some registered, some not, generally unsupervised	Not recognized, regulated, or supervised
Subsidies	Donor subsidies to MFI itself	Subsidies to NGO providers	Subsidies to NGO providers	No direct subsidies

Sources: NGO and microfinance client interviews; Banco Nacional Commercio de Timor-Leste (2014), Coulibaly (2014), Solano (2013), Seeds of Life (2016), UNCDF (2014), Coulibaly (2014), Wronka (2015).

Essentially, four kinds of institutions offer microfinance in Timor-Leste (Table 6.1). Formal microfinance is provided by the two MFIs and the microfinance unit of the Timorese national bank, Banco Nacional Commerçio de Timor-Leste (BNCTL). Second, self-help group (SHG) microfinance is provided by credit unions and financial cooperatives (SHGs). These are also called savings and loans cooperatives, Usaha Bersama Simpan Pinjam (literally, Business Together Saving Lending), or credit cooperatives.[4] The third type of microfinance is provided by nonfinancial cooperatives, usually agricultural cooperatives. Finally, moneylenders provide informal microfinance.

In the first case, a field officer from an MFI attracts a group of eight to ten clients, trains them, and disperses the first loans. The officer organizes a governance system, usually holding an election for a leader and treasurer, and subsequently returns weekly or monthly to collect repayments. The MFI charges interest, which it uses to cover overhead. The group decides which members receives loans and in what order. Because the group must cover individual defaults and the loan officer will not disperse new funds until previous loans have been repaid, the group exerts strong pressure on individual members to repay in order to secure the next tranche of loans. Microfinance is thus famous for its high repayment rates of uncollateralized loans (Mader 2015).

In SHG microfinance, the process is similar. Initial capital comes from the group's savings or from an external grant (Credit Unions Australia 2011; FIELD-Support 2014). An officer trains women and forms a group, but first the SHG members as a whole undergo a process of compulsory savings until enough capital has been amassed. Members decide the interest rate, usually higher than that charged by MFIs. International NGOs pushed this model in many developing countries on the assumption that SHGs are more equitable than MFIs because members control the groups and profits return to them rather than to shareholders. SHGs are credit-driven models, however, and people join in order to access loans (Isern et al. 2007; Seeds of Life 2016). They are also subject to little regulation or supervision; in Timor-Leste, some SHGs are supervised by their NGO partners, and some are only nominally supervised by Law 16/2004 Governing Cooperatives (Democratic Republic of Timor-Leste 2004).

Advocates for microfinance hold that an economic dimension to women's empowerment can have a flow-on effect to political or social dimensions (Cornwall 2014). Microfinance using the basic group model could create social bonds between women, leading to greater social solidarity and empowerment (Kabeer 2001; 2005; Mayoux 2001; Rankin 2002). As microfinance alone did not transform gender relations, microfinance programming sometimes contained additional features, such as training or resources for group members on women's leadership, domestic violence, challenging male authority, and group organizing (Drolet 2010; Mayoux 2000).

Once marginal, from the late 1990s microfinance was included in donors' poverty reduction programs targeted at women. On the positive side, this focus drew attention to the fact that poverty is gendered, with significant burdens for women (Chant 2008, 167, 171–172). Women's incorporation into the World Bank's "inclusion" agenda starting in 1995 largely took the form of market inclusion efforts, and chief among these was microfinance (Bedford 2007). Women would be given the opportunity to empower themselves by being included in labor markets and credit markets, and as entrepreneurs. In promoting microfinance, donors took the view that women's empowerment was efficient for the economy as a whole; it could "lift economies, drive growth, improve infant and child health, enhance women's skills as mothers ... [and] open up opportunities for women's economic and political engagement" (Eyben, Kabeer, and Cornwall 2008, 1). Women's economic empowerment was also a good investment, because women would spend their new income on their families, providing a general boost to development (Chant and Sweetman 2012, 519). Microfinance was thus a smart investment for development, welfare, and the economy.

Poverty Reduction and Women's Empowerment

After decades of qualitative and quantitative measurement, it is now clear that microfinance does not reduce poverty. Banks and microfinance providers often measure success in terms of outputs such as uptake of loans, numbers of people trained, and repayment rates. Critics respond that these types of data do not measure poverty reduction or women's empowerment (Vik 2013). Randomized controlled trials gauging impact have not found increases in household incomes, business profits, or saving rates (Angelucci, Karlan, and Zinman 2015; Bauchet et al. 2011). A systematic review of evidence from sub-Saharan Africa shows that microfinance has had a mixed impact on incomes: some people grew richer, but others became poorer because of microfinance, leading to zero overall change in the poverty rate (Stewart et al. 2010). On the question of encouraging broader economic growth, Nega and Schneider (2014) argue that social entrepreneurship using microfinance has had no impact on growth. Other authors suggest that without broader service provision in health, welfare, and housing, microfinance does not positively affect development (Ahlin and Jiang 2008; Ahlin, Lin, and Maio 2011). The systematic review concludes with an explicit recommendation that donors should not promote microfinance as a means to achieve the UN Millennium Development Goals (Stewart et al. 2010, 7).

Providing microfinance to women does not necessarily transform gender relations, but it most certainly relies on existing gender dynamics in the household and society to function (Eyben, Kabeer, and Cornwall 2008; Goetz and Gupta 1996; Elyachar 2002; Isserles 2003; Kabeer 2001; 2005; Mayoux 2001). Studies show that microfinance intersects with the gendered division of labor and unequal access to and control over resources. For instance, although women did the work to acquire and repay loans, evidence showed that they did not always get to use the loan or benefit directly from it (Goetz and Gupta 1996; Rahman 1999). Some authors argue that microfinance instrumentalizes an ideology of empowerment—of self-help and self-actualization—that cannot address structural inequalities (Elyachar 2002).

Likewise, because VAW is rooted in unequal power relations between men and women, the consequences of providing access to material resources depend on a variety of factors and can be difficult to predict (Kabeer 2014, 12). The evidence shows that providing women with greater access to and control over resources in communities and households, including through microfinance, can be contested and actually increase violence against them (Eves and Crawford 2013; Malhotra, Schuler, and Boender 2002; Rahman 1999). A study on Bangladesh revealed comparable domestic violence perpetration rates by husbands of microfinance clients and nonclients. However, husbands of microfinance clients in urban areas refer to their wives' access to financial resources to justify their own violence. Considering that Bangladeshi women receiving microcredit report higher rates of domestic violence than other women do, the destabilizing effect of these resources is alarming (Murshid 2016, 146–147).

Charging high interest rates to the poor is the most controversial aspect of microfinance because of the implication of usury. Liberalized microfinance sectors charge high interest rates, globally averaging 26.6 percent per annum, although in individual cases percentages can run into the hundreds (CGAP 2003; Mader 2014, 608). High interest rates have effects at the individual and social level because the resulting debt shapes both current and future power relations between people, creating conditions of "domination and subordination between creditor and debtor, and it has both a financial and a social component" (Graeber 2011; Karim 2011, 37; Rankin 2004). Thus, in a study by Guérin, Kumar, and Agier (2013), microfinance was shown to be part of the reproduction of unequal access to, and control over, power and resources by giving some women power over others.

The Financialization of Development

Despite such mixed or negative evidence, the promotion and growth of microfinance have continued apace. In countries around the world, a neoliberal push to liberalize agricultural credit markets precipitated what Robinson (2002) called the "microfinance revolution." Since the 1970s, international organizations and experts have pushed microfinance toward a financially sustainable model, starting with the Ohio school.[5] This approach argued that providing micro- and group loans to the poor through banks at commercial rates, rather than through the state, would avoid the inefficiency and corruption that permeated subsidized agricultural credit in state-led development and the bureaucratic aid industry (Gonzalez-Vega 1977). The Ohio school of thought was instrumental to the Indonesian government's embrace of "sustainable" microfinance, in which loan providers cover their overhead and become profit-making using the yield on interest. In this view, MFIs that rely on government or donor money to subsidize client interest rates are unsustainable (Ravicz 1998; Rahman 1999). Critics have termed the microfinance industry's move away from poverty reduction or women's economic empowerment to focus on financial sustainability as a "mission drift" (Augsburg and Fouillet 2013).

From the late 1990s, and concurrent with the use of microfinance in poverty reduction programs, the role of commercial finance and financial intermediaries (FIs) in microfinance expanded. FIs are specially created investment banks and managed funds that invest in microfinance. By 2009, at least half of commercial loans (or guarantees for loans) offered by MFIs globally were sourced through the international financial sector—that is, through FIs (Reille and Glisovic-Mezieres 2009). Financial intermediaries such as the Grameen Trust, Blue Orchard, and Oiko Credit have accelerated the expansion of financially sustainable microfinance by increasing the availability of commercial loans for MFIs (Reille, Forster, and Rozas 2011).[6] Investors put capital into FIs that supply these loans to MFIs because their historically low cost has meant that microfinance portfolios have consistently returned 5 percent per annum, higher than many other forms of investment. This is made possible by the gap between the cost of the wholesale loans and the price of credit given to the poor. Another factor in the expansion of microfinance has been public offerings of shares in MFIs such as Bank Rakyat Indonesia and Banco Compartmentos, which have made billions of dollars for shareholders and state-owned enterprises (Lieberman et al. 2008; Mader 2015, 67–68). Accordingly, microfinance facilitates surplus extraction from poor citizens in developing countries for the benefit of capital owners in developed countries.

As a result of its investment appeal, the sources of funding for microfinance increasingly found their way into the hands of financial asset managers. Internationally, the donor percentage of capital in microfinance institutions declined rapidly, from 30 percent in 2002 to just 3.4 percent in 2007 (Augsburg and Fouillet 2013). The funding sources are now almost wholly controlled by financial asset managers in FIs, not by development organizations, although donor governments continue to make transfers to microfinance FIs. Microfinance is part of a new "deep marketization" or financialization of development, wherein the financial market sets the conditions for development. The money invested in microfinance by donors and banks changes the relationship between citizens, states, and markets (Carroll 2015).

Microfinance works politically by playing down its adverse social implications (Weber 2014, 545). Foremost, microfinance functions as a political safety valve by providing marginalized people with small amounts of cash and creating opportunities for labor in precarious informal markets, where organization is difficult (Weber 2002). Debt itself becomes a political tool, whether by trapping poor people in debt cycles, creating neoliberal subjects, or limiting citizens' claims on the state for resources and infrastructure (Elyachar 2005; Gehlich-Shillabeer 2008; Karim 2008; Mader 2015; Weber 2014).

In order to create the conditions for liberalized (micro)finance markets, interveners work through, with, and around the state. Through the state, donors draft laws (de)regulating microfinance. Especially since the 1970s and 1980s, interveners have disciplined governments into crafting liberalized policies for the financial sector and used microfinance politically to mediate the adverse effects (Weber 2004; 2014). Microfinance interventions are, as geography and planning specialist Katharine Rankin (2001, 20) notes, "a highly contested planning activity through which global economic processes articulate with local cultural-political structures via the mediating power of the state." Donors also work with the state to promote and domesticate liberalized markets using microfinance, such as in efforts to minimize individual resistance to large-scale structural adjustments in Latin America. Working around the state, interveners such as the UNCDF, active in Timor-Leste, now promote microfinance as a form of "financial inclusion," muting the bad reputation of microfinance (and previously microcredit) for charging high rates.[7] Financial inclusion brings together SHGs, microfinance, and loans to small and medium-sized enterprises, but it also usually involves the expansion of microfinance to pay for public goods such as water, sanitation, and power, along with the use of insurance and derivatives to protect against losses (Mader 2016; Soederberg 2014).

Advocates and policymakers have always been at pains to differentiate between empowering microfinance vehicles and rapacious moneylenders. Given recurrent crises of microfinance and its role in suicides, violence, and debt cycles, however, its supporters are now on the back foot (Guérin, Labie, and Servet 2015). Echoing earlier distinctions between microfinance and moneylending, those who are critical of MFIs or financially sustainable microfinance likewise wish to differentiate between market-driven microfinance and "grassroots" SHG microfinance (Duggan 2016). SHGs are seen as providing an independent, localized, and more beneficial form of finance, but for borrowers there may be little difference in these various lenders and a great deal of overlap in their personnel.[8] Moreover, SHGs in Timor-Leste charge higher interest rates than MFIs, anywhere from 24 to 120 percent per annum (see Table 7.1). MFIs, SHGs, and moneylenders are all based on credit- and interest-driven models and have overlapping historical roots. The nature of debt, obligation, and control over financial resources has important implications for class and gender relations, as the colonial and neo-colonial lineage of microfinance in Timor-Leste demonstrates.

Militarized Microfinance in Timor-Leste

Although microfinance is now the policy of choice for poverty reduction and women's empowerment in Timor-Leste, it was not introduced by international donors in the postconflict era. This type of financial arrangement was a part of the Indonesian occupation and rural development strategy, which in turn was derived from Dutch colonial policy. The structure of Indonesian village microfinance and the interplay of patrimonial relationships and cooperatives continue to influence microfinance in Timor-Leste today. Current SHG and MFI microfinance organizations in the country are referred to as cooperatives: *kooperativa* (Tetun) or *Kooperasi simpan pinjam* (Indonesian). Under the 2004 Law on Cooperatives, citizens can start cooperatives dealing with trade, education, factories, fishing, or culture. The most common form is a financial cooperative, and in practice the term has become synonymous with microfinance, driven by the overlap of agricultural credit with the expansion of profit-driven finance over the last three decades. This legacy shapes class and gender relations and sets the parameters within which microfinance gender interventions take place.

For the Timorese independence movement, notably the left-wing FRETILIN, "cooperative" signified a particular, independent mode of development, compatible with Timorese culture and distinct from market capitalism. After declaring independence in 1974, FRETILIN began organizing the rural economy into cooperatives that would run nationalized land, believing that these arrangements would form the basis of a social economy (Aditjondro 2001, 109; Guterres 2006; Rocamora 1980, 19; Democratic Republic of Timor-Leste 2002).[9] FRETILIN Central Committee member Abilio Araújo, who was later expelled from the party, described cooperatives in 1980 as having two goals: to conscientize the population and to mobilize it (Rocamora 1980, 19). Timorese leader Nicolau Lobato admitted to a journalist in 1974 that the Timorese remained "suspicious" of the new FRETILIN cooperatives, because earlier, similar collectives established by the Portuguese and the Japanese had drawn them in and then left them dispossessed (Budiardjo and Liong 1984, 55). The fighting and displacement resulting from Indonesian annexation in 1975 disrupted the foundations of the colonial economy and with them FRETILIN's nascent cooperatives.

Although the Indonesian New Order had a vastly different vision of the state and society, cooperatives funded through microfinance during the occupation were also a crucial aspect of control over the rural economy. In Indonesia itself, the antecedents of microfinance are rural credit programs introduced by the Dutch colonial government in 1901 as part of Holland's so-called ethical colonial policy (Maurer 1999). The policy directed that rural banks provide subsidized agricultural credit to smallholders grouped in cooperatives. A major creditor was the state-owned Hulp en Spaarbank der Inlandsche Bestuurs Ambtenaren in Java, established in 1895 (Robinson 2002). The thinking was that agricultural credit to smallholders would reduce famine in two ways. First, it would help groups to stockpile emergency food supplies and foster "mutual cooperation," or *gotong royong*.[10] Second, agricultural credit to smallholders would combat moneylenders, whom the Dutch made scapegoats for the impoverishment of the population under the earlier high-taxing and brutal Cultivation System, which had required a portion of agricultural production to be devoted to export crops (Prawiranata 2013). Agricultural credit was aimed at the household level, as part of what anthropologist Ann Laura Stoler (2001, 833) calls the "microphysics" of colonial subjugation and control that spread across Asia in the early twentieth century.

After 1945, in independent Indonesia, President Sukarno (1945–1965) introduced credit cooperatives, and these became a hallmark of New Order development policy under President Suharto (1965–1998). Credit cooperatives were aligned with economic organization according to "family principles" and "self-sufficiency" (Republic of Indonesia 1945, art. XXXIII). In 1968, under Suharto, the Indonesian government transformed the former Dutch colonial bank Hulp en Spaarbank der Inlandsche Bestuurs Ambtenaren into the Bank Rakyat Indonesia (BRI) (Maurer 1999; Robinson 2004). BRI provided credit to distribute seed, fertilizer, technical assistance, and pesticides through a network of compulsory Kooperasi Unit Desa (KUD), or village unit cooperatives, a central institution in the New Order (Suradisastra 2006). Farmers who needed government resources such as seeds and credit were obligated to be members of the KUD.

War shaped Indonesian microfinance in occupied East Timor because rural credit overlapped with powerful military institutions. Members of the Indonesian military used cooperatives operating with rural credit to accumulate wealth. PT Denok and PT Batara Indra Group were Chinese-Indonesian logistics companies that operated in the initial military invasion of East Timor and had connections to Indonesian general Benny Murdani. After the invasion, PT Denok took over Portuguese-owned coffee plantations, marble, and sandalwood exports (Aditjondro 1996). The company exercised a monopoly over the coffee industry using the KUD cooperative organizations to manage production, storage, and profit. Most of the five million to fifteen million dollars in yearly profits accrued to military leaders in East Timor, but Timorese elites also benefited, especially those in Timorese-Indonesian military units. The wealthy Carrascalão family's plantations were returned to them in 1980, for example, and PT Denok gave higher per-kilo prices to them than to farmers working in the KUDs (Budiardjo and Liong 1984, 104–105; Danzer 2008, 183–184). The KUD structure and the interplay of patrimonial relationships and cooperatives continue to shape microfinance in contemporary Timor-Leste. For example, generally speaking, village heads usually become the heads of village cooperatives and microfinance groups of all kinds today (Ravicz 1998, 3).[11]

From the mid-1980s and throughout the New Order, international finance institutions (IFIs) promoted the financialization of microfinance and poverty. Falling oil prices in the 1980s allowed the World Bank to pressure Indonesia to liberalize agricultural credit (Holloh 1998). Sustainable or commercial microfinance became a model for a World Bank–backed "new wave" of microfinance in Indonesia, in the context of increasing economic liberalization supervised by IFIs (Tilley 2017). Changes to rural credit were made on the advice of academics from the Harvard Institute of Development who argued that existing models of subsidized rural credit did not benefit the rural majority because elites captured the benefits (Mader 2015; Mosley et al. 2012; Robinson 2002). As a solution, US advisers wanted the Indonesian government to reduce the need for subsidies, or even eliminate them, using three tools: "charging real (market set) interest rates, aggressively pursuing repayments, and achieving a significant volume of business" (Ravicz 1998, ix).[12]

In the 1990s, the microfinance terrain changed again when the United States began pushing Indonesia to open up occupied East Timor to trade while also increasing pressure to liberalize agriculture. At the same time, in line with IFI ideas, the Indonesian state-owned bank BRI launched commercial microfinance products with commercial interest rates. It also expanded the numbers of borrowers, which was a condition of self-sustaining microfinance, and the subsidized KUDs provided a large customer base to convert to financially sustainable MFI microfinance. By 1988, Indonesian East Timor had over 172 village cooperative units, with over thirty-two thousand members (BAPPENAS 1988, 832). These KUDs, largely controlled by the Indonesian military, were opened up to commercial competition.

In 1994 the East Timor Centre for Village Cooperative Units, PUSKUD, received a $6.8 million grant from USAID to promote organic coffee production for export and established its own network of village cooperative units (Piedade 2003). This group challenged the military-connected PT Denok and PT Batara Indra Group and their KUDs. The chair of the centrally controlled PUSKUD at that time was Herminio da Costa. He was also third-in-command of Pasukan Pro-Intergrasi, a pro-integration umbrella grouping of militia, and leader of the Aitarak militia, which killed many and razed Dili in 1998.[13] After independence and with the help of USAID, PUKSUD cooperatives were rebranded as Cooperativa Café Timor, still the biggest coffee producer in the country and the largest sector of the non-oil export economy (Piedade 2003; USAID and Mendez England 2013).

Under Suharto's New Order, gender ideology and the state apparatus reinforced the gendered division of labor, affecting the way in which microfinance worked on the ground in both Indonesia and East Timor. The state controlled access to microfinance for women's craft, trading, and farming groups through the Family Welfare Movement (PKK), a state organization of public servants' wives (Suryakusuma 2011). The PKK had a hierarchical chain of command that incorporated every public servant's wife; each woman was assigned a title and responsibility reflecting the importance of her husband, extending from the wife of the president to the wife of a hamlet leader. Together with other key organizations such as Dharma Wanita, the PKK propagated an ideology of gender relations that defined women by their role as wives and mothers looking after their family's welfare. Critics have termed this doctrine "state *ibuism*," or state mother-ism (Stivens 1990; Syamsiyatun 2007; Wieringa 1992). Accordingly, elite women managed activities such as family planning, hygiene, and welfare, but all of these started with savings and loans (Holloh 1998, 74). These elites ran village microfinance groups for women along with the compulsory rotating savings and loan associations known as *arisan* (Holloh 1998, 40, 69).

In the context of New Order authoritarianism, the PKK, always tightly linked to the militarized state, together with the state family planning agency Badan Koordinasi Keluarga Berencana Nasional (BKKBN), thus ran microfinance groups that ensured state supervision of family life, reproduction, and the gendered division of labor (Wieringa 1993). Most concretely, the New Order linked population control to microfinance. From 1979, microfinance groups started by the BKKBN required women to use contraceptives before they could get loans (Shiffman 2002, 1209).[14] Further, in East Timor, the BKKBN and the PKK helped with government family planning programs that were in effect part of a military strategy of population control. Timorese women were coerced into sterilization and other types of birth control, mirroring the use of SGBV as a weapon of war (Aditjondro 1998, 116; Budiardjo and Liong 1984).

The Visible Hand of Microfinance Intervention

During the peacebuilding era, interveners supported the existing microfinance industry in the newly independent Timor-Leste, seeking to expand and reshape it. From 2002 to 2017, donors spent nearly $45 million on various projects promoting microfinance. Agricultural cooperatives absorbed almost $33.8 million, MFI projects took $9.8 million, and SHG projects received over $1.3 million. So significant is the microfinance industry today that it shapes the Timorese economy. The broad economy and microfinance specifically have experienced interconnected crises associated with liberalization, in which material support from interveners has played a crucial role.

East Timor province had been economically dependent on Indonesia, and after independence, the economy contracted around 40 to 45 percent, bankrupting many petty traders and microfinance groups. Moving into the gap, the World Bank, the ADB, the UNCDF, and a variety of NGOs all founded new MFIs. The World Bank's Community Empowerment Program (CEP) used microfinance to recapitalize shops, businesses, and infrastructure destroyed in the militia violence of 1998–1999. Other microfinance schemes included same-day (payday) loans offered through Opportunidade Timor Lorosa'e; the MFI Moris Rasik, supported by the Grameen Bank investor network; and the MFI Tuba Rai Metin, started by Catholic Relief Services (Marino 2006). In 2001, the ADB set up the Institute of Microfinance of Timor-Leste (IMfTL), which quickly attracted many new clients.

Interveners saw microfinance as a way to address economic losses from the war, alleviate poverty, and foster social cohesion. In Timor-Leste, the UN mission believed that the expansion of microfinance would have a beneficial effect on incomes, reduce poverty, and loosen the credit bottleneck impeding rural development (UNMIT 2009). Microfinance could help achieve the UN Millennium Development Goal 2015 targets on poverty reduction by extending market access—increasing "financial services for the poor and low-income people, both women and men" (UNCDF 2014, 5). It would do so by remedying the market's failure to provide "sustainable" (profitable) sources of credit to the poor, thereby allowing a poor individual to earn income through entrepreneurial activities or interest on savings. In addition to MFI credit, SHG microfinance would help build savings and social capital. For example, Credit Unions Australia (2011, 6–7), which worked with the financial cooperative Hanai Malu in Timor-Leste on the expansion of credit cooperatives, suggested that the joint liability of group members fostered social cohesion and strengthened social ties.

Dealing with Crisis

Yet the microfinance industry in Timor-Leste faced successive crises. From 1999 to 2002, UN staffing levels drove Dili's service economy and real estate market. But in 2002 the withdrawal of international troops caused a severe economic contraction and a related microfinance crisis. Repayment rates in the CEP credit scheme fell to 40 percent, and it was declared a failure and abandoned (Conroy 2004; Hughes 2009). A few years later, during the political crisis of 2006, violent upheaval and fear of army and police rivalry caused thousands to flee, and non-oil GDP contracted by at least 5 percent. Microfinance-supported businesses such as small retail shops and credit unions went bankrupt, and microfinance providers across Timor-Leste shut their doors.[15] IMfTL had large numbers of defaulters who were unlikely to repay (Day 2010).

After the microfinance collapse, IFIs took three steps to consolidate the sector. First, ADB gave the debt-plagued IMfTL to the government of Timor-Leste, transforming it into the state-owned Banco Nacional Commerçio de Timor-Leste (BNCTL). The notional rescue of IMfTL thus transferred MFI debt to the Timorese state. The second step donors took was to recapitalize the MFIs through Inclusive Finance for the Underserved Economy (INFUSE), a project jointly funded by IFIs and the Timorese government. Between 2008 and 2015 INFUSE made a series of grants and soft loans to only two MFIs, Moris Rasik and Tuba Rai Metin, amounting to nearly $8 million (De Sousa Shields 2011; UNCDF 2014).[16]

The third step was regulation, not to protect borrowers but to ensure that Timorese microfinance conformed to market principles. INFUSE provided capacity building and expertise to draft a law regulating MFIs (Democratic Republic of Timor-Leste 2010d). Public Instruction No. 06/2010—Licensing and Supervision of Other Deposit Taking Institutions—thus adhered to liberalized financial market ideals: high interest rates, commercial borrowing, no subsidies directly to clients, and collateralizing the moveable property of the poor (UNCDF 2014). Timorese MFIs are now legally required to source their loans from international credit markets. For example, Moris Rasik borrowed from the financial intermediary Blue Orchard. Under these conditional grants, the MFIs are evaluated on the basis of expansion of their client base, rather than their impact on either poverty or women's empowerment (Day 2010; Vik 2013). The law also makes MFIs subject to supervision by the Timorese central bank to ensure that their interest rates are high enough to be financially sustainable or profitable.[17] Currently, that means the two Timorese MFIs have effective interest rates of around 35 percent a year (see Table 7.1).

The bailouts show that microfinance in Timor-Leste is not a financially sustainable development. Rather, instead of donors or governments subsidizing the poor directly through grants or transfer programs, the public sector and donors subsidize private-sector MFIs (Mader 2015, 56). Microfinance is most materially valuable to the NGOs, government, and private groups that own and run microfinance and benefit in the form of jobs and grants. The injection of tens of millions of dollars from donors and government enabled the two MFIs to survive and come to dominate the Timorese credit market.

Financial Liberalization through SHGs

International donors also encouraged the liberalization of the financial sector in another area, by promoting the expansion of SHG microfinance and thus effectively adding another layer of finance. The links between liberalization and both SHG and MFI microfinance have been overlooked in the literature. Particularly after the 2006–2007 political crisis, NGOs such as Oxfam, Seeds of Life, and UNDP Compasis began training SHGs to mobilize savings to use as loans within the group. As explained earlier, microfinance can work with and through the state to deliver aid and development, and SHGs have become a dominant form of delivery for development goods to poor rural women (Jakimow 2009, 473). At least ten NGOs and other government departments currently run SHG groups in Timor-Leste. These groups have thousands of customers, although it is unclear how many there are because they are not registered or supervised (Wronka 2015).

SHG advocates argue that because the groups are organized and run for members, they represent a form of self-empowerment (Cameron and Ananga 2015; Dichter and Harper 2007). Donors and IFIs promote SHGs as a natural and authentic response of communities to poverty, but it is neither. The perception of SHGs and other forms of informal credit, such as arisan, as "natural" or "traditional" or "voluntary" is longstanding, although there is little empirical evidence that they predate colonialism (Holloh 1998). A similar view can be seen in a recent USAID report on agricultural finance. The authors caution against government regulation of SHGs or subsidies for agricultural cooperatives because such involvement would "hinder the spontaneous expansion of informal UBSP village savings and loan associations [SHGs] as entry-level financial service providers that are not ready or willing to convert into formal financial cooperatives" (FIELD-Support 2014, 11). The demonization of subsidies and regulation echoes the advice of US academics to the Indonesian government to foster commercial microfinance in the 1980s.

In fact, I assert that SHGs are not about self-help as much as they are about financial intermediation within a given group or community. Although more evidence is needed to confirm this, I believe we need to change the view of SHGs as mutual assistance groups to one of groups of debtors and creditors—in other words, of class-led accumulation. Research on SHGs in Uganda and Laos reports problems of over-indebtedness and lack of distinction between microfinance, pyramid schemes, and moneylending (Duggan 2016; Koichi 2015). Detlev Holloh (1998, 97), writing on SHGs in Indonesia, found that each group contained half lenders and half borrowers. Regardless of their internal workings, it is well established that unregulated expansion of SHGs can lead to credit market volatility—with extreme peaks and troughs in interest rates, and sudden problems with (too much) access to credit—which ought to be cause for concern for poverty reduction programs (Duggan 2016; Holloh 1998; Low 1995, 10).

The Local Turn and Microfinance

Politically, MFI and SHG microfinance blossomed at the confluence of two policy ideals: one from the leftist party of independence, FRETILIN, referring to credit groups as "cooperatives," and the other from neoliberal approaches to poverty reduction, referring to them as "microfinance." Whatever the name, the social credentials of these groups as a bottom-up intervention resonated with Timorese elite political ideology, while their neoliberal focus on market-led development suited donor and government policy (Budiardjo and Liong 1984, 55; Hughes 2015, 917). The local turn in peacebuilding was also satisfied by this prioritizing of local needs and bottom-up measures. In Caroline Hughes's analysis, development strategies such as funding cooperatives through microcredit gave FRETILIN and local-turn proponents common cause despite very different ideological foundations.

Support for the coexistence of public and private cooperatives was written into the Timorese constitution in 2002, although neither the specific terms of coexistence nor the role of the financial sector in cooperatives is clarified in the document (Democratic Republic of Timor-Leste 2002). Other documents developed in the postindependence era demonstrate a suspicion of state interventionism. For example, the 2004 Law on Cooperatives, drafted during FRETILIN's term, states that Indonesian occupiers "distorted" cooperatives in order to "prevent their associates' self-reliance. Cooperatives came to be an organized form of creating and *strengthening the spirit of dependence of the community on subsidies and assistance granted by the occupying State*, as a way of fostering alienation and buying social peace" (Democratic Republic of Timor-Leste 2004, emphasis added). FRETILIN and the Indonesian occupiers both promoted cooperatives as part of a rural development strategy, yet the view of Timorese lawmakers was that the involvement of the state fostered dependence, not community empowerment. Thus, what Julia Elyachar (2002, 496) calls a "pro-people, anti-state" ideal is the aspect of microfinance that has resonated with the Timorese elite, as it has with neoliberal interveners.

Successive Timorese governments have supported market-led approaches to poverty reduction, regarding microfinance as an effective way to resolve a perceived bottleneck to private-sector growth by providing access to finance (Wronka 2015). Indeed, support for microfinance is now formalized in "soft law"—the Timorese government's accession to the Maya Declaration on Financial Inclusion (Soederberg 2014). The government's Strategic Development Plan 2011–2030 identifies the private sector as the appropriate primary source of income and employment growth in rural areas (Democratic Republic of Timor-Leste 2011b). In this plan, the Central Bank of Timor-Leste (BCTL) promotes the provision of credit to the private sector in order to enhance national development goals (BCTL 2013). Further, in 2015 Prime Minister Rui Araújo confirmed that his government would continue to encourage the central bank to give micro-, small, and medium-sized companies access to credit, and cooperatives run with microfinance are now seen as a major aspect of private investment in rural areas. Within the broader Strategic Development Plan, Araújo's program explicitly pledged government support for the formation of cooperatives "to encourage private sector growth in rural areas" (Democratic Republic of Timor-Leste 2015a, section 3.12).

Since independence, microfinance has been one of the fundamental ways in which Timorese governments have envisaged integrating women into the market economy. Responsibility for monitoring and sometimes implementing programs for women's economic empowerment lay with the office titled the Socio-Economic Promotion for Women (SEM). Women's groups active in the productive sector are formalized and registered as businesses in order to receive one-off grants from SEM. A senior male manager described the process: "Groups of five to ten can apply for the grant. These are pure grants. We encourage them to deal with the banks because there is no second phase of funding. Initial capital only."[18]

The Oecusse free trade zone illustrates the links between microfinance and economic growth. The ZEESM "frontloaded" government spending on infrastructure such as roads, an airport, hotels, and a harbor to service foreign private-sector companies. That is, by spending big on infrastructure, the government hoped to attract private investment in the future. The ZEESM had stated social goals, including reducing poverty by increasing employment and incomes.[19] According to policymakers, the ZEESMs would provide jobs and growth directly in construction and export industries, and microfinance for small enterprises in the zone would aid in the integration of social and gender goals. During my fieldwork in 2015, a senior staff member told me of a plan for the ZEESMs to link the three hundred existing MFI and SHG groups in Oecusse with export processing, such as strawberry farming.[20] However, the intended outcomes for poverty reduction and women's empowerment were nebulous. Other scholars have similarly noted a lack of coordination and cohesion across the four ministries that implement microfinance policy (Day 2010; Lyman, Shrader, and Tomilova 2015; Wronka 2015).

Endorsement of the potential of microfinance to reduce poverty in Timor-Leste has ignored the effects of earlier microfinance crises and minimized the risks of expanding low-return, petty-trade businesses in a volatile economy. Microfinance markets are prone to crisis from both endogenous and exogenous factors (Guérin, Labie, and Servet 2015). At least eight countries around the globe experienced destabilizing microfinance crises between 2008 and 2015.[21] In Timor-Leste, publicly available evaluation reports on microfinance performance through crises are mixed. The IFC, UNCDF (2014), and USAID (USAID and Mendez England 2013) are upbeat on the subject, and some reports do not mention the risks for clients and local credit markets associated with the expansion of MFI or SHG microfinance (Day 2007; 2010; FIELD-Support 2014; Solano 2013). None take into account the widely acknowledged problems regarding the limited ability of governments to regulate and limit default risk, loan arbitrage, and market saturation or to ensure a realistic capital-to-loan ratio, especially in SHGs (Staschen 2002).

Only an independent evaluation of the microfinance component of the World Bank's CEP is pessimistic (Conroy 2004). The report explains how emergency micro- and midi-loans were supposed to promote postconflict reconstruction by recapitalizing retail shops and using credit to fund village infrastructure. It concludes that microfinance was not suited to the high-risk postconflict environment because of the fragility of the economy and the vulnerability of Timorese citizens during downturns.[22]

When microfinance groups went bankrupt during an economic downturn, IFIs, donors, and governments attributed the problem to the rural poor's lack of capacity or training in money management. Poverty was reframed as an agential issue, solved or exacerbated by the actions and "mentality" of the poor, although fieldwork data point instead to the external risks that microfinance brings for borrowers. Hughes (2015) showed that microfinance groups in the Timorese district of Liquisa collapsed because of stagnating economic growth. A manager in a Timorese NGO retold this common story regarding its program: "When the UN mission was still in Timor-Leste [in 2012], there were many foreigners, and they bought many pieces and textiles and then women got money. They could have money for basics. Now that the UN has left, there is not enough business."[23] Without foreigners buying cloth at the markets, microfinance clients were unable to increase their incomes or repay their debts.

Despite these structural and historical causes of poverty, elites such as civil servants and NGO workers tend to view citizens as responsible for their own poverty. In the words of the director of the donor-supported Hanai Malu, "In my opinion, the problem we face is one of mentality. The population's lives are conservative, in particular, they do not adapt to reality. . . . For example, the people have a base, a cow or a goat. They do not sell the cow in order to develop the cow that it might become two cows, but instead, they slaughter it for an animist sacrifice" (Ferreira 2012, 24). Ferreira's opinion illustrates how the "inability or unwillingness" of the poor to "adapt" and join the market to overcome poverty is seen as "individual weakness"—in this case, a weak mentality (Soederberg 2014, 204). In another example, a Timorese microfinance expert reported that policymakers believed ordinary Timorese put no value on self-sufficiency, and instead "the government must always come to the rescue" (Allden 2009, 278). Even the former national director of micro cooperatives and small business, Jacinta dos Santos, remarked, "The problem is a mentality where people just ask [for handouts]. However, because there is a different attitude of helping yourself in a cooperative, they know a cooperative needs to be independent and do things to help themselves. It is not just that someone else should continue to come and give them support" (*Timor Post* 2015b).

For policy elites, microfinance stands in for welfare. Consumer credit provided through microfinance—or "debtfare"—is promoted in order to avoid the requirement to provide welfare (Soederberg 2014, 196). Microfinance also shifts the responsibility for poverty from structures to agents by entrenching the idea that the core problem facing people is their lack of assets. By this logic, the solution is to extend credit, shifting attention away from the structural nature of poverty. That is, poverty is borne of "rampant inequality and of rotten relationships that are rife with coercion, discrimination, exploitation and powerlessness" (Copestake et al. 2015, 5). As a policy to reduce poverty, microfinance thus puts the onus for income growth on the poor, which corresponds with elite interests in centralizing spending in Dili. This repeats the elite-focused distribution of state resources that veterans' pensions have facilitated, as I described in Chapter 3.

Since independence, the microfinance industry has expanded, collapsed, and expanded again. The IFC and financial intermediaries set the conditions and rules for the microfinance industry, which was only possible using donor funds. In other words, microfinance in Timor-Leste is not financially sustainable, as interveners claim, because it has required donor funding and state subsidies over a long period. These subsidies primarily benefit MFIs and NGOs, not microfinance clients. Instead, during times of economic downturn, underregulated microfinance can pose risks to clients in the form of over-indebtedness and the resultant social stress. At the same time, donors have encouraged the expansion of SHG microfinance, with substantial consequences, as the following chapter discusses. Most significantly, support of both MFI and SHG microfinance has continued without robust evidence that it reduces poverty or empowers women.

7
Gendered Circuits of Debt and Violence

Why have gender interventions for microfinance been so qualified? We know that MFI microfinance extracts money from the poor through high interest rates and transfers it to international financial institutions. This credit-led accumulation has been repeated in miniature in MFI and SHG microfinance at the village level. And by encouraging the expansion of both these forms of microfinance as a way to advance women's economic empowerment, gender interventions have in fact facilitated class-based strategies of credit-led accumulation.

Instead of increasing access to capital and therefore improving incomes, microfinance has strengthened the economic control of the liurai-dato class over poor villages by formalizing kinship and social debt relations and reconfiguring heavy social debts into interest-bearing loans. Because Timorese microfinance occurs in the context of complex networks of exchange and obligations that encourage and coerce repayment, meager but significant sums are transferred through sky-high interest rates from poorer to relatively wealthier sections of Timorese communities. This transfer happens because SHG and MFI microfinance overlap with one another and with moneylending, and none of these activities are properly regulated. Moreover, the co-occurrence of these three underregulated activities has created an unstable shadow financial system.

Rural elites use microfinance as a way of controlling economic life in the village and bolstering their historical, political, and cultural domination. Economies of debt and exchange are fundamental to power in villages with low levels of monetization and a tradition of brideprice. Timorese social and gender relations are expressed in terms of debt, as I explained earlier with respect to brideprice, and debts from microfinance thus fit within an already established repertoire of social domination. Women's empowerment through microfinance is constrained by the centrality of male authority in kinship relations and by the role microfinance plays in brideprice. Debt also sets the

Building Peace, Rebuilding Patriarchy. Melissa Johnston, Oxford University Press. © Oxford University Press 2023.
DOI: 10.1093/oso/9780197637999.003.0008

166 BUILDING PEACE, REBUILDING PATRIARCHY

conditions for high levels of violence against women. Finally, pursuing a rural development policy based on the so-called cooperative model (actually microfinance) mixed with donor goals for women's economic empowerment shifts risks and responsibility from the central government onto women and the rural poor.

Village Political Economy

A case study of a Manufahi village, supplemented with observations from fieldwork in microfinance-saturated Oecusse, illuminates the failure of microfinance in postconflict Timor-Leste.[1] The village of Mota has a population of around a thousand across seven hamlets in Manufahi. Fehuk is the highest-ranked hamlet and is high up (*leten*), or closer to the mountain, reflecting its elevated status. The leading family in Fehuk is the founding liurai lineage, and its leaders have ultimate authority over who may farm the productive land across Mota. As elsewhere in the country, all leadership positions are occupied by members of liurai and dato lineages. Bonifacio, the village chief of the village of Mota, is a dato married to a female liurai. Their lineage is matrilineal; Bonifacio's wife, Lucia, is the niece of the liurai (king), who also has a

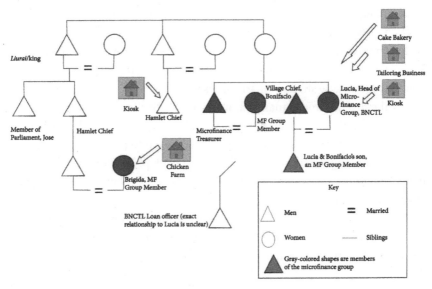

Figure 7.1 Overlapping kinship and microfinance in Mota

son, Jose, who is a member of parliament (Figure 7.1). Bonifacio was elected village chief (*xefe suku*) in 2009 and leads the Mota village council, whose members comprise his relatives and members of higher-lineage houses.

Liurai and dato lineages have businesses buying and selling cattle, chickens, and clothes or operating small shops or kiosks (*kios*), in addition to running family farms. The village and hamlet chiefs own all the kiosks except one, and microfinance has funded most of this small retail expansion. Others have noted that these microfinance-funded kiosks are now so numerous in Timor-Leste that the market is saturated (Moxham 2005; Seeds of Life 2016). At least two of the Mota kiosks are supplied with government-subsidized imported rice by the MP Jose, from the liurai family. Like many villages in Timor-Leste, Mota has very poor access. River flooding makes the road to the district capital impassable in the wet season, so residents have to buy items such as oil, salt, and rice from the kiosks. Their dependence on these retail outlets means that owners can overcharge. Indeed, press reports showed that government-subsidized rice has been sold under monopolies by village leaders in these small shops for double and triple the stipulated price (March 2012).

Members of higher lineages can afford to hire lower-ranked (more distant) relatives to work their fields during busy periods. The majority of Mota's villagers are peasants and subsistence farmers who usually pay for consumer items and school costs by raising and selling a few animals a year, but they sometimes own small businesses (Democratic Republic of Timor-Leste 2011a). Members of the lowest (poorest) peasant lineages generally survive solely on subsistence farming and animal husbandry of pigs and chickens. A few men in this group can earn small incomes working as day laborers.[2]

In sum, the village of Mota comprises a group that dominates animal husbandry, small shops, and businesses, and another group engaged mostly in subsistence farming of corn and a few vegetables on more marginal land. This poorer group, the lower-ranked lineages, are often referred to as *ema araska* or *ema susar* (people with hardships or problems). Adult literacy is 46 percent in Mota, and only 62 percent of children are enrolled in primary school. There is no access to electricity. Nevertheless, the Asian Development Bank (2012) ranks the village as having a living standard just below average compared with others in Timor-Leste.

Economic Activity and Power

In this context, I spoke at length to Lucia about her experiences with microfinance in Mota. Lucia is married to Bonifacio, and her maternal uncle is the liurai. The liurai's son, Jose, her cousin is a member of parliament. She founded a Moris Rasik microfinance group in 2007. The loans she received allowed her to start three businesses: a kiosk, a bakery, and a tailoring service. In 2012 the state-owned bank BNCTL opened an office in the district capital, and government-subsidized microfinance expanded to Manufahi. Lucia was tired of the weekly repayment schedule and interest of around 35 percent at Moris Rasik, so that year she and her brother Antonio, a schoolteacher, received training from the Ministry of Commerce and Industry in managing a cooperative through BNCTL. Because Antonio is a schoolteacher, he had already participated in a public servants' loan program to refurbish his house, buy a car, and start a business. Together, they founded a new microfinance group to give them access to better loan conditions. Lucia's loan from BNCTL has a government-subsidized interest rate of 12 percent per annum and the fifteen members of her group, all relatively wealthy, use it to borrow for large expenses. Lucia's group consider their experiences with microfinance to have been very positive. Her cooperative is successful, and she has a reputation in the village as an empowered, hardworking, and resourceful entrepreneur. Lucia is a microfinance success story.

Lucia's success in building her businesses stems from her ability to tap into her network of relations in positions of power. Her husband, Bonifacio, restricts use of his signature, which is needed on government paperwork because of his position as village chief, and he can also prevent citizens from complaining to higher levels of the district administration. In addition, he controls access to public programs such as solar energy, Bolsa da Mãe cash transfers, and water facilities, and to traditional dispute resolution.[3]

Contrary to the cooperatives law, Lucia's microfinance group sells credit as a moneylending business. One of her relatives is a loan officer at the local district branch of BNCTL. We can surmise that loan officers also act as mediators between moneylenders and microfinance organizations in Timor-Leste, as they do in India, mirroring Isabelle Guérin's findings in India that certain women are able to use microcredit groups to position themselves more advantageously within clientelist networks (Guérin 2014, 46, 48). Table 7.1 shows that Lucia's group procures the BNCTL loan at 12 percent and sells the credit at 120 to 360 percent (0.5 to 1 percent per day) to nonmembers.[4]

Table 7.1 Interest rates, volumes, and lending to nonmembers

Name	Date founded	Mode	Repayment	Loan portfolio (US$)	Interest per annum (%)	Number of Borrowers	Borrower profile	Average loan size (US$)	Evidence of lending to nonmembers	Interest to nonmembers	Headed by village leaders?
Moris Rasik	2001	MFI	weekly	$4,525,162	35.16%	7,373	99.30% women	$542	No	n/a	Yes
Tuba Rai Metin	2001	MFI	weekly	$9,727,499	36.04%	7,265	98.50% women	$748	No	n/a	n/a
BNCTL microfinance	2000	MFI	monthly	$290,210	10% (+ 2% late fee)	n/a	Targeted at women	>$1000	Yes	Up to 360%	n/a
Oxfam Savings and Loans	2006	SHG	monthly	n/a	n/a	1,500	Mixed	n/a	Yes	n/a	Yes
Alola Foundation	n/a	SHG	n/a	n/a	n/a	111	Women victims of gender-based violence	$1000 initial grant	No	n/a	n/a
UNDP Compasis	2005	SHG	monthly	n/a	30% to 120%	213	98% women in Oecusse; focus on vulnerable	Approx. $100	Yes	Greater than 30% to 120%	Yes

(continued)

Table 7.1 Continued

Name	Date founded	Mode	Repayment	Loan portfolio (US$)	Interest per annum (%)	Number of Borrowers	Borrower profile	Average loan size (US$)	Evidence of lending to nonmembers	Interest to nonmembers	Headed by village leaders?
Seeds of Life	2008	SHG	monthly	$1,154,786.50 (Oecusse only)	24% to 60% (nonflat rate) + fines + collateral	925 (Oecusse only)	n/a	$439	Yes	n/a	Yes
Timorese NGO Oecusse	n/a	SHG	monthly	$2,000	240%	n/a	Women	n/a	No	n/a	n/a

Sources: Moris Rasik data from www.mixmarkets.org, accessed 5 January 2016. Tuba Rai Metin data from www.mixmarkets.org, accessed 5 January 2016. BNCTL data from Audit Report 2014 BNCTL Banco Nacional Commercio de Timor-Leste (2014) and Interviews with Antonio ET130, Lucia ET131, Manufahi, 1 September 2015, and Brigida ET146, 7 September 2015. Alola Foundation data from Annual Report Alola Foundation (2014, 18) and interview with a male senior manager at Alola ET083, Dili, 9 June 2015. UNDP Compasis data from UNDP Compasis evaluation (Coulibaly 2014). Seeds of Life data from Seeds of Life evaluation reports 2013 and 2016 (Seeds of Life 2016; Solano 2013). Timorese NGO Oecusse data from focus group interview with Timorese Women's NGO ET096, ET097, ET098, ET099, Oecusse, 27 July 2015.

Note: Interest rates are reported on www.mixmarkets.org as "yield on gross profit." Most MFIs do not report their actual interest rates (Rosenberg et al. 2013). Both of the Timorese MFIs report that they have a "flat interest rate" of 12% per annum. However, as Wronka stated in her report on Access to Finance, "Interest paid every month is calculated based on the total loan amount instead of the outstanding balance" (Wronka 2015, 14). This translates to a doubling of the interest rate over time. As a result, she estimates Moris Rasik and Tuba Rai Metin to have an interest rate of 30.16% per annum. Even so, Wronka does not include fees and charges. These account for the extra 5% yield on portfolio profit recorded in the mixmarkets data as I report here, which I take to be a more accurate reflection of the actual rate paid by borrowers.

In fact, Lucia was elected group president because her experience with Moris Rasik had taught her "a lot about giving people credit," the implication being that she had used a Moris Rasik loan to float a moneylending business in prior years.[5] Currently, she chooses borrowers based on people's character: "You must look at their background. If you give it to them and they have a good history, all is well; if they don't have a good history, then that's bad."[6] Lucia told me that a prospective borrower's character was particularly important when lending for cultural ceremonies such as weddings and brideprice.[7]

Village elites thus dominate the most profitable area of the economy, consumer credit. Table 7.1 shows that many SHG and MFI groups are controlled by village leaders, and Figure 7.1 shows the kinship network underlying Lucia's microfinance group. Guérin notes the same phenomenon in her field sites in India: those who control political power and interaction with the state are also those who lend money to the lower-status members of their communities. In Timor-Leste, as in South India, women have a greater interest in negotiating their involvement in state and political networks than in challenging them, as those networks provide access to resources (Guérin 2014, 47). Taken together, microfinance and preferential access to state resources such as subsidized rice and subsidized credit help the elected leaders of Mota to control many aspects of economic life in the village.

The monopoly of village leaders over state resources has led to resentment in Mota. Those who are not directly connected with the village chief's family believe that its members have used their power and position to enrich themselves.[8] I conducted interviews with members of the hamlet of Feto-Kiik, where villagers are members of lower lineages and in-migrants. The hamlet is located near the river and is subject to malaria and flooding. Rosita, a female villager, complained that leaders ought to "provide shade"—that is, protect the residents as a large tree provides a canopy for coffee crops. Instead, she said, they "haven't taken care of us, however many years they've been in charge."[9] Sancio, who also lives in Feto-Kiik, explained that its residents had applied for an electricity connection but been denied access by either the village chief or the state: "Some of us borrowed money from our family, from our neighbors, gave our electoral cards and money and photocopies to the village chief, and until today we still don't have it. The electricity hasn't arrived. Why not? We people of Mota, we take care of our lands, our lives, and our work, but the State doesn't value us: they don't consider us [*la foo konsiderasaun*]."[10]

Using Microfinance for Moneylending

Microfinance literature is at pains to make a sharp distinction between microfinance as benevolent and pro-poor while moneylending is abusive and exploitative, but across Timor-Leste, as elsewhere, these categories are blurred. Monitoring and evaluation reports show lending to nonmembers in four NGO programs for SHGs that together cover most districts in Timor (Coulibaly 2014, 23; Solano 2013). The UNDP Compasis, Seeds of Life, and Care International SHGs have all reported lending to nonmembers. Most UNDP Compasis SHGs in Oecusse were found to be lending money to nonmembers at a higher interest rate, at least 30 to 120 percent per year (Coulibaly 2014). Loan arbitrage was also discovered in two Compasis SHG groups in the district of Ermera (Table 7.1). Although program evaluators have reported this unsanctioned lending, they have not recognized the implication that higher interest rates extract money from nonmembers for members.

The use of microfinance to finance moneylending businesses has also been recorded by researchers working in Bangladesh, India, and Senegal (Guérin 2014; Karim 2011; Koichi 2015; Perry 2002). During the Andhra Pradesh microfinance crisis, the overlap was noted in the global press: "Traditional moneylenders, the *Wall Street Journal* reported, were not being displaced by MFIs but rather were thriving, thanks to them" (Mader 2015, 172). Similarly, Donna Perry (2002, 31) documented the overlap of microcredit in rural Senegal, as women opted to invest their loans not in artisanal activities or petty trade but in moneylending.

Where other forms of entrepreneurship are risky and crowded, the demand for loans is a smart investment. One of Lamia Karim's interlocutors who used microfinance to float moneylending described it simply: "I realised that this was a lucrative business. All I had to do was raise money and give it to someone else to invest. I decided to join different NGOs to raise money" (2011, 108). Karim found that women in the home had few opportunities to be entrepreneurial except as moneylenders: "In their social world, money lending proved to be a particularly viable option. As moneylenders, women could stay at home and lend to traders who could not get microfinance loans" (Karim 2014, 159). In Timor-Leste, lending money at higher interest rates has proved to be an easy way to make money and convert the capital and labor of the lower lineages into cash.

New Order Gender Legacies

The dominance of the village leader's wife in microfinance groups and resulting patterns of debt relations builds on systems created during the authoritarian Indonesian occupation of Timor-Leste. During the New Order era, as I explained in the previous chapter, microfinance for women was organized under the PKK. The role of PKK members was to promote government interventions in village life, especially in the areas of hygiene and family planning. PKK conducted arisan (lottery) and microfinance groups. Today, the location of power within microfinance groups closely resembles the PKK model, in which each male official's wife had a corresponding place in the institutional hierarchy.[11]

A senior manager at Moris Rasik was aware of the issue: "I know the PKK, and I try to get away from this system. When I began at Moris Rasik, in the majority of the centers the leaders were the wives of the Xefe Suku [village chief]."[12] She noted that changing this practice took time, describing how a typical village chief's wife behaved as leader of a microfinance group: "She doesn't allow others to get bigger loans. When she does, some of the loans have to be for her. She keeps them subdued. She says, 'You don't help me, you don't cover up for me, I won't approve you.'"

This general trend represents a continuation of the exercise of control over poorer women by wives of village chiefs, as was common under the PKK. Such an outcome is not unusual for women's empowerment in microfinance generally (Guérin, Kumar, and Agier 2013, 76). Domination is required because microfinance involves internally hierarchical groups of women who can exert peer pressure to enforce payments. Coulibaly found that SHG treasurers and presidents in Ermera and Oecusse exercised pronounced control over the other group members, concluding, "It is possible that members are not aware of the profit made by the group" (2014, 17).

These elite women are in turn dominated by their male relatives, as Lucia's case demonstrates. Even though she exercises control over the economic activities of both men and other women through her monopolization of small shops and lower-interest loans, her male relatives evidently consider her subordinate. Her brother Antonio is treasurer of the microfinance group. He insisted that although she is the president, as her older brother he is still her superior in kinship and adat:

Antonio: There is some agreement [between adat in Suku Mota and women's rights], but women's rights are a bit less. Men have to be a bit higher. Men cannot be lower than women. . . . Because of this, women have to be subordinate to men. Like me. I have a younger sister, Lucia. According to adat, she has to listen to me. I am a man. She is a woman. That's simply how it is for them: they all have to be a little lower. They have to listen to men.

Melissa: But according to universal human rights, people are all the same.

Antonio: I agree with the human rights—then it is just one system. However, when it comes to implementing your adat, then women have to be a little lower.[13]

Antonio was happy to support women's equality intuitively and at the national level, but not in terms of his own privileges. The division between public and domestic spheres means that although Lucia has authority in her work for the microfinance group, she must be subordinate within the kinship group and household.

The Pressure of Debt

Moris Rasik, which means "independent life," has earned the unflattering and punning nickname *Mate Rasik* (die alone). Poor people with no economic power, or *forsa la iha* (no force), have turned to Lucia for moneylending services. Her group has lent to poorer members when illness prevented them from working in the fields to support their families, and the group members then receive profits from interest.[14] In this way, a debt relation between higher- and lower-ranked villagers is established. Through interest, the village leader's microfinance group is able to extract capital from poorer villagers, reflecting the real relation of debt: "The lack of sufficient capital to satisfy needs among one class, poor people, becomes the basis for a contract with members of another class who are willing (for whatever reasons, whether 'social' or 'financial') to rent out capital" (Mader 2015, 104). Guérin (2014, 45) similarly notes that debt in India is asymmetric between higher and lower castes, with borrowing flowing in only one direction.

Collateralization and Repossession

Poor Timorese fear microfinance because of its high interest rates and attendant risk of repossession and over-indebtedness. The Law on Other Deposit Taking Institutions, which regulates MFIs, makes it possible to collateralize debts using meager belongings, movable property, and land (Democratic Republic of Timor-Leste 2010d, art. D). The fear of microfinance thus comes from the fear of having to forfeit vital assets. In Oecusse, which is saturated with microfinance, interviewees explained as follows:

Michaela: Yes, we have microfinance people here—people from Moris Rasik, from Tuba Rai [another MFI], many people from Oecusse. Our family doesn't use it. Because you get problems from it.
Elisabetha: Your money will go. The state will come and take your house!
Michaela: You don't have to give everything to the state, but you must pay. We know about this because we heard about it. It has already happened here before.[15]

Another Oecusse interviewee reported that she knew an MFI client whose husband had killed himself after having sold their house and land to repay their debt.[16] Interviewees in the Manufahi district capital of Same also described financial stress from microfinance: "In Same, you have Moris Rasik; they have a very high interest rate. Some people can't pay, because the interest rate is very high and their money is already gone."[17] An evaluation of NGO impacts on local communities on the Timorese island of Atauru reported similar views (Trembath, Grenfell, and Noronha 2010). Back in Suku Mota, in Manufahi, Lucia pointed to the financial pressure of borrowing: "If you borrow a lot of money, and you use it well, that's fine . . . but if you don't know how, you just have debt. Then the fear never ends. It's just a struggle against death/collapse."[18] Mota residents reported furniture being taken as collateral by SHG and MFI members.[19] Seeds of Life, an Australian Aid–funded agricultural cooperative and microfinance organization, requires SHG members to sell collateral to pay overdue debts (Solano 2013, 9).[20] Repossession of household items in this fashion in Timor-Leste supports Heloise Weber's argument that microfinance disciplines the poor by making possible the collateralization of their belongings, preventing debt strikes and protests (2014, 548).

Debts and Domestic Violence

As explained earlier, kinship organizes social inequality into a four-tier system in Timor-Leste, enforced through brideprice. Although reciprocity and cohesion are part of social life, focus on the reciprocal aspects of kinship debt has romanticized the role that debt and obligation play in Timorese class and gender stratification. Guérin's argument regarding the South Indian case applies equally well in Timor: "Debt may produce solidarity and social cohesion but also exploitation, hierarchy, and domination" (2014, 41). To reiterate, debt is not merely an idiom with symbolic significance but a crucial part of material social relations with critical distributive outcomes and associated power imbalances.

The creation of significant indebtedness can lead to girls and women being sold to pay debts: "In rural areas, heavily indebted parents sometimes provided their children as indentured servants to settle debts. If the child was a girl, the receiving family could also demand any dowry payment normally owed to the girl's parents" (United States Department of State 2013). Ann Wigglesworth (2010, 127) similarly notes the sale of daughters through marriage to a creditor as a way to repay a preexisting debt, although she suggests that the practice has become more infrequent in Timor-Leste. Thus, the association of brideprice with debts between lineages is linked to human trafficking.

The use that microfinance borrowers make of loans is another aspect of gender relations (Rahman 1999). Women are often the "holders of the money" in Timorese households, but this is a fraught responsibility because they must manage the family budget while having little control over income or significant areas of spending. That can force them to find new sources of debt, which as Guérin notes are often strictly feminine (Guérin 2014, 46). A report on the economic dimensions of domestic violence in Timor-Leste acknowledged the double-edged nature of household fund management for women: "It gives them an important measure of influence, yet can also place them at risk of violence when they are not seen as sufficiently compliant by an abusive spouse" (Grenfell et al. 2015, 13). I saw this dynamic often in my fieldwork, as the following quote demonstrates: "Sometimes women get a loan but they don't use it for a business; they use it for the household, for the children. Then, when it comes time to repay the money, they have to sell household items. Then it leads to strife in the household. This is one of the problems.... When the money is finished, and you have no things left, then you have problems in the household."[21] The widespread use of microfinance to pay for food or school uniforms and supplies creates debts that in turn put economic pressure on households already below the poverty line. Many interlocutors blamed domestic violence on household poverty and economic stress.

Microfinance organizations generally claim that they make loans to women entrepreneurs only for productive activities, but lending for brideprice is common in Timor-Leste. This should be unsurprising; microcredit has been a source for dowry payments for some time (Rozario 2002, 68). Employing a feminist political economy perspective makes it clear that funding brideprice through microfinance incorporates the practice into the formal and international financial markets and makes brideprice interest bearing. Because brideprice payments are so large, they are most often manifested as debt, creating a great affinity with microfinance. Importantly, brideprices are owed in perpetuity and when brideprice is monetized through cash and microfinance loans are used to pay them, the loans that extend over decades are also subject to very high interest. Moreover, when a brideprice loan is made by a microfinance provider, the profit from the interest is channeled to a microfinance institution connected to the international financial market.

Microfinance debt relationships flow in the same direction as brideprice debts; they mirror the obligations of lower lineages to higher lineages. In the case of brideprice, high-status lineages—liurai and dato—can charge more money for brides than lower-status lineages can. Thus, they accumulate brideprice or, more commonly, debts owed to them through brideprice obligations. And because microfinance is dominated by members of the liurai-dato class, both microfinance and brideprice result in ordinary citizens owing debts to higher-ranked lineages. In that sense, microfinance is not separate from the broader political economy of debt in Timor-Leste. Wealthy families, usually from high-status lineages, lend money to lower lineages, which accumulate debt. Debts and reciprocity are framed in terms of "looking after" lower lineages, as in the case of Lucia's microfinance group loaning money to villagers too ill to work.[22]

Risks of Microfinance

A monitoring report by Seeds of Life suggests that its sponsored SHGs are not reaching the target population of the very poorest, especially in hamlets where "microfinance groups are bigger, have raised greater capital and are asking for higher monthly compulsory savings to their members" (Solano 2013, 32). These findings are similar to other studies showing that microfinance tends to reach the most economically active poor, not the very poorest. In India, for example, the majority of new clients for microfinance do not come from the bottom 30 percent of a village (Kabeer 2005, 4711). This concurs with the results of a randomized evaluation of microfinance in Ghana, in which "it was only the larger female-owned businesses that benefited in terms of profit. Women from the general population are not always, nor, indeed, more likely to be, able to convert capital into profits, and men tend to be more successful overall" (Bauchet et al. 2011, 11).

The Andhra Pradesh crisis highlights the endogenous and exogenous risks faced by poor borrowers, overexposed moneylenders, and the microfinancial market, risks that also apply in Timor-Leste. Mader (2015, 164–168) describes four endogenous causes of the Andhra Pradesh microfinance collapse: first, rapid growth in the number of loans because of, second, the withdrawal of state-sponsored agricultural credit. Third, the earlier direct state credit to poor sectors of the community was replaced by state-sponsored MFI loans, and fourth, MFIs were able to "poach" new clients from older programs of subsidized credit and existing SHGs. The crisis occurred in the context of wider economic pressures: a shortage of land that squeezed farmers onto smaller and smaller plots, the promotion of cash crops and subsequent dependence on volatile markets, greater living expenses following the withdrawal of state welfare subsidies, and a degraded environment and climate risks. Increased lending and NGO privatization were coupled with extensive shareholder investment in microfinance, which also created a boom in the Indian microfinance market. All these factors contributed to increased borrowing from MFIs.

The Timor-Leste case carries comparable endogenous risks. In the stagnant agricultural sector, farmers who have suffered through persistent droughts, floods, landslides, and other natural disasters do not have the income to repay their loans and must either borrow more or sell assets to do so. A shift from state-subsidized to MFI microfinance has already taken place, although uneven pockets of state support for microfinance still exist (Wronka 2015). The exogenous risks are the low levels of stable government spending on agriculture, patrimonialism in the allocation of veterans' pensions, political instability, and decreasing oil receipts that increase dependence on aid and reduce state spending (Drysdale 2007; Scambary 2015). Microfinance in

Timor-Leste has been vulnerable to such risks and crises before, and as the poor know only too well, many risks remain.

The expansion of SHGs of MFIs, promoted by donors under the rubric of financial inclusion, does not take into account the key factors that are intensifying microfinance risks. In addition to conflict and economically driven instability, financial markets are inherently unstable. MFIs and SHGs are no different. Risks to microfinancial markets include "contagious" defaulting, loan arbitrage, market saturation, unsustainable or distorted SHG capital-to-loan ratios, stagnant economic conditions, lack of consumer credit protection, and borrower over-indebtedness (Staschen 2002; Wronka 2015). Further, moneylenders operating SHGs in the shadow market need to be able to threaten severe or violent sanctions in order to ensure repayment, and any government wishing to expand microfinancing options should note that supervision of such activity is a daunting task (Duggan 2016). If microfinance principal is not repaid—because of over-indebtedness or external shocks—the system can collapse. Microfinance is a risky business, and the crises to which it is prone have real, material effects.

Advocates for the use of microfinance to reduce poverty have ignored the risks involved in offering underregulated, high-interest credit products and failed to take into account the limited ability of governments to regulate and limit default risk, loan arbitrage, and market saturation, or to ensure a realistic capital-to-loan ratio (Staschen 2002). Levels of over-indebtedness in Timor-Leste have not been measured quantitively, and qualitative findings of resulting stress, domestic violence, and other problems deserve greater attention. Moneylending is rarely mentioned explicitly in the practitioner literature covering Timor-Leste, while assessments of microfinance have minimized the endogenous risks associated with the expansion of MFI or SHG microfinance (e.g., Day 2007; 2010; FIELD-Support 2014; Solano 2013). Moreover, Timorese MFI regulations do not provide consumer credit protection (Day 2010). Yet when microfinance groups go bankrupt after external shocks or economic downturn, donors and government officials lay the blame at the rural poor's lack of capacity or assert that culture is an obstacle to development. At a policy level, microfinance facilitates the shifting of responsibility for poverty from the political elite onto the poor, at the same time satisfying neoliberal donor demands and freeing budgets to buy support from veterans.

Microfinance thus does not work *for* the people it is meant to target, precisely because it works for other groups of Timorese. But it does work *at* the (re)production of inequality through class-based accumulation at the village level. It reproduces gendered economies of debt and brideprice and the gendered division of labor. Microfinance is materially valuable to NGOs, government, and private-sector groups that own and run microfinance groups and benefit in the form of jobs and international aid funding.

The way microfinance works in Manufahi and Oecusse undoes donor and government assumptions. First, many loans are used for consumption and for moneylending, the main entrepreneurial activity. Microfinance has helped village elites to be economically active, reproducing class relations rather than functioning as a bottom-up development tool. The (re)growth of microfinance in the postindependence era did not trickle down in villages and raise living standards for all. Instead, it allowed elites to retain control of the village economy and extract wealth from poorer members, mirroring historical patterns and political economies of domestic violence. The legacy of colonial and neo-colonial economic governance is evident in Timorese microfinance, constituted through material relations of inequality and strengthened through war and militarization during the New Order and earlier Portuguese mercantilism, slavery, and plantation-driven economies.

Finally, microfinance offers another way to reckon intergenerational and community debts. Despite prevailing rhetoric that declares access to credit to be empowering to the poor and to women, in reality microfinance strengthens debt-regulated inequality. Microfinance also intersects with gender through brideprice in a concrete fashion, as microfinance programs reinforce gender order and village leaders' control despite some economic empowerment for some women in the families of village leaders. Microfinance thus transforms the basis of densely woven kinship relations from debt relations into loan relations. They are two sides of the same coin.

Conclusion

Over the last two decades, and especially since UNSCR 1325 on Gender, Peace and Security, peacebuilding interventions have increasingly incorporated gender perspectives. These interventions use both gender mainstreaming and development programs for women's empowerment. On the whole, however, they have had qualified results.

My central aim in this book has been to explain this disappointing outcome in Timor-Leste. This is a matter of measuring results not only against interveners' aims but more crucially against the yardstick of gender justice. To do so involves evaluating the distribution of resources and power, a measure that has allowed me to move beyond the successes and failures of specific interventions to encompass redistributive aspects. In other words, by considering gender justice I was able to ask who got what, when, and how. I was also able to look at the material relations of power driving domestic violence, which is significant given the prevalence and severity of violence against women after conflict in many countries, not just Timor-Leste.

Scholars associated with the local turn have made timely and essential critiques of liberal peacebuilding, but both the local turn and hybridity approaches have proven to be inadequate tools with which to examine gender interventions. This comes in part because the assumptions guiding the local turn are, ironically, insufficiently attentive to class and gender hierarchies *within* local societies. What's more, an alliance of domestic and international support has contributed to aspects of the local turn being incorporated into peacebuilding in practice in Timor-Leste. Although surely an unintended consequence, the local turn has provided a veneer of legitimacy to the continuation and reinvigoration of highly unequal gender relations in the critical areas of state resource distribution following peace settlements, traditional dispute resolution, and brideprice.

This study has pushed forward the analysis of gender interventions by identifying gender relations as a crucial aspect of broader processes through which the dominant class, the liurai-dato, secures its position in independent Timor-Leste. Structural relations of class and gender are the cause of uneven outcomes of gender intervention in no small measure because these gender and class are mutually constitutive. In some senses, it's obvious that gender relations between men and women are crucial to class reproduction over time although both feminist and structural political economy theoretical approaches have largely neglected it. For this reason, I added kinship to my framework. In the book I showed how close control over kinship has enabled the liurai-dato class to retain its power in villages and has also provided a means of wealth accumulation.

Unlike other studies focused on contests between local and international, my analysis thus considers international interveners to be just one of a number of groups in competition over the sociopolitical order. Control over women, reproduction, and the gender division of labor are fraught areas of gender intervention that feature contests and coalitions within and across categories of local and international.

The gendered nature of state resource distribution, traditional dispute resolution, and debt relations in Timor-Leste is key to understanding why gender interventions have had qualified outcomes. The distribution of state resources is gendered in three ways. First, at an individual level, the valorization of armed masculinity has been used to justify allocating state resources—both cash transfers and infrastructure contracts—to men. This ideology is deeply gendered because it privileges heroes over victims. Around 87 percent of veterans' pensions go to men, as do lucrative government contracts. Transfers to women through the Bolsa da Mãe are small and conditional, and they reinforce gender roles.

Second, focusing state resources on men detracts from spending in areas of high import to women's well-being and leads to gender injustice. The Timor-Leste case confirms that peacebuilding can involve concessions to, and buying off, armed groups of men, and this is particularly relevant with respect to personal law and the distribution of resources (Goetz and Jenkins 2016). Gender-responsive budgeting (GRB) in postconflict states ought to have considerable positive outcomes for gender justice, yet more radical forms of GRB, inspired by social justice, have been stymied by the interest of men of the liurai-dato class in monopolizing state resources.

Third, the nature of the postconflict Timorese state has set the boundaries of gender interventions. Namely, allocating resources to well-connected men rather than using them for state infrastructure, health, welfare, and education has increased burdens on women with negative consequences for their well-being. The postconflict distribution of resources has been profoundly shaped by second-generation neoliberal reform agendas. Approaches inimical to the everyday welfare of the majority—patrimonial projects, cash transfers to the elite, microfinance, and lack of state support for health, education, and welfare—have ruled government programming from 2007 onward, continuing a dearth of welfare spending during the neoliberal UN era from 1999 to 2006. The resulting impoverishment of rural areas has had flow-on effects. Poverty and scant resources are linked to the practice of brideprice, because cash, goods, and reciprocal networks provide some material security for families. But these networks and brideprice itself drive violence against women, meaning that material reciprocity comes at the cost of gender justice. Poverty also encourages over-indebtedness through microfinance—which transfers wealth to MFIs and on to international financial institutions, and creates exorbitant debts owed to higher-ranked lineages.

The analysis of resource distribution leads me to my first conclusion: that *gender interventions cannot be measured according to program-level aims because this misses the broader political implications of state resource distribution.* Evaluating interventions according to who gets what from interventions is more accurate than looking at internal goals. Who gets what permits a more accurate assessment of the outcomes of peacebuilding for women. Gender intervention must be conceptualized as an inherently political activity for all groups and alliances. Moreover, the fact that the most vulnerable women are the most negatively affected by the lack of gender interventions in state resource distribution, brideprice, and microfinance points to the need to use gender justice as an assessment tool.

The co-constitutive nature of class and gender relations can be seen not only at the level of the state but also at the level of the village. The implementation of the Law Against Domestic Violence (LADW) in Timor-Leste has had only limited success because liurai-dato villagers rely on their control over marriage and traditional dispute resolution as a means of accumulation. Thus, my second conclusion is that *historically specific power relations between dominant and subordinate classes shape outcomes of gender intervention.* These material considerations, not culture per se, form the basis for objections to changes to traditional law, culture, marriage customs, and institutions.

The gender ideology inherent in brideprice undergirds these material relations of class, leading to a third and critical inference: that *brideprice connects the dominant class vertically across the state and is a vital part of class-based accumulation and interests.* The emergence and dominance of the liurai-dato class has depended on gender relations, and brideprice is not a peripheral aspect of cultural practice but a central feature of the political economy of Timor-Leste. Brideprice establishes status—wealthy families charge higher brideprices—and allows higher ranks to accumulate wealth, shoring up their political power and dominance. In that sense, brideprice is a basis of social structure, connecting gender and class, not some anachronistic aspect of cultural practice but an essential part of contemporary processes of class formation and class conflict. Brideprices benefit dominant groups and are detrimental to subordinate ones because they initiate accumulation and debt relations. At an individual level, they create obligations between powerful fathers-in-law and less powerful sons-in-law. At the group level, they create a series of material obligations whereby resources flow upward from lower to higher ranks in return for brides.

My fourth conclusion is that *various international and national groups support, while others resist, gender interventions, and their support depends on their interests and ideology.* Coalitions of peacebuilders and national elites have made concessions in areas of personal law—the realm of the local –involving particular compromises for the benefit of powerful, patriarchal groups and traditions (Goetz and Jenkins 2016). By promoting traditional dispute resolution and legal pluralism in the courts, interveners have inadvertently fueled a political economy of domestic violence. Village leaders' interests in using traditional dispute resolution have aligned with the interests of ordinary men, because the subordination of their wives, daughters, and sisters has conferred a patriarchal dividend on ordinary men from the gender division of labor.

Finally, I conclude that *gender interventions in finance require historical and gendered analysis* that places them within the context of expansion of state development and neoliberal globalization. Kinship relations—defined through debts—play out through gender interventions on microfinance, although the mutually constitutive relationship of debts, kinship, and finance is not a new phenomenon. Under Indonesian occupation, microfinance-linked cooperatives were heavily implicated in the Indonesian military's extraction of money from the occupied country, and the same microfinance groups were also linked to a shift from state-subsidized credit to "financially sustainable" microfinance. In the postindependence period, the liurai-dato class is able to control local resources in villages through both microfinance debts and brideprice debts.

The major reason for the failure of gender interventions, as I outline here, is the rebuilding of patriarchy that takes place during peacebuilding. For many women and girls of Timor-Leste, independence is a theoretical notion, with gender injustices at multiple levels constraining women's full and free citizenship of their country. Denied any significant share of state petroleum resources, the labor of women and girls—farming, cooking, cleaning, and caring—is the main buttress of households. The devaluation of women's labor is experienced in an everyday way when men who fought are valorized and given the lion's share of resources, while women's labor is not considered work at all. Peace has cemented the gender division of labor in Timor-Leste.

Gender interventions seek to reduce, among other things, violence against women, but they have been largely ineffective. My shock at seeing VAW every day in so-called peacetime propelled me to do the long-term fieldwork for this study. For too many Timorese women, violence from men in their lives is part of daily living; the power, control, and lack of options shapes women's decision-making at nearly every moment. It is not enough for peacebuilders to stop men's public violence while domestic violence and everyday control over women is justified at every turn as "not serious," cultural, part of local exchange economies, and necessary to keep kinship networks together in the name of peace and stability. Given the links between experiences of violence in the family and the wider use of violence, preventing violence against women is both the only course for justice but also foundational to peace.

Accelerated spending on brideprice in peacetime is not some sign of increased mutual aid and reciprocity, but of the liurai dato class flexing their economic power by increasing patriarchal control. Brideprice dominates the everyday lives of young Timorese, limiting their choices of romantic partners and reifying inequality between the rich and the poor.

Gender interventions will play bigger roles in peacebuilding missions in the future. Beyond programs that seek to change laws and strengthen civil society, interveners should be clear that many of their measures intended to build peace instead rebuild patriarchy. The rebuilding of patriarchy after peace sets the conditions for high levels of VAW and imperils peace itself.

Methodological Notes

This book is grounded in an extended period of fieldwork in Timor-Leste and Indonesian West Timor: five months in each place in 2015, as well as an earlier month in 2011. The work in West Timor informs elements of the study—in particular, my understanding of brideprice, traditional dispute resolution, and microfinance among sociologically and culturally similar groups of Timorese—but it is not referred to explicitly. Likewise, preliminary work in 2011 is referred to but does not constitute the bulk of the data used in this analysis.

Thus the present study principally employs a variety of qualitative data from Timor-Leste collected in 2015: interviews, observations, newspaper articles, reports, and brochures. The work was conducted in Oecusse, Manufahi, and Dili. These places were chosen to reflect different rural and urban settings, class divisions, patrilineal and matrilineal groups, and physical environments. Oecusse has received high levels of gender intervention, while Manufahi has had relatively few. Oecusse was also undergoing a period of intensive infrastructure development during the period of my fieldwork. Time in Dili was necessary to allow me to interview elites, government workers, and nongovernment workers. I stayed at field sites for weeks or months, boarding with Timorese families in both Dili and Manufahi, and living and working closely with families in Oecusse, using the Tetun language for everyday communication and interviews.

I designed the research using feminist frameworks that draw attention to hierarchies and power (Ackerly, Stern, and True 2006). Feminist methods are also attentive to gaps and silences in the data and include these lacunae in the research design (Reinharz and Davidman 1992). Wide-ranging, long-term fieldwork facilitated in-depth interviews with elites and non-elites, with particular critical attention given to gender, class hierarchies, and engagement with Timorese women's organizations (Nentwich and Kelan 2014, 132).

Semistructured interviews form the central, constitutive part of the study. From May to September 2011, I conducted eighteen interviews in Timor-Leste. These interviews were obtained under ethical standards applicable at the University of Vienna, Austria, and taught through the Institute for Social and Cultural Anthropology (KSA). I was required to inform research participants of possible adverse outcomes, protect their privacy by anonymizing their data, and explain the scope and aims of the research in order to receive their oral consent. From January to May 2015, I conducted seventy-five interviews in West Timor, Indonesia. Finally, I gathered my principal data through eighty interviews in Timor-Leste from June to November 2015. Some subjects in this last group also participated in the 2011 round, and this time I used signed forms to obtain their consent to be interviewed again, following the Australian National Statement on Ethical Conduct in Human Research (Murdoch University Permit Number 014/188).

The interviews conducted in 2015 had four main types of participants: national experts (at the national and district level, with some NGO participants), gender experts (international, national, and local NGOs), local leaders (village and hamlet chiefs, spiritual leaders), and ordinary people with no links to local or national leaders (predominantly women). More than double the number of women than men were interviewed to ensure

Table A.1 Timor-Leste interviewees, 2015, by gender

	Women	Men
Citizens in rural communities	16	3
Leaders or members of village councils	5	5
People connected to the village or subnational leadership by close kin ties	7	2
Timorese gender experts	13	4
International gender experts	4	0
National or subnational policymakers, experts, or NGO workers	4	14
International policymakers or experts	1	2
Total	50	30

that a variety of women's voices were heard. Tables A.1 and A.2 summarize and provide profiles of the main informants cited in the study. An additional area of data collection was newspaper monitoring, in particular articles in the *Timor Post* from June to September 2015. Articles were selected on the basis of the following themes: gender, violence against women, local governance, NGOs, human trafficking, state resource distribution, corruption, and microfinance.

As described at the outset of this work, the three gender interventions on which the study focuses—gender-responsive budgeting, the LADV, and microfinance—are part of a larger set of fourteen (Table 1.2). These comprised gender mainstreaming in UN missions and national institutions, gender quotas, work on conflict-related SGBV through the Commission for Truth Reception and Reconciliation, new laws on domestic violence, funding to Timorese women's organizations, microfinance, and conditional cash transfers. All fourteen are discussed to varying degrees, but close analysis of each intervention is outside the scope of my study. One reason for selecting these particular three gender interventions to examine in detail is that although extant scholarship on postconflict Timor has covered gender mainstreaming (Joshi 2005; Olsson 2009; True 2009), reparations (Kent 2016), and political participation quotas (Cummins 2011; Ospina 2006), the political economy aspects of gender remain little examined. The other reason is that material power is central to the outcomes of interventions, and those chosen for analysis strongly reflect the themes of control over state resources, over women, and over local resources. They are thus particularly relevant to an evaluation of power relations.

Table A.2 Cited interviewees

Number	Pseudonym	Description	Age	District interviewed	Language of interview	Social status	Date interviewed	First language
ET076		Female international manager at UN	–	Dili	English	Elite	6 June 2015	French
ET077		Female Timorese NGO senior manager	–	Dili	Tetun	Elite	5 June 2015	–
ET078		Female Timorese NGO senior manager	–	Dili	Tetun/English	Liurai	6 June 2015	Portuguese
ET079		Female Timorese NGO senior manager	–	Dili	Tetun/English	Liurai	11 July 2015	Mambai
ET082		Female Timorese NGO senior manager	36	Dili	Tetun	Elite	8 June 2015	Tetun Praça
ET083		Male manager at Alola	43	Dili	English	Dato	9 June 2015	Makkassae
ET085		Female member of GMPTL	57	Dili	Tetun	Elite	11 June 2015	Tetun Praça / Portuguese
ET089		Senior manager, Timorese women's organization	–	Dili	Tetun	Liurai	17 July 2015	Mambai

(*continued*)

Table A.2 Continued

Number	Pseudonym	Description	Age	District interviewed	Language of interview	Social status	Date interviewed	First language
ET096		Female Timorese NGO director	32	Oecusse	Tetun/Indonesian	Liurai	27 July 2015	Meto
ET097		Male Timorese NGO program manager	32	Oecusse	Tetun/Indonesian	Elite	27 July 2015	Meto
ET098		Female Timorese NGO finance officer	29	Oecusse	Tetun/Indonesian	Elite	27 July 2015	Meto
ET099		Female Timorese NGO program manager	30	Oecusse	Tetun/Indonesian	Elite	27 July 2015	Meto
ET102	Lina	Female villager	43	Oecusse	Tetun	Citizen	30 July 2015	Meto
ET103		Female volunteer with veterans' group, Housewife	59	Oecusse	Tetun	Liurai	30 July 2015	Meto
ET104		Male village chief	61	Oecusse	Tetun/Indonesian	Elite	30 July 2015	Meto
ET105		Male hamlet chief and farmer	62	Oecusse	Tetun/Indonesian	Dato	2 August 2015	Meto
ET108	Eugenio	Senior government official	–	Oecusse	Tetun/English	Elite	4 August 2015	Meto/Portuguese
ET110	Serafina	Female secretary of the village	32	Oecusse	Tetun/Indonesian	Dato	4 August 2015	Meto

ID	Name	Role	Age	Location	Language	Status	Date	Local Language
ET112		Female senior manager, women's shelter	34	Oecusse	Tetun	Liurai	4 August 2015	Meto
ET113	Michaela	Female farmer	29	Oecusse	Tetun/Indonesian	Citizen	5 August 2015	Tetun
ET114	Elisabetha	Female farmer	60	Oecusse	Tetun	Citizen	5 August 2015	Meto
ET120		Female senior manager, microfinance institute	–	Dili	English	Elite	16 August 2015	Tetun/Portuguese
ET122		Catholic nun in a leadership role	–	Dili	English	Elite	18 August 2015	Portuguese
ET127	Bonifacio	Male village chief Suku Mota	~50	Manufahi	Tetun	Dato	1 September 2015 and June 2011	Laklae
ET130	Antonio	Male teacher	43	Manufahi	Tetun	Dato	1 September 2015	Tetun Therik
ET131	Lucia	Wife of village chief and businesswoman	47	Manufahi	Tetun	Dato	1 September 2015	Tetun Therik
ET137	Sancio	Female villager	35	Manufahi	Tetun	Village Elite	4 September 2015	Tetun
ET138	Rosita	Female villager	29	Manufahi	Tetun	Citizen	4 September 2015	Tetun Therik

(continued)

Table A.2 Continued

Number	Pseudonym	Description	Age	District interviewed	Language of interview	Social status	Date interviewed	First language
ET139		Female villager	45	Manufahi	Tetun	Citizen	4 September 2015	Tetun Therik
ET146	Brigida	Female villager Suku Mota	31	Manufahi	Tetun	Dato	7 September 2015	Tetun Therik
ET147		Female villager Suku Mota	22	Manufahi	Tetun	Dato	8 September 2015	Tetun Therik
ET148		Female villager Suku Mota	28	Manufahi	Tetun	Dato	8 September 2015	Tetun Therik
ET150		Male Student	–	Manufahi	Tetun	Citizen	8 September 2015	–
ET151		Male Student	–	Manufahi	Tetun	Citizen	8 September 2015	–
ET152		Female UN senior manager	–	Dili	English	Elite	9 September 2015	–
ET158-2011		Daughter of a village chief	55	Dili	Tetun	Elite	7 July 2011	Tetun Therik
Not recorded		Male government researcher	–	Dili	English	Elite	23 July 2015	Meto
WT042		Hamlet chief	50	Belu, West Timor, Indonesia	Indonesian	Elite	16 March 2015	Tetun Therik
WT071		Male East Timorese ex-militia member, residing in West Timor, Indonesia	46	Timor-Tenggah Selatan, West Timor, Indonesia	Indonesian	Citizen	31 March 2015	Tetun Praça

Note: Elites include liurai, parliamentarians, and so on. Dato are not included in elite classes, although they have greater status than the ordinary citizenry.

METHODOLOGICAL NOTES   193

Interviewee Selection

Readers should note that interviews from earlier fieldwork in Timor-Leste in 2015 are cited as ET followed by a three-digit number (e.g., ET010), and some information on the gender, social status, and affiliation is listed in the accompanying notes. More detailed information is given in Table A.1. The few participants from West Timor are cited as WT, followed by a three-digit number (e.g., WT010). The few interviews from 2011 append the year to the citation (e.g., ET156—2011).

Locating interviewees (sampling) was done purposively. Names of national policymakers, experts, and gender experts were gathered from websites, the Timorese news, documentary research, and established and emergent Dili-based networks. For example, the Oecusse subnational contact list was drawn up with the help of an international gender and police capacity building expert. To establish contact with village leaders and subnational leaders in rural areas, I drew initially from the network of contacts I had developed from 2011 fieldwork in Timor-Leste. Interlocutors included village leaders, liurai and dato, veterans, and members of NGOs and women's organization networks. These initial interviews were instrumental in introducing me to other potential participants. In other words, I used purposive snowball sampling to identify appropriate interviewees. This is deemed the most efficient method when researchers become a temporary feature of the rural community in which they are working (Kerstan and Berninghausen 1992). However, the use of elite networks and snowball sampling introduces bias. Partiality arises in part because elite or male or educated interlocutors/participants act as gatekeepers, intentionally or unintentionally controlling the terms on which researchers can talk with other citizens.

With this in mind, a principal aim of my 2015 fieldwork was to avoid one-sided sampling of the patrimonial networks within which I had to operate. The broad range of interlocutors is evidenced in Table A.1. Roll (2014) gives a good account of problematic bias in qualitative snowball sampling in Timorese patrimonial networks. I compensated for this common problem by attempting to sample beyond the networks of "gatekeepers" and "patrons." At all sites, I initially approached higher-status formal and informal gatekeepers, seeking formal and informal approvals while conducting interviews. Next, at each field site, I employed one or two younger, educated people from the area. These research assistants introduced me to the community and acted as informal key informants (Rabinow 1977). Walking around with these assistants—who, as young people, were often considered to be of low status—allowed me to reach lower-status community members, because the familiar faces of my assistants reassured them that I was under someone's supervision and protection. This "supervised" freedom allowed me to move beyond gatekeepers' networks to talk to people unrelated to village chiefs, hamlet chiefs, or other subnational leaders.

Interview Processes

Getting beyond gatekeepers' networks provided vital insights into hierarchy and subordination in Timor-Leste. Methodologically, I looked critically at elites' historical narratives, and social scientists' reproduction of them, to sketch the material and structural implications. I assessed who benefited, and by what means, from the gender division of labor, economic processes, war and militarization, and international intervention.

The interview process followed a set format. Interviewees were given an information letter, in Tetun, Indonesian, or English, describing the scope of the study, its aims, their role, and possible risks. Those with low levels of literacy had the letter read out and explained to them. We then discussed the information letter and the aims of my research and my background, after which participants were nearly always happy to sign the consent form. The interviews were all audio-recorded except one or two informal ones, which were transcribed. At the same time, with the help of the researcher and research assistant, participants completed biodata forms. These forms aided recordkeeping and collation, in particular with respect to substantive data on social status.

Next, participants were engaged in face-to-face, semistructured interviews of about forty to sixty minutes. I conducted nearly all the interviews myself, in Tetun, Indonesian, or English. Nonetheless, in rural areas, research assistants were crucial in smoothing communication and overcoming considerable gaps in understanding. Rural Timorese citizens' first language is not typically Tetun. Tetun is a creolized and nonstandard language and reflecting the use of Tetun in practice, many participants spoke a version of Tetun heavily influenced by another language or dialect such as Indonesian, Portuguese or in this research, Meto, Tetun Therik, or Laklei (cf. Ross 2016, 73).

Questions were drawn from a menu, and only some are discussed briefly here. Answers to the initial questions established and described the social status of the participants and their social group, as well as the social relations and gender relations surrounding them. Social status was also elicited through biodata forms asking about first language, education level, occupation, number of people living with the participant, and so on. Additionally, the biodata forms helped clarify oral information during the interview. The forms asked interviewees to assess whether they considered themselves of ordinary class (*ema bai bain*), farmers (*toos nain*), or upper middle class (*kelas menengah atas*); of liurai or dato rank; or indeed whether they considered themselves elite (*ema boot*).

Next, the interview itself established biographical narratives and kinship affiliations. I drew kinship diagrams to establish individuals' affiliations across administrative bodies and families. Social status, biography, and affiliation were particularly useful for understanding interests, benefits, and access to resources. Other areas of discussion also centered on kinship, authority, adat, and extralegal institutions. It established common ground and definitions, and who exercises (extra)legal authority with regard especially to transactions, problems with legitimacy and authority, and brideprice. It also elicited opinions about ideal types of authority, ideal types of romantic partners, problems in family relationships, marriage, brideprice, and dispute resolution.

The penultimate area of discussion was gender and violence, probing the juncture of gender, class, and the "local" to analyze systemic issues. Discussion topics included definitions of gender and violence, women's organizations, typical circumstances in which domestic violence occurs, traditional dispute resolution, and transactions of goods and cash associated with it. These issues were handled with care, drawing on my professional experience working with the European NGO network Women Against Violence Europe. Discussing these issues in the Timorese context often involved interviewees asking me questions about VAW in other countries. I replied that VAW occurred all over the world because of gender relations, but that different countries and communities experienced different drivers of VAW, different legal processes, and different outcomes. The results of these discussions—particularly participants' experience of the intersections of brideprice and traditional dispute resolution—are presented in Chapters 4 and 5. The final part of each interview often moved back to the political economy of the everyday: looking at who gets what, when, and how—and at feelings of justice or fairness in the family, village, organization, or nation, or between and among these levels.

Interview data were collated and analyzed using Nvivo qualitative research software. Not all interviews were transcribed; some were merely annotated. Two coding schemes were developed to identify and analyze themes. First, an a priori coding scheme was developed based on the research question and the structural political economy of Southeast Asia (Hughes 2009; Hutchison et al. 2014; Jayasuriya and Rodan 2007; Rodan, Hewison, and Robison 2006) and feminist political economy (True 2012). Coded data from interviews, reports, and newspaper articles were organized according to thematic areas such as control over resources, elites, class formation, and so on. Second, a coding scheme emerged out of the data itself, or in vivo (Bernard and Ryan 2003). Over time, themes emerged that formed the main empirical areas of the study: control over state resources, development and infrastructure, veterans' payments and welfare, poverty and inequality, marriage and brideprice, microfinance, and village elites.

Glossary

Note that I use the term "Tetun," not "Tetum," reflecting how Tetun sounds when spoken (Ross 2016).

Term	Language	Definition
A luta continua	Portuguese	A FRETILIN slogan meaning "the struggle continues." FRELIMO in Mozambique uses the same revolutionary calp.
Acar	Fataluku	Slave
Adat	Tetun/ Indonesian	Customary law governing inheritance of property, spouse eligibility, ritual etiquette, *tara bandu* (taboo observance), land ownership, political authority, sanctions, oral literature, and cosmology
Administrador	Tetun	District administrator
Affine	English	Relative by marriage
Akan	Fataluku	Commoner/farmer
Akanu	Fataluku	Slave caste
Aldeia	Tetun	Hamlet
Amaf Naek	Meto	Noble
Angotta DPR	Indonesian	Member of Indonesian Parliament
Arisan	Indonesian	Lottery finance, or rotating savings and loan associations (ROSCAs)
Asuliar	Tetun	Servant
Atan	Tetun	Slave

Term	Language	Definition
Auxiliar	Portuguese	Help
Auxiliar	Tetun	Auxiliaries/servants
Babinsa	Indonesian	Noncommissioned guidance officer or team
Baikeno, baiqueno	Tetun	Language of Oecusse
Baino	Tetun	Noble. See *dato*
Bapak	Indonesian	Man or mister, used in Tetun to refer to Indonesian men in Timor during the occupation
Barlake, barlaki, barlaque	Tetun	Brideprice; less commonly, Common-law marriage
Bee manas ai tukan	Tetun	Literally, hot water and firewood, a payment made by the groom's family to the bride's at a couple's engagement to recognize the bride's parents' efforts in raising their daughter
Belak	Tetun	Gold, silver, or bronze disk worn as jewelry on the chest and used in brideprice
Belis	Eastern Indonesian	Brideprice
Bua malus	Tetun	Areca nut and betel leaf chewed to produce a narcotic effect
Budak	Indonesian	Slave
Buibere	Tetun	Woman, a term used among FRETLIN and FALINTIL but also meaning a female farmer who is a revolutionary subject. See also *Maubere*.
Bupati	Indonesian	District head
Camat	Indonesian	Subdistrict head
Capitacão	Portuguese	Head tax

GLOSSARY

Term	Language	Definition
Chattel slavery	English	A system whereby the enslaver has rights of ownership over the slave, with the intent to exploit through the use, management, profit, or transfer of that person
Clandestinos	Tetun	Members of the clandestine nationalist front for independent Timor-Leste, many of whom were women
Cooperativa credito	Tetun	Credit cooperative
Corvée	French	A form of labor tax exacted by a lord or local authority
Dato	Tetun	Noble
Debt bondage	English	Debtors pledging their labor, or the labor of a dependent, as security for a debt
Deportardu	Tetun	Deported political prisoners
Deputada	Tetun	Female parliamentarian
Desa	Indonesian	Village
Village administrative area		
Differend	French	An injustice that arises because the colonizer's hegemonic discourse actively precludes the possibility of this wrong being expressed
Distriktu	Tetun	District administrative area
Dom	Portuguese	King
Ekonomia	Tetun	National economy; household economy
Ema boot	Tetun	Important or "great" person
Ema kiik	Tetun	Ordinary or "little" person
Ema reino	Tetun	Commoner

GLOSSARY

Term	Language	Definition
Ema susar	Tetun	Poor people with difficulties
Endogamous	English	The practice of marrying within a clan, tribe, or family group
Estado do India	Portuguese	Indian state, the name for the Portuguese colonial empire
Feto nia folin	Tetun	Literally, woman's price or brideprice (see *Barlake*)
Folin	Tetun	Price, brideprice
Gotong royong	Indonesian	Literally, mutual cooperation, a form of community labor on local public works popularized by Suharto's New Order
Grau	Tetun	Grade or seniority in military rank
Hafolin	Tetun	To appreciate, value, or esteem; to negotiate; a brideprice or arranged marriage
Hypogamous	English	Marriage type, between a high-status or high-class woman and a low-status or low-class man
Ianjo	Japanese	Military brothel
Kadeira	Tetun	Chair, as a political position
Kampung	Indonesian	Village
Katuas/Ketuas	Tetun	A male elder or leader or male elders
Kepala desa	Indonesian	Head of the village; village chief
Ketua	Indonesian	Leader
Ketua adat	Indonesian	Male spiritual leader
Kios	Tetun	Small shop selling small amounts of everyday items such as oil, rice, salt, cigarettes, cola
Kodim	Indonesian	District military command
Kooperativa	Tetun	Cooperative
Koramil	Indonesian	Subdistrict military command

Term	Language	Definition
Kore metan	Tetun	Literally, cutting/lifting the black cloth, a ceremony marking a death, anniversary of a death, or end of mourning
Koremetan naçional	Tetun	National memorial ceremony
Korperasi simpan pinjam	Indonesian	Savings and loans cooperative
Kostumes	Tetun	Customs
Kultura	Tetun	Culture
Lafurana hi kare	Makassae	Literally, hearth and knife, a sister
Lia loos	Tetun	Truth
Lia nain	Tetun	Literally, owner of the voice, an elder
Lisan	Tetun	Customary practice
Liurai	Tetun	Literally, more land, a king or landowner
Lulik	Tetun	Sacred or taboo
Lutu-hum	Tetun	Literally, dwellers at the bottom of the pale (i.e., wooden fence), retainers of a *liurai*
Mate rasik	Tetun	Die alone
Matrilocal residence	English	Married couple residing with the wife's family
Maubere	Tetun	Male Timorese farmer, a term repurposed by FRETILIN to symbolize a revolutionary subject. See also *Buibere*.
Meo	Baikeno	Noble warrior class in Oecusse
Mestiço	Portuguese	Timorese, Portuguese, Mozambican, Angolan, Brazilian, Hakka Chinese, Macanese, Arab, Indonesian-Malay, or Dutch
Mikrokredit	Indonesian	Microcredit
Moris naroman	Tetun	Enlightened life; enlightenment

Term	Language	Definition
Naizuf	Baikeno (Meto)	King
Ordinença	Portuguese	Ordnance, military logistic support
Paca	Fataluku	Noble
Patrlineages	English	Kin groups related through males
Patrilocal residence	English	Married couple residing with the husband's family
Pembantu	Indonesian	Maid, home help
Pensaun veteranus	Tetun	Veterans' pension
Pensaun vitalisia	Tetun	Life pension, paid for life to former members of parliament
Petani	Indonesian	Farmer
Piastres	Portuguese	Portuguese currency
Preman	Indonesian	Strongmen or gangsters
Rai lulik	Tetun	The spiritual world
Ratih (short form of Rakyat Terlatih)	Indonesian	Trained civilians, civilian militia
Ratu	Fataluku	King
Regulo	Portuguese	Petty king
Reino	Portuguese	Peasant, kingdom, realm, tribe, subjects, commoners, people
Rubrica orçamental separada	Portuguese	Separate budget lines
Rukun tetangga	Indonesian	Neighborhood association
Rukun warga	Indonesian	Administrative unit
Saun	Tetun	The material world
Secretaria suko	Tetun	Secretary of the suku. See *Suku*.
Serfdom	English	Land system whereby a tenant is bound by law, custom, or agreement to live and labor on land belonging to a landlord, to render a service to the landlord, and that tenant is not free to change their status

GLOSSARY

Term	Language	Definition
Serralhos	Portuguese	Harem
Servile marriage	English	Marriage form whereby a woman, without the right to refuse, is married on payment to her parents, guardian, or family of an amount of money or goods
Servo, servi, servidor	Tetun	Serf
Sirih pina	Indonesian	Areca nut and betel leaf combination, chewed to produce a mild narcotic effect; used in many ceremonies
Subdistriktu	Tetun	Subdistrict administrative area smaller than a district
Suku, suco, suko	Tetun	Village, village administrative area; Portuguese rendering of modern Indonesian *suku*, meaning tribe.
Tais	Tetun	Traditional Timorese woven cloth, worn as skirts and scarfs and used in marriage and mortuary ceremonies
Tama	Tetun	Enter, interfere
Tara bandu	Tetun	Official prohibition (e.g., on entering a plot of land)
Tau korenti, tau morteen	Tetun	Literally, put on a necklace; a ceremony to mark an engagement
Tenaga bantuan operasi	Indonesian	Military operation assistants, known as TBO
Temukung	Atoni	Head of the lineage
Tob, tobe	Baikeno	Noble
Toos nain	Tetun	Farmer
Topasses	Indonesian	Portuguese-speaking people in Oecusse, Flores, and Solor, from the Indonesian *topi*, or hat. Also commonly called Black Portuguese.

Term	Language	Definition
Tua haraki	Tetun	Palm liquor
Tuur hamutuk	Tetun	Sit together to resolve a problem or to celebrate
Ulun-houris	Tetun	Chattel slave, usually a war captive. The name means "living head" owing to the tradition of headhunting in Timor
Uma	Tetun	House, lineage group
Umane	Tetun	Wife's family, wife givers
Usif	Meto (Baikeno)	King
Violensia bai-bain	Tetun	Normal or everyday (domestic) violence
Violensia boot	Tetun	Serious (domestic) violence, usually involving blood
Wanra (Perlawanan Rakyat)	Indonesian	People's resistance, civilian militia
Wife giver	English	Lineage group providing a wife to another group
Wife taker	English	Lineage group receiving a wife from another group
Xefe aldeia	Tetun	Hamlet chief
Xefe posto	Tetun	Chief of the post

Notes

Introduction

1. I use the term "East Timor" to refer to the period of Indonesian occupation (1975–1998), during which it was officially the province of Timur-Timor, Indonesia. I use "Timor-Leste" to refer to the independent country after 1998.
2. Interview with a male ex-militia member from East Timor residing in West Timor, Indonesia, WT071, Timor Tenggah Selatan, 31 March 2015. Due to the large numbers of interviews conducted and the need to preserve anonymity in data collection, an alpha numeric system is used throughout, with WT referring to interviewees in West Timor, and ET referring to interviewees in Timor-Leste. Readers should note that interviews from earlier fieldwork in Timor-Leste in 2015 are cited as ET followed by a three-digit number (e.g., ET010), and some information on the gender, social status, and affiliation is listed in the accompanying notes. A full anonymized list of interviewees cited in this book can be found in the methodological notes in Table A.1.
3. Class fractions are a unit of Marxist analysis that can distinguish between nationally orientated groups of the ruling class, for example, and the internationally focused groups of the ruling class. Both are members of the same ruling class, but their material interests may be competing. In this case, the *liurai-dato* is one historically contingent class, but some members belong to purely domestic patrimonial groups (their power and interest lies in their links to the rural heartland and the national legislature), while others are embedded within the international system (such as returnee leaders and those working within the United Nations, or for Chinese business interests).
4. Interview with Timorese gender expert, ET082, Dili, 8 June 2015.

Chapter 1

1. Academics and policymakers in the early 2000s developed the Responsibility to Protect (R2P) doctrine, which argued that countries ought to intervene militarily to protect people at risk of gross human rights abuses and war atrocities (Chandler 2012).
2. UN family organizations active in Timor-Leste from 1999 to 2017 included the UN Development Program (UNDP), UN Capital Development Fund (UNCDF), UN Development Fund for Women (UNIFEM, renamed UN Women in 2012), and UN Population Fund (UNFPA).
3. Gender mainstreaming is an approach to policy that assesses the implications of legislation, policies, or programs for gender relations. It advocates for

consideration of gender relations to be an "integral dimension of the design, implementation, monitoring and evaluation of policies and programs in all political, economic and societal spheres so that women and men benefit equally and inequality is not perpetuated" (United Nations ECOSOC 1997).
4. Interview with UN Women, senior manager ET076, Dili, June 6, 2015. From 2012 to 2015, this office was called the Secretary of State for the Promotion of Equality (SEPI), and then became known as the Secretary of State for the Support and Socio-Economic Promotion for Women (SEM) from 2015 to 2017.
5. Chopra worked for UNTAET as a district administrator. Hohe worked first for UNAMET as a district electoral officer and then later a district field officer for UNTAET.
6. Magalhães was elected to the national parliament in 2017 as second on the list for Taur Matan Ruak's People's Liberation Party (PLP). Taur Matan Ruak is the commonly used nom de guerre of former guerrilla leader José Maria Vasconcelos.
7. Although Cummins used the term *patriarchal*, the correct term to describe the type of descent and inheritance of a particular kinship group is *patrilineal*. Patriarchal refers to a system of male dominance of social, economic, and political life, originating in the family.
8. For a full discussion of UNSCR 1325 and the six subsequent UNSCR "Women, Peace, and Security" Resolutions, see the special issue of *International Political Science Review* "Women, Peace and Security: Exploring the Implementation and Integration of UNSCR 1325" (George and Shepherd 2016) and the special issue of the *International Feminist Journal of Politics* "Critically Examining UNSCR 1325 on Women, Peace and Security" (Shepherd 2011).
9. See True (2012, 30) and Meillassoux (1975, 4). The household is not a particular place or group of people, nor confined to heterosexual couples and their children, but stands for "the bundle of relationships ... through which primary reproductive activities are organised, recognising that these frequently involve principles of kinship and residence" (Kabeer 1991, 7).
10. In Timor-Leste, domestic work signifies work associated with the private sphere and the household, covering not only child rearing, cleaning, and cooking but also tending to household gardens, raising small animals, and running small shops or businesses from the home. Public work includes both paid work and any work associated with the public sphere, such as tending faraway fields and staple crops, raising communal houses, transporting goods, heavy lifting, driving, politicking, and negotiation between families. This is common in rural areas in developing countries. The gender division of labor is normative, rather than actual, because in Timor-Leste women regularly perform "public" work. See Grenfell et al. (2009, 2015) for a more detailed description of the gender division of labor in Timor-Leste.
11. I use the UN definition of violence against women as "any act of gender-based violence that results in, or is likely to result in, physical, sexual or psychological harm or suffering to women, including threats of such acts, coercion or arbitrary deprivation of liberty, whether occurring in public or in private life" (UN Women 2013). Until relatively recently, women's experiences of intimate partner violence were dismissed

by turns as exceptional or normal. In the 1980s, new research on prevalence established how pervasive, multifarious, and extensive VAW was (Kelly 2005, 475). In the 1990s, following successful lobbying by anti-VAW activists armed with new data and a new strategy to make "women's rights, human rights," the study of VAW moved in the academy from margin to mainstream (Kelly 2005, 475). Networking and coalition building by activists on a single anti-VAW message generated support and resources for the anti-VAW movement and has been a wellspring for much feminist activism (Kelly 2005, 475).

12. *Harmful practices* is the term employed by the United Nations to refer to a range of issues pertinent to family law, including but not limited to forced marriage, child marriage, child enslavement by kin members, brideprice, female genital mutilation, and forced birth or marriage following rape.

Chapter 2

1. Unless otherwise specified, non-English words in this work are Tetun, and translations are based on the *Standard Tetun-English Dictionary*, 2nd ed. (Sydney: Allen & Unwin, 2001). Here "liurai" means "king; Timorese native chief," and "dato" means "native chief, nobleman; nobility, nobles." Compare "dato" with the Indonesian term *datu*, meaning "title of headman." Where Indonesian terms are translated, they are based on *Kamus Indonesia Inggris: An Indonesian-English Dictionary*, 3rd ed. (Sydney: Allen & Unwin, 2001).
2. The specific relationship between kinship and class in Timor is explained in Chapters 4 and 5.
3. The colonial empire was termed the *Estado do India* (the Indian state). Despite claiming Timor in 1515, Timor-Leste was not named as a Portuguese overseas dominion until 1681 (Andaya 2010).
4. In Timor, in general, many families have mixed ethnic backgrounds with Timorese, Portuguese, Mozambican, Angolan, Brazilian, Hakka Chinese, Macanese, Arab, Indonesian-Malay, or Dutch ancestry. "Topasses" is probably derived from *topi*, Indonesian for "hat." (Hägerdal 2012).
5. The word "*suco*" is a Portuguese rendering of *suku*, which in modern Indonesian means "extended family, ethnic group, or tribe." Three spellings exist today in Tetun—*suku, suko*, and *suco*—and the term generally signifies a collection of hamlets constituting a spread-out village, although can also be used to refer to someone's family background. I translate the word "*suku*" as "village" throughout this study.
6. In the 1960s, when Timorese were granted Portuguese citizenship, Portugal expanded education for children of liurai and dato in Catholic seminaries. These were the only literate Timorese. For a discussion of the influence of church education on the formation of this intelligentsia, see Carey (1999).
7. For an overview of political parties in 1975, see Gunn (2011; 1999) and Dunn (2003).
8. FRETILIN began in 1974 as the Associação Social-Democratica Timorense (ASDT), or Timorese Social Democratic Association. Other leaders of the 1975 generation

from *liurai* families included Vicente Sahe and Borja da Costa, both members of the FRETILIN Central Committee (Guterres 2006).

9. Brothers Mario and João Carrascalão were sons of a wealthy coffee plantation owner. Mario, who died in 2017, was a member of the Portuguese fascist National Union party (United Nations 1976). The family of Domingos de Oliviera, who was a member of the military-administered customs office, had coffee interests.
10. This chapter relies heavily on the work of the Comissão de Acolhimento, Verdade e Reconciliação (CAVR; Commission for Reception, Truth and Reconciliation). The UN-initiated CAVR was tasked by the East Timor government with investigating past human rights violations and finding factual and objective information to determine whether a pattern of abuses took place, and of what kind (Roosa 2007, 569–570).
11. Interview with the daughter of a village chief, a young girl at the time of the invasion, ET158-2011, Dili, 7 July 2011.
12. Estimates suggest that from 1975 to 1999, up to a quarter of all Timorese people (250,000) were killed as a result of fighting or deliberate famine, or in concentration camps (CAVR 2006).
13. Yoder (2005), for example, states that the eighteen suku listed in 1952 in Oecusse became eighteen desa under Indonesian administration.
14. See Budiardjo and Liong (1984, 100) for greater explanation of these examples. PT Denok's role in the occupation is described in greater detail in Chapter 6.
15. Liurai Gaspar Nunes, who supported the UDT, was appointed speaker of the Indonesian provincial legislature (Kammen 2016, 135). In another example, one of my interviewees who was a member of the Indonesian parliament representing East Timor in the 1990s was demoted to village chief at the end of Indonesian rule. Interview with village chief, ET104, Oecusse, 30 July 2015.
16. Established Procedure (Protap) on Intelligence no. 01/IV/1982, cited in Budiardjo and Liong (1984, 194). GPK refers to Gerakan Pengacau Keamanan.
17. The dual structure of Indonesian civilian and military command was the same in the rest of New Order Indonesia (Turner 2005; Crouch 2007).
18. Much later, in 2008, do Amaral asserted that he had been deposed because of his suggestion that FRETILIN members living in the forests should look to "new ideas," principally that they should stop having children. Klaak Seminal, "Hau nee ema FRETILIN" [I am a FRETILIN person], 22 September 2008.
19. The term "conscientization" is taken from the work of Brazilian education theorist Paulo Freire. For a description of the application of Freire's theories of consciousness raising by FRETILIN during this period, see da Silva (2012).
20. Ular Rihi was the nom de guerre of Commander Virgílio dos Anjos of the FALINTIL.
21. Interview with a Catholic nun who was exiled in Portugal during the Indonesian occupation but is in a leadership role today. ET122, 18 August 2015.
22. The CNRM was later also called the CNRT, not to be confused with Gusmão's post-2007 National Council for the Reconstruction of Timor, also called CNRT.
23. Slavery exists when a slaveholder or slaveholder agent exerts personal and physical domination over the slave. It is based on ownership and characterized by absolute

power backed up by physical or psychological violence (Patterson 2012, 323). "Unfree labor" is a generic term to encompass chattel slavery, dependency, indenture, domestic slavery in marriage, and modern slavery (Hägerdal 2010, 20–21; Allain 2012).

24. Da Silva's (2012) interlocutor was a member of FRETILIN who ran education programs in occupied East Timor. Antero da Silva won the Student Peace Prize in 1999 for work on nonviolent struggle for independence from Indonesian occupation. The practice of slaves being killed or committing suicide on their master's death was also observed in Sumba, a culturally similar area of eastern Indonesia (Hoskins 2004, 107).
25. For a discussion of the problems of defining modern slavery, see Patterson (2012). Patterson uses the term "traditional slavery" to refer to slavery that occurs as a part of social hierarchies.
26. Taur Matan Ruak, part of Gusmão's 2017 alliance, was named as Timor-Leste's new prime minister in 2018.
27. Sources on sexual slavery in the Indonesian period do not talk about brideprice, and neither does the CAVR report. The lacuna is likely because violence was the only coercive force used by Indonesian military men, so brideprice was not paid in these forced marriages. Discussion of brideprice might also have been avoided because survivors, interviewers, and the CAVR authors understandably want to focus on the violent coercion present in domestic sexual slavery and forced marriage. A report on Japanese sexual slavery written by Akihisa Matsuno and José-Luis Oliviera (2016) does mention such payments occurring in Timor during the Second World War.
28. I also recorded the Indonesian military practice of paying compensation for rapes in the border areas of West Timor, Indonesia, in 2015. A hamlet chief told me that sexual violence did not provoke further violence between community members and soldiers stationed among them so long as the soldiers followed West Timorese tradition and paid compensation. Interview with hamlet chief, WT042, Tasi Feto Timor, Indonesia, 16 March 2015.
29. A women in a forced marriage or sexual slavery was sometimes termed *feto nona*. *Feto* is Tetun for woman; *nona* is a term common in eastern Indonesia for "unmarried woman" or "girl." Another term was "TNI [Indonesian army] wife."
30. The three female members were Rosa "Muki" Bonaparte Soares, Maria do Céu Pereira, and Guilhermina Araújo. Bonaparte Soares was head of the OPMT. For an overview of women in the Timorese nationalist struggle, see Loney (2015; 2016), Cristalis and Scott (2005), and Cristalis (2002).

Chapter 3

1. The F-FDTL was established on 1 February 2001 despite the earlier belief within the resistance that no army would be needed and FALANTIL would be disbanded upon independence (Kingsbury 2007).
2. The first was the Law on Veterans' Pensions No. 3/2006, which was revised twice: once to make one-off payments of thirteen hundred dollars prior to the 2009 village chief

elections, and again in 2011 to establish Veterans' Councils to regulate pension claims. The legislation was followed by the Decree Law on the Pensions of the Combatants and Martyrs of the National Liberation No. 15/2008, as amended by Decree Law Amending Decree Law No. 15/2008 of 4 June No. 25/2008 (Roll 2015).
3. Important sections of the donor community agreed, notably UN Millennium Project director Jeffrey Sachs, who visited Timor-Leste in 2010 (Goldstone 2013, n18, 225).
4. In the same fashion, most village and hamlet chiefs are from the liurai-dato class. As a result, many village leaders have retained their roles in the postindependence period.
5. Vicente Sahe, Borja da Costa, Xavier do Amaral, Nicolau Lobato, Rosa Bonaparte, Justino Mota, José Ramos-Horta, and Xanana Gusmão all come from FRETILIN. From the UDT come Francisco Lopes da Cruz, Gaspar Nunes, Domingos de Oliveira, Mario Carrascalão, and João Carrascalão. José Abilio Osorio Soares is associated with the Indonesian-era APODETI, and Clementino dos Reis Amaral, who served in parliament from 2001 to 2007, belonged to the pro-Indonesian party KOTA (Guterres 2006; Bovensiepen 2014a; Gunn 2011; 1999; Kammen 2016).
6. Interview with a member of the Women's Cross-Party Caucus (GMPTL), ET085, 11 June 2015.
7. In Government Decree No. 10/2010, on veteran data verification, the commissioners were all male FALINTIL leaders with long service records. They were (noms de guerre in quotation marks): Faustino dos Santos, "Renan Selak"; João Miranda "Aluk Descartes"; Justo Bernardino da Costa "Lari Mau"; Camilo Tibúrcio Hornay "Larcy"; Vidal de Jesus, "Riak Leman" (FALINTIL regional secretary and currently vice commander of F-FDTL); Calisto Santos "Koliati" (vice secretary of Ainaro region); Pedro Alves Carlos "Raituto" (responsible for Caixa Ramelau); Gil da Costa Monteiro "Oan Suro" (second rank commander of Covalima); Félix Amaral "Sakari"; Edmundo Amaral; Justino da Costa "Fitun Mesak" (secretary of NUREP Bobonaro); Jacinto Viegas Vicente "Roke"; Agostinho Soares Carvalheira "Samarusa"; Francisco dos Réis Magno "Loco Meo" (secretary of the Liquiçá subregion); César dos Santos da Silva "Merak"; Filinto Fátima Marques "Marconi"; Ernesto Fernandes "Dudo"; Eduardo de Deus Barreto "Du Sahe"; Afonso Martins "Aten Brani"; Martinho da Cunha "Mala"; and Zeferino da Cruz Sal "Papa Teme". It is beyond the scope of this study to determine the sociopolitical status of all these men or to confirm whether they received the highest pension amounts.
8. Interview with male senior bureaucratic Eugenio, ET108, Oecusse, 4 August 2015.
9. Interview with Eugenio's mother, ET103, Oecusse, 30 July 2015.
10. Interview with female village secretary Serafina, ET110, Oecusse, 4 August 2015.
11. *Naizuf* is the Meto equivalent to *liurai*. (Meto is the language of Oecusse.) See Table 6.3.
12. Fieldwork notes, Oecusse, 30 July 2015.
13. Fieldwork notes, discussion with researchers from Lao Hamutuk, Dili, 13 August 2015.
14. Interview with male senior bureaucratic Eugenio, ET108, Oecusse, 4 August 2015
15. Interview with female village secretary Serafina, ET110, Oecusse, 4 August 2015.

NOTES   211

16. Ibid.
17. Conditional cash transfer (CCT) programs are common worldwide. For instance, nineteen out of twenty-three Latin American countries have a CCT program. The payments in Latin America are always quite small, although all are much greater than the Timor-Leste program (Fernandes 2015). For instance, CCT programs include Bolsa Familia, in Brazil (started in 2003), with an average payment of fifty dollars per month; Juntos, in Peru (started in 2005), with an average payment of seventy dollars per month; Oportunidades, in Mexico (started in 1997); Solidario, in Chile (started in 1992); and Asignación Universal por Hijo, in Argentina (started in 2009) (Saad-Filho 2015).
18. World Bank Development Indicators 2016: Fertility rate, total (births per woman), https://data.worldbank.org/indicator/SP.DYN.TFRT.IN?locations=TL.
19. Interview with a village chief, ET104, Oecusse, 30 July 2015.
20. Some Bolsa da Mãe funds went missing after being transferred to bank branches. Of the $9 million total budget for 2014, $89,222 was not received by families although it was paid into the BNCTL banks (da Cruz 2014). This is referred to as "leakage."
21. *Timor Post* (2015a).
22. Antonia da Cruz's report for the Ministry of Social Solidarity states the following: "Sistema selesaun ba benefisarias nebe balun sidauk tuir kriterius Bolsa Mae (Ex. Inan-Aman Funsionariu publiku hetan benefisiu husi Programa Bolsa Mae" [The system of selection of some beneficiaries does not follow the criteria of Bolsa Mãe (e.g., Both male and female public servants receive benefits from the Bolsa Mãe program)] (da Cruz 2014, 21).
23. In the Timorese political system, parliamentary commissions are permanent standing committees with jurisdiction over specific areas of lawmaking.
24. Interview with a female international manager at the UN, ET076, 6 June 2015.
25. Interview with a member of the Women's Cross-Party Caucus, ET085, 11 June 2015.
26. Interview with a female Timorese NGO senior manager, ET077, 5 June 2015.
27. Interview with a member of the Women's Cross-Party Caucus, ET085, 11 June 2015.
28. Interview with a female international manager at the UN, ET076, 6 June 2015.
29. Interview with a female Timorese NGO senior manager, ET077, 5 June 2015.
30. Interview with a female Timorese NGO senior manager, ET078, 6 June 2015.
31. Interview with a female Timorese NGO senior manager, ET082, 8 June 2015.
32. Ibid.
33. Interview with a female international manager at the UN, ET076, 6 June 2015. See also Costa, Sharp, and Austen (2009); Costa (2010).
34. Interview with a female Timorese NGO senior manager, ET082, 8 June 2015.
35. Interview with a female Timorese NGO senior manager, ET082, 8 June 2015.
36. Interview data, June to September 2015.
37. Interview with a female Timorese NGO senior manager, ET077, 5 June 2015.
38. Interview with a member of the Women's Cross-Party Caucus, ET085, 11 June 2015.
39. Interview with a member of the Women's Cross-Party Caucus, ET085, 11 June 2015.
40. Interview with female international manager at the UN, ET076, 6 June 2015.

41. Interview with female international senior manager at the UN, ET152, 9 September 2015.
42. One female international manager at the UN (ET076, 6 June 2015), noted that she and other international staff "didn't know what was going on."

Chapter 4

1. Ever-partnered women are those who currently have a male sexual partner or who have ever been married or lived with a man.
2. Earlier estimates of the prevalence and severity of domestic violence in Timor-Leste were probably underestimated (Asia Foundation 2016).
3. Debate has taken place over which term best describes traditional law and practice in Timor-Leste. The Indonesian-derived term "*adat*" has wide currency, while the Tetun term "*lisan*" is preferred by some writers, including a key proponent of the local turn, Josh Trindade (2008). I concur with cultural anthropologist David Hicks that the term "*adat*" denotes customary law governing "inheritance of property, spouse eligibility, ritual etiquette, *tara bandu* (taboo observance), land ownership, political authority, sanctions, oral literature and cosmology" (2013, 27). *Lulik* (sacred) describes specific aspects of customary practice regarding sacred and profane objects, especially things that might be subject to a *bandu* (official prohibition). Portuguese speakers favor the term *kostumes* (customs). Lastly, *kultura* (culture) is used to speak about material culture and custom in general.
4. For example, a female village secretary stated that villagers vote for the liurai or the liurai's family "because they believe in the liurai. They look within the liurai's family, then they vote accordingly." Interview with Serafina, ET110, Oecusse, 4 August 2015.
5. Interviews with a village chief, ET127, Manufahi, 8 June 2011 and 31 August 2015; a village chief, ET104, Oecusse, 1 August 2015; a hamlet chief, ET103, Oecusse, 30 July 2015.
6. Domestic violence was not a crime under New Order–era Indonesian law (Hall 2009).
7. Interview with a female Timorese NGO senior manager, ET077, 2 June 2015.
8. In turn, passage of the penal code was delayed because of a debate between Alkatiri and Gusmão over the authority of parliament to pass decree laws on, for example, defamation, without any public debate (Shoesmith 2008, 77).
9. Interview with a senior manager of a Timorese women's organization, ET082, Dili, 8 June 2015.
10. Ibid. The accusation against Florindo also appeared on a Facebook message board on 17 September 2012: "Member of Parliament from FRETILIN—slept with a second wife, then beat his wife named **** Director of FOKUPERS until bloody." Copy archived with author.
11. The Commission for Anti–Violence Against Women was established in Indonesia after 1998 and the fall of Suharto.

12. In 2012, after acting as an expert witness for those advocating for the use of traditional dispute resolution in the courts, Babo-Soares was appointed minister of justice because of his expertise in "customary law" (Grenfell 2013, 266).
13. Village elections in 2016, 21 out of 442 village chiefs elected were women. This was despite the existence of a quota and donor and NGO support for 319 female candidates.
14. For examples concerning politics and economics, see Hughes (2009, 208).
15. Interview with the wife of a village chief, ET130, Manufahi, 1 September 2015.
16. Fieldwork notes, 2011 and 2015. Also reported in an interview with two young male citizens, ET150 and ET151, Manufahi, 9 September 2015.
17. Interview with two young female citizens, ET147 and ET148, Manufahi, 8 September, 2015.
18. Ibid.
19. Interview with ET131, Manufahi, 1 September 2015.
20. Interview with female villager Brigida, ET146, Manufahi, 8 September 2015.
21. Interview with a village chief, ET104, Oecusse, 1 August 2015.
22. Interview with village chief Bonifacio, ET127, Manufahi, 1 September 2015.
23. Interview with the senior manager of a women's shelter, ET112, Oecusse, 5 August 2015.
24. The observation that they resemble a "fault-finding process" has also been made regarding rape sentencing in formal courts in Papua New Guinea (Zorn 2012).
25. Interview with a hamlet chief, ET105, Oecusse, 30 July 2015.
26. Interview with male teacher Antonio ET131, Manufahi, 1 September 2015; and village chief Bonifacio ET127, 1 September 2015.

Chapter 5

1. Interview with a male village chief, ET104, Oecusse, 30 July 2015. He is using the term "adat," generally traditional law, in the specific sense of brideprice and indicating that the prices have risen now.
2. The median income figure of $384 per year attempts to quantify noncash portions of income. This is problematic, however, as the figure includes an imputed value for rental costs, even though most Timorese do not rent their houses. Therefore, the actual amount of cash used by an individual is much lower (Democratic Republic of Timor-Leste 2011a). See Inder, Cornwell, and Datt (2015) for a discussion.
3. Word Finder: English-Tetun/Tetun-English, 2nd ed., s.v. "*barlaki*." (Note the different spelling in the Dili Institute of Technology Dictionary.)
4. *Hafolin* as a transitive verb means to appreciate, to value or esteem, or to negotiate. As a noun, it means brideprice or arranged marriage. In West Timor, Indonesia, the term *belis* is used instead (Hägerdal 2010). "*Belis*" is possibly derived from the Indonesian *beli* or to buy. "*Belis*" is used throughout Nusa Tenggara Timur province on the islands of Timor, Rote, Sabu, and Flores (Hägerdal 2010). Compare the standard Indonesian for brideprice, *mahar*, which is derived from the Islamic tradition. "*Mahar*" means "expensive" in Tetun.

5. Interview with a male hamlet chief, ET105, Oecusse, 1 August 2015.
6. Fieldwork notes from a brideprice negotiation ceremony, Dili, 14 August 2011, at which the highest-ranked man sat with four or five older men and one woman. Thus, the brideprice negotiation was conducted primarily between male lineage heads, not between women.
7. Jolly (2015) and Tarney (2017) provide more examples of high brideprice rates internationally.
8. My argument on this issue applies a political economy of domestic violence that combines the work of feminist anthropologist Jane Fishburne Collier (1988) on the co-constitutive nature of marriage and social hierarchy with that of international relations scholar Jacqui True (2012) on the political economy of violence against women. Using a combination of these two materialist frameworks explains how brideprice in the Timorese political economy has limited the effectiveness of the LADV as a gender intervention.
9. Interview with a male village chief, ET104, Oecusse, 30 July 2015.
10. Dualisms are identified in kinship (wife-giving and wife-taking houses) (Fox 1980); in the ranked hierarchy between higher aristocrats and lower nobles (Trindade 2008); in colonial relations (Shepherd and McWilliam 2013); in interactions with the church (Therik 2004); and in marriage, childbirth, and death, chiefly identifying women with nature, inside, the raw, blood, and ritual pollution—and men with culture, outside, the cooked, and the clean (Clamagirand 1980; Forman 1980; Fox 1980). Feminist anthropologist Michelle Rosaldo's critique of *The Flow of Life* (Fox 1980), a collection of essays describing dualisms found in Timor and eastern Indonesia, is salutary here: "What high-rank and power *mean* are nowhere entertained nor is rank treated systematically in relation to actual marriage" (Rosaldo 1982, 214).
11. A key academic proponent of the local turn, Josh Trindade (2008), has argued that the Timorese focus on women and fertility signifies that women are highly valued.
12. Some marriage payments transfer the valuables to the bride, not to her family. These are dower systems and are common in Islamic marriage payment (*mahr*). They are intended as an economic buffer for wives in case of divorce or death.
13. Interview with a female villager, ET146, Manufahi, 7 September 2015. See Thu, Scott, and Van Niel (2007) for a discussion on the inconsistencies of matrilineal land inheritance in Timor-Leste.
14. Brideprice may have decreased in Oecusse, and there may be less society-wide support for it, but it is not clear from the present research that the amounts have decreased in any meaningful way.
15. Interview with a male hamlet chief, ET105, Oecusse, 1 August 2015. He never went to school.
16. Although the interviewee mentions a government program to reduce the amount of money paid in engagement ceremonies, I did not find any evidence of such a program. Interview with a female farmer, ET113, Oecusse, 5 August 2015. She had finished high school.
17. Interview with a female Timorese senior manager in a women's organization, ET089, Dili, 11 July 2015.

18. Interview with Serafina, female village secretary, ET110, Oecusse, 4 August 2015. She had finished high school.
19. Khan and Hyati (2012, 34) note that female members of patrilineal groups that do not pay barlake are subject to less domestic violence.
20. Interview with Lucia, wife of a village chief, ET131, Manufahi, 1 September 2015.
21. Interview with a male village chief, ET104, Oecusse, 30 July 2015.
22. These claims have massive implications for the development of the social market free trade zone in Oecusse. A government historian told me that the government's decision to research the "true history" of Oecusse in the lead-up to the five hundredth anniversary of the Portuguese arrival in Lifau led to problems because at least three families claimed to be the true rulers of Oecusse. Interview with a government researcher from Oecusse, Dili, 23 July 2015.
23. Interview with Antonio, ET130, Manufahi, 1 September 2015. Name of village and hamlet changed to deidentify data.
24. Debt is a major organizing principle of human social and political relations (Graeber 2011).
25. Fieldwork notes, 8 September 2015.
26. Interview with a female farmer, ET113, Oecusse, 5 August 2015.
27. In *The Moral Economy of the Peasant*, Scott (1976) argued that because peasant households in Southeast Asia were always close to hunger, they formed reciprocal bonds with other households to ensure survival through crisis. At the same time, reciprocity instantiates social judgment on nonreciprocity, the "moral economy."
28. Grenfell et al. (2015) explore the role of brideprice in a "discourse" to justify domestic violence.
29. Interview with female farmer Rosita, ET138, Manufahi, 4 September 2015.
30. Interview with young men, ET150 and ET151, Manufahi, 8 September 2015.
31. Similarly, in a report on the economic dimensions of violence against women, respondents frequently cited poverty as a cause of arguments and conflict within the household (Grenfell et al. 2015, 36).
32. Interview with Antonio, ET130, Manufahi, 1 September 2015.

Chapter 6

1. This figure includes only two MFIs. The amount is no doubt higher, as the total microfinance portfolio of Banco Nacional Commerçio de Timor-Leste (BNCTL) is not known.
2. The loan should be small relative to a person's annual income, no more than 250 percent (CGAP 2003).
3. I use the term "microfinance" as it covers savings and insurance parts of programs, but it principally refers to microloans.
4. As do other writers on Timorese microfinance, I classify all of these kinds of self-help groups together.

5. The Ohio school, based at Ohio State University, was influential in promoting liberalized agricultural credit markets, microfinance, and deregulated, competitive credit markets in the Global South.
6. Blue Orchard, for example, is a Swiss-regulated, Luxembourg-based microfinance investment bank that the United Nations started in 2000.
7. UNCDF is the primary UN-run financial intermediary active in Timor-Leste. Its mission shift to microfinance and financial inclusion has been particularly acute since the Bill and Melinda Gates Foundation and the Mastercard Foundation became major donors in 2008 and 2010, respectively. See http://www.uncdf.org/contributions-to-uncdf.
8. There is also little to differentiate SHG and MFI microfinance and rotating savings and loans associations (ROSCAs), called *arisan* in Indonesian. These are sometimes held to be more innocuous than SHG microfinance, but in fact many ROSCAs charge interest, some use violence to enforce payments, and some lend to others outside the group at higher interest rates. Thus, ROSCAs too may be indistinguishable from other forms of informal credit (Low 1995).
9. It is unclear what kind of "social economy" FRETILIN aspired to, and its meaning is quite diffuse. In general, a social economy tries to prioritize just social outcomes, rather than purely market profit.
10. Likewise, *gotong royong* became an important part of the New Order's political toolkit, at once justifying unpaid work gangs and promoting community cohesion and order (Bowen 1986).
11. Interview with a senior manager of a Timorese MFI, ET120, Dili, 16 August 2015.
12. Interest rates needed to achieve this goal varied from 81 to 550 percent per annum (Ravicz 1998, ix).
13. Although implicated in the destruction of Dili and in a massacre at the Liquiçá Church in which about two hundred people were killed, da Costa has never been tried for war crimes and remains a political functionary in West Timor. See the Masters of Terror database, http://www.syaldi.web.id/mot/Herminio%20da%20Costa.htm.
14. Shiffman (2002) discusses linking of loans to contraception in Indonesia, which during this period includes East Timor, but independent evidence of this happening in East Timor is scant.
15. The commercial banking sector was also severely disrupted. The Portuguese-owned Banco Nacional Ultramarino (BNU), which operated in Timor-Leste during the colonial period and carried a $97 million portfolio of loans averaging around $12,000 each, experienced major repayment problems. Around half of its loan portfolio remains nonperforming (FIELD-Support 2014, 11).
16. Data on project donor, title, aims, results, and disbursed funds (2002–2017) collected from https://aidtransparency.gov.tl/portal.
17. One MFI struggled to meet the requirements of the law, especially with respect to international capital, profits, and minimum staff qualifications of tertiary education. Interview with a senior manager of an MFI, ET120, Dili, 16 August 2015.
18. Interview with a senior government official, ET108, Dili, 4 August 2015.

NOTES 217

19. The budget preamble for ZEESMs states that the economic zone will "give priority to social economic activity which could propagate a good life for the whole community in the region" (Democratic Republic of Timor-Leste 2016a, my translation).
20. Interview with a senior government official, ET108, Dili, 4 August 2015.
21. The press reported microfinance crises in Nicaragua (2008), Bosnia-Herzegovina (2008–2009), Morocco (2009), Kolar, India (2009), Uganda (2009), Andhra Pradesh, India (2010), Pakistan (2010), Ghana (2015), and Cambodia (2017). See Bateman (2017); Boateng et al. (2016); Chen, Rasmussen, and Reille (2010); and Lyman, Shrader, and Tomilova (2015).
22. Emergency microfinance loans were similarly used by the World Bank in Bolivia. See Weber (2004).
23. Interview with an NGO manager, ET082, Dili, 10 June 2015.

Chapter 7

1. The following information is drawn principally from four months of fieldwork, interviews, and participant observation: over six weeks in Mota in 2011, three weeks in Oecusse in 2015, and six weeks in Mota, Manufahi, in 2015. Place names have been changed.
2. Government benefits do not reach the poor, because the veterans' pension is not means-tested and is rather a regressive form of welfare. To reiterate, the Bolsa da Mãe payment for mothers reaches both wealthier and poorer Timorese (Fernandes 2015).
3. Interviews with the village chief Bonifacio, ET127, Manufahi, 1 September 2015, and Rosita, ET138, Manufahi, 4 September 2015.
4. Interview with Brigida, ET146, Manufahi, 7 September 2015.
5. Interview with Lucia, ET130, and Antonio, ET131, Manufahi, 1 September 2015.
6. Interview with Lucia, ET130, Manufahi, 1 September 2015.
7. Interview with Lucia, ET130, and Antonio, ET131, Manufahi, 1 September 2015.
8. Interview with Rosita, ET138, Manufahi, 4 September 2015.
9. Interview with Rosita, ET138, Manufahi, 4 September 2015, and Sancio, ET137, Manufahi, 4 September 2015.
10. Interview with Sancio, ET137, Manufahi, 4 September 2015.
11. The other mass women's organizations affiliated with the government during the New Order were Dharma Wanita, for wives of officials, and Dharma Pertiwi, for wives of military and police personnel.
12. Interview with the senior manager of an MFI, ET120, Dili, 16 August 2015.
13. Interview with a schoolteacher, Antonio, ET130, Manufahi, 1 September 2015.
14. Interview with Brigida, ET146, Manufahi, 7 September 2015.
15. Interview with a villager, Michaela, ET113, and her mother, Elisabetha, ET114, Oecusse, 5 August 2015.
16. Interview with a villager and laundress, Lina, ET102, Oecusse, 7 July 2015. Similar experiences with microfinance and micro-insurance suicides were reported in Bangladesh in 2010 (Weber 2014) and in Andhra Pradesh the same year (Mader 2015).

17. Interview with a schoolteacher, Antonio, ET130, Manufahi, 1 September 2015.
18. Interview with Lucia, ET131, Manufahi, 1 September 2015.
19. Interview with a schoolteacher, Antonio, ET130, Manufahi, 1 September 2015.
20. Article 4(d) on collateralizing debts (Democratic Republic of Timor-Leste 2010d).
21. Focus group interview with managers at a Timorese women's NGO, Oecusse, 27 July 2015: female director, ET096; male program manager, ET097; female finance officer, ET098; female program manager, ET099.
22. Interview with Brigida, ET146, Manufahi, 7 September 2015.

References

Ackerly, Brooke, Marilyn Stern, and Jacqui True. 2006. *Feminist Methodologies for International Relations*. Cambridge: Cambridge University Press.

Aditjondro, George. 1996. "Man with the Right Mates." *West Australian*, January 3.

Aditjondro, George. 1998. "The Silent Suffering of Our Timorese Sisters: A Report to the UN Special Rapporteur on Women." In *Free East Timor: Australia's Culpability in East Timor's Genocide*, edited by Jim Aubrey, 243–267. Sydney: Vintage/Random House.

Aditjondro, George. 2000. "Mapping the Political Terrain." *Arena Magazine*, (46) April. https://arena.org.au/mapping-the-political-terrain/.

Aditjondro, George. 2001. *Timor Lorosa'e on the Crossroad: Timor Loro Sae's Transformation from Jakarta's Colony to Global Capitalist Outpost*. Jakarta: Center for Democracy and Social Justice Study.

Agarwal, Bina. 1994. *A Field of One's Own: Gender and Land Rights in South Asia*. Cambridge: Cambridge University Press.

Ahlin, Christian, and Neville Jiang. 2008. "Can Microcredit Bring Development?" *Journal of Development Economics* 86 (1):1–21.

Ahlin, Christian, Jocelyn Lin, and Michael Maio. 2011. "Where Does Microfinance Flourish? Microfinance Institution Performance in Macroeconomic Context." *Journal of Development Economics* 95 (2):105–120.

Alanamu, Temilola. 2015. "'You May Bind Me, You May Beat Me, You May Even Kill Me': Bridewealth, Consent and Conversion in Nineteenth-Century Abẹ́òkúta (in Present-Day Southwest Nigeria)." *Gender & History* 27 (2):329–348.

Allain, Jean, ed. 2012. *The Legal Understanding of Slavery*. Oxford: Oxford University Press.

Allden, Susanne. 2007. "Internalising the Culture of Human Rights: Securing Women's Rights in Post-conflict East Timor." *Asia-Pacific Journal on Human Rights and the Law* 1:1–23.

Allden, Susanne. 2009. "Microfinance and Post-conflict Development in Cambodia and Timor-Leste." *SOJOURN Journal of Social Issues in Southeast Asia* 24:269–284.

Alola Foundation. 2014. *Annual Report*. Dili: Alola Foundation.

Alves, Ubalda Maria Felipe, and Teresa Verdia Alita. 2009. "NGOs Alternative Report: Implementation of the Convention on the Elimination of All Forms of Discrimination Against Women (CEDAW)." Dili: FOKUPERS.

Andaya, Leonard. 2010. "The 'Informal Portuguese Empire' and the Topasses in the Solor Archipelago and Timor in the Seventeenth and Eighteenth Centuries." *Journal of Southeast Asian Studies* 41 (3):391–420.

Anderson, Benedict. 1993. "Imagining East Timor." *Arena Magazine*, May (4):23–27.

Anderson, Siwan. 2007. "The Economics of Dowry and Brideprice." *Journal of Economic Perspectives* 21 (4):151–174.

Angelucci, Manuela, Dean Karlan, and Jonathan Zinman. 2015. "Microcredit Impacts: Evidence from a Randomized Microcredit Program Placement Experiment by Compartamos Banco." *American Economic Journal: Applied Economics* 7 (1):151–182.

Araujo, Abilio 1975. *Timorese Elites*. Canberra: Canberra Technical College.

Arnold, Matthew B. 2009. "Challenges Too Strong for the Nascent State of Timor-Leste: Petitioners and Mutineers." *Asian Survey* 49:429–449.

Asian Development Bank. 2012. *Least Developed Sucos: Timor-Leste*. Mandaluyong City, Philippines: Asian Development Bank.

Asian Development Bank and UNIFEM. 2005. *Gender and Nation Building in Timor-Leste: Country Gender Assessment*. Asian Development Bank South East Asia Regional Office.

Asia Foundation. 2016. *Women's Experiences of Intimate Partner Violence in Timor-Leste. Fact Sheet 1*. Dili: The Asia Foundation.

Asia Justice and Rights. 2017. *Joint Shadow Report at the UN Committee Against Torture's 62nd Session*. Dili: United Nations.

Aspinall, Edward, and Greg Fealy. 2010. "Introduction." In *Soeharto's New Order and Its Legacy: Essays in Honour of Harold Crouch*, edited by Edward Aspinall and Greg Fealy, 1–14. Canberra: ANU E-Press.

Augsburg, Britta, and Cyril Fouillet. 2013. "Profit Empowerment: The Microfinance Institution's Mission Drift." In *The Credibility of Microcredit*, edited by Dwight Haase, 199–226. Leiden: Brill.

Austen, Siobhan, Monica Costa, Rhonda Sharp, and Diane Elson. 2013. "Expenditure Incidence Analysis: A Gender-Responsive Budgeting Tool for Educational Expenditure in Timor-Leste?" *Feminist Economics* 19 (4):1–24.

Autesserre, Séverine. 2010. *The Trouble with the Congo: Local Violence and the Failure of International Peacebuilding*. Cambridge: Cambridge University Press.

Babo-Soares, Dionísio 2004. "*Nahe Biti*: The Philosophy and Process of Grassroots Reconciliation (and Justice) in East Timor." *Asia Pacific Journal of Anthropology* 5 (1):15–33.

Ban Ki-Moon 2012. *Conflict-Related Sexual Violence. Report of the Secretary-General. S/2012/33*. New York: United Nations.

BAPPENAS. 1988. *Regional, Village and City Development*. Jakarta: Republic of Indonesia.

Bateman, Milford. 2017. "Don't Fear the Rate Cap: Why Cambodia's Microcredit Regulations Aren't Such a Bad Thing." NextBillion.com. https://nextbillion.net/dont-fear-the-rate-cap-why-cambodias-microcredit-regulations-arent-such-a-bad-thing/.

Bauchet, Jonathan, Cristobal Marshall, Laura Starita, Jeanette Thomas, and Anna Yalouris. 2011. *Latest Findings from Randomized Evaluations of Microfinance*. Washington, DC: CGAP.

Bedford, Kate. 2007. "The Imperative of Male Inclusion: How Institutional Context Influences World Bank Gender Policy." *International Feminist Journal of Politics* 9 (3):289–311.

Belloni, Roberto. 2012. "Hybrid Peace Governance: Its Emergence and Significance." *Global Governance* 18:21–38.

BELUN. 2013. *The Social Impact of Veterans Payments Processes EWER Policy Brief VI*. Dili: Centre for International Conflict Resolution.

Bernard, H. Russell, and Gery W. Ryan. 2003. "Techniques to Identify Themes." *Field Methods* 15 (1):85–109.

Bexley, Angie, and Maj Nygaard-Christensen. 2014. "From Poet to Despot: The Changing Face of Xanana Gusmão." *Sydney Morning Herald*, December 22.

Bhabha, Homi K. 2004. *The Location of Culture*. Oxon: Routledge.

Blomberg, Matt. 2019. *Cambodia and China Can't Stop 'Bride Trafficking' without More Funding*. Phnom Penh: Global Citizen, April 2. https://www.globalcitizen.org/en/content/cambodia-urged-to-end-bride-trafficking/.

BCTL. 2013. *Timor-Leste Financial Development Master Plan*. Dili: Banco Central de Timor-Leste.

BNCTL (Banco Nacional Commercio de Timor-Leste). 2014. *Financial Statements and Independent Auditor's Report*. Dili: Syarief Basir and Rekan.

Boateng, Festival Godwin, Stephen Nortey, Jonas Asamanin Barnie, Peter Dwumah, Martin Acheampong, and Eunice Ackom-Sampene. 2016. "Collapsing Microfinance Institutions in Ghana: An Account of How Four Expanded and Imploded in the Ashanti Region." *International Journal of African Development* 3 (2):37–62.

Boege, Volker, Anne M. Brown, and Kevin Clements. 2009. "Hybrid Political Orders, Not Fragile States." *Peace Review: A Journal of Social Justice* 21 (1):13–21.

Boege, Volker, Anne M. Brown, Kevin Clements, and Anna Nolan. 2008. *On Hybrid Political Orders and Emerging States: State Formation in the Context of "Fragility."* Berghof Handbook. Berlin: Berghof Research Center for Constructive Conflict Management.

Boomgaard, Peter. 2003. "Bridewealth and Birth Control: Low Fertility in the Indonesian Archipelago, 1500–1900." *Population and Development Review* 29 (2):197–214.

Boserup, Ester. 1989. *Women's Role in Economic Development*. Trowbridge, UK: Cromwell Press.

Bovensiepen, Judith. 2014a. "Installing the Insider 'Outside': House Reconstruction and the Transformation of Binary Ideologies in Independent Timor-Leste." *American Ethnologist* 41 (2):290–304.

Bovensiepen, Judith. 2014b. "*Lulik*: Taboo, Animism, or Transgressive Sacred? An Exploration of Identity, Morality, and Power In Timor-Leste." *Oceania* 84:121–137.

Bowen, J. R. 1986. "On the Political Construction of Tradition: *Gotong Royong* in Indonesia." *Journal of Asian Studies* 45 (3):545–561.

Brahimi, Lakhdar. 2000. *Report of the Panel on United Nations Peace Operations*. New York: United Nations. https://peacekeeping.un.org/en/report-of-panel-united-nations-peace-operations-brahimi-report-a55305.

Brown, M. Anne. 2012a. "Entangled Worlds: Villages and Political Community in Timor-Leste." *Local Global* 11:54–71.

Brown, M. Anne. 2012b. "Hybrid Governance and Democratisation: Village Governance in Timor-Leste." *Local Global* 11:156–164.

Brown, M. Anne, and Alex Gusmão. 2009. "Peacebuilding and Political Hybridity in East Timor." *Peace Review* 21 (1):61–69.

Brown, M. Anne, and Alex Gusmão. 2012. "Looking for the Owner of the House: Who Is Making Peace in Rural East Timor?" In *Hybrid Forms of Peace from Everyday Agency to Post-liberalism*, edited by Oliver Richmond and Audra Mitchell, 107–130. Basingstoke: Palgrave Macmillan.

Budiardjo, Carmel, and Liem Soei Liong. 1984. *The War against East Timor*. Sydney: Pluto Press.

Budlender, Debbie 2015. *Budget Call Circulars and Gender Budget Statements in the Asia Pacific: A Review*. Bangkok. UN Women.

Burgess, Patrick. 2006. "A New Approach to Restorative Justice: East Timor's Community Reconciliation Processes." In *Transitional Justice in the Twenty-First Century*, edited by Naomi Roht-Arriaza and Javier Mariezcurrena, 176–205. Cambridge: Cambridge University Press.

Cameron, Stuart, and Eric Daniel Ananga. 2015. "Savings Groups, Livelihoods and Education: Two Case Studies in Ghana." *Journal of International Development* 27 (7):1027–1041.

Carey, Peter. 1999. "The Catholic Church, Religious Revival, and the Nationalist Movement in East Timor, 1975–1998." *Indonesia and the Malay World* 27:77–95.

Carey, Peter. 2003. "Third-World Colonialism, the *Geração Foun*, and the Birth of a New Nation: Indonesia through East Timorese Eyes, 1975–99." *Indonesia* 76 (October):23–67. https://www.jstor.org/stable/3351348.

Carroll, Toby. 2010. *Delusions of Development: The World Bank and the Post-Washington Consensus in Southeast Asia*. Basingstoke: Palgrave.

Carey, Peter. 2015. "'Access to Finance' and the Death of Development in the Asia-Pacific." *Journal of Contemporary Asia* 45 (1):139–166.

CAVR. 2006. *Chega! The Report of the Commission for Reception Truth and Reconciliation in Timor-Leste*. Dili: Commission for Reception, Truth and Reconciliation in Timor-Leste (CAVR).

CEDAW. 2009. *Concluding Observations of the Committee on the Elimination of Discrimination Against Women*. New York. United Nations.

Centre for Women and Gender Studies. 2014. *Gender Assessment of the Special Social Economy Market Zone for Oecusse*. Dili: ZEESMs and UN Women.

CGAP. 2003. *Microfinance Consensus Guidelines: Definitions of Selected Financial Terms, Ratios, and Adjustments for Microfinance*. Washington, DC: CGAP.

Chandler, David. 2012. "Resilience and Human Security: The Post-interventionist Paradigm." *Security Dialogue* 43 (3):213–229.

Chant, Sylvia. 2008. "The 'Feminisation of Poverty' and the 'Feminisation' of Anti-poverty Programs: Room for Revision?" *Journal of Development Studies* 44 (2):165–197.

Chant, Sylvia, and Caroline Sweetman. 2012. "Fixing Women or Fixing the World? 'Smart Economics,' Efficiency Approaches, and Gender Equality in Development." *Gender & Development* 20 (3):517–529.

Chappell, Louise. 2016. *The Politics of Gender Justice at the International Criminal Court*. Oxford: Oxford University Press.

Charlesworth, Hilary. 2008. "Are Women Peaceful? Reflections on the Role of Women in Peace-Building." *Feminist Legal Studies* 16 (3):347–361.

Charlesworth, Hilary, and Mary Wood. 2001. "'Mainstreaming Gender' in International Peace and Security: The Case of East Timor." *Yale Journal of International Law* 26 (2):313–319.

Charlesworth, Hilary, and Mary Wood. 2002. "Women and Human Rights in the Rebuilding of East Timor." *Nordic Journal of International Law* 71:325–348.

Chaudhary, Torunn W., Orzala Ashraf Nemat, and Astri Suhrke. 2011. "Promoting Women's Rights in Afghanistan: The Ambiguous Footprint of the West." In *A Liberal Peace? The Problems and Practices of Peacebuilding*, edited by Susanna Campbell, David Chandler, and Meera Sabaratnam, 106–120. London: Zed Books.

Chen, Greg, Stephen Rasmussen, and Xavier Reille. 2010. *Growth and Vulnerabilities in Microfinance*. Washington, DC: CGAP.

Chesterman, Simon. 2002. "East Timor in Transition: Self-determination, State-Building and the United Nations." *International Peacekeeping* 9 (1):45–76.

Chesterman, Simon. 2004. *You, the People: The United Nations, Transitional Administration and State-Building*. New York: Oxford University Press.
Chopra, Jarat. 2002. "Building State Failure in East Timor." *Development and Change* 33:979–1000.
Chopra, Jarat, and Tanja Hohe. 2004. "Participatory Intervention." *Global Governance* 10 (3):289–305.
Clamagirand, Brigitte. 1980. "The Social Organisation of the Ema of Timor." In *The Flow of Life: Essays on Eastern Indonesia*, edited by James J. Fox, 134–151. Cambridge, Massachusetts: Harvard University Press.
Cockburn, Cynthia. 2013. "War and Security, Women and Gender: An Overview of the Issues." *Gender & Development* 21 (3):433–452.
Connell, R. 2005. *Masculinities*. London: Polity Press.
Conroy, John D. 2004. *Timor-Leste: Independent Review of the Credit Component of the Community Empowerment Project*. Washington, DC: The World Bank Conflict Prevention and Reconstruction Unit.
Cooke, B. 2003. "A New Continuity with Colonial Administration: Participation in Development Management." *Third World Quarterly* 24 (1):47–61.
Copestake, James, Mateo Cabello, Ruth Goodwin-Groen, Robin Gravesteijn, Julie Humberstone, Susan Johnson, Max Nino-Zarazua, and Matthew Titus. 2015. "Towards a Plural History of Microfinance." *Bath Papers in International Development and Wellbeing* 40:1–28.
Corcoran-Nantes, Yvonne. 2009. "The Politics of Culture and the Culture of Politics: A Case Study of Gender and Politics in Lospalos, Timor-Leste." *Conflict, Security & Development* 9 (2):165–187.
Cornwall, Andrea. 2007. "Revisiting the 'Gender Agenda.'" *IDS Bulletin* 38 (2):69–78.
Cornwall, Andrea. 2014. *Women's Empowerment: What Works and Why?* Sussex: Institute of Development Studies.
Costa, Monica. 2010. *"Following the Money" to Gender Equality: The Role of Non-governmental Organisations in Timor-Leste*. Buenos Aires: International Association for Feminist Economics.
Costa, Monica. 2015. "Gender Equality, Economic Policy and State Resilience in the New State of Timor-Leste." PhD diss., School of Communication, International Studies and Languages, University of South Australia.
Costa, Monica. 2018. *Gender Responsive Budgeting in Fragile States: The Case of Timor-Leste*. Abingdon: Routledge.
Costa, Monica, Marian Sawer, and Rhonda Sharp. 2013. "Women Acting for Women." *International Feminist Journal of Politics* 15 (3):333–352.
Costa, Monica, Rhonda Sharp, and Siobhan Austen. 2009. *Unlocking the Potential for Gender-Sensitive Public Finances in Timor-Leste*. Heterodox Economics' Visions. Australian Society of Heterodox Economists 8th Annual Conference, Sydney, December 7.
Coulibaly, Abdoul Karim. 2014. *Evaluation of UNDP COMPASIS Saving Groups as Financial Service Providers*. Dili: UNDP.
Cox, Robert W. 1981. "Social Forces, States and World Orders: Beyond International Relations Theory." *Millennium—Journal of International Studies* 10 (2):126–155.
Credit Unions Australia. 2011. *Timor-Leste: Building Institutional Capacity: Project Plan 2008–2011*. Sydney: National Directorate of Cooperatives, Credit Union Foundation Australia.

Cristalis, Irena. 2002. *Bitter Dawn: East Timor: A Peoples' Story*. London: Zed Books.
Cristalis, Irena, and Catherine Scott. 2005. *The Story of Women's Activism in East Timor*. London: Catholic Institute for International Relations.
Crouch, Harold. 2007. *The Army and Politics in Indonesia*. Politics and International Relations of Southeast Asia. Ithaca, NY: Cornell University Press.
Cummins, Deborah. 2010. "Local Governance in Timor-Leste: The Politics of Mutual Recognition." PhD diss., School of Social Sciences and International Studies, University of New South Wales.
Cummins, Deborah. 2011. "The Problem of Gender Quotas: Women's Representatives on Timor-Leste's *Suku* Councils." *Development in Practice* 21 (1):85–95.
Cummins, Deborah. 2013. "A State of Hybridity: Lessons in Institutionalism from a Local Perspective." *Fletcher Forum of World Affairs* 37 (1):144–160.
Cummins, Deborah, and Michael Leach. 2012. "Democracy Old and New: The Interaction of Modern and Traditional Authority in East Timorese Local Government." *Asian Politics & Policy* 4 (1):89–104.
da Cruz, Antonia Carmen. 2014. *Relatoriu Implementasaun Planu Asaun Anual DNRS 2014: Relatoriu Narrativu* [Report on the implementation of the annual action plan for DNRS 2014]. Dili: Ministry of Social Solidarity (MSS).
Dale, Pamela, Lena Lepuschuetz, and Nithin Umapathi. 2014. "Peace, Prosperity and Safety Nets in Timor-Leste: Competing Priorities or Complementary Investments?" *Asia & the Pacific Policy Studies* 1 (2):287–296.
Danzer, Erick M. 2008. "From Farmers to Global Markets: The Politics of Commodity Supply Chains in Indonesia." PhD diss., University of Wisconsin.
da Silva, Antero Benedito. 2012. "FRETILIN Popular Education 1973–1978 and Its Relevance to Timor-Leste Today." PhD diss., School of Education, University of New England.
Davidson, Katharine G. 1994. "The Portuguese Colonisation of Timor: The Final Stage 1850–1912." PhD diss., University of Melbourne.
Davies, Sara, and Jacqui True. 2015. "Reframing Conflict-Related Sexual and Gender-Based Violence: Bringing Gender Analysis Back In." *Security Dialogue* 46 (6):495–512.
Day, Milissa. 2007. *Leveraging Remittances with Microfinance: Timor-Leste Country Report*. Brisbane. The Foundation for Development Cooperation.
Day, Milissa. 2010. *Microfinance in Timor-Leste (East Timor)*. Singapore: Citi Foundation.
Democratic Republic of Timor-Leste. 2002. *Constitution of the Democratic Republic of Timor-Leste*. Dili: Democratic Republic of Timor-Leste.
Democratic Republic of Timor-Leste. 2006. *Decree Law No. 6/2006 on the Election of the National Parliament*. Dili: Democratic Republic of Timor-Leste.
Democratic Republic of Timor-Leste. 2009. *Parliamentary Law No. 3/2009 Community Leaderships and Their Election*. Dili: Democratic Republic of Timor-Leste.
Democratic Republic of Timor-Leste. 2010a. National Parliament Resolution 12/2010 *Relativa à Preparação de um Orçamento que Tenha em Consideração a Igualdade de Género* [Concerning the preparation of a budget that takes into account gender equality]. Dili: Democratic Republic of Timor-Leste.
Democratic Republic of Timor-Leste. 2010b. *Parliamentary Law No. 7/2010 Law Against Domestic Violence*. Dili: Democratic Republic of Timor-Leste.
Democratic Republic of Timor-Leste. 2010c. *Presidential Decree 13/2010 for a Gender Responsive Budget*. Dili: Democratic Republic of Timor-Leste.

Democratic Republic of Timor-Leste. 2011a. *Timor-Leste Household Income and Expenditure Survey 2011*. Dili. National Directorate of Statistics.
Democratic Republic of Timor-Leste. 2011b. *Timor-Leste Strategic Development Plan 2011–2030*. Dili: Office of the Prime Minister.
Democratic Republic of Timor-Leste. 2014. *Second and Third Periodic Reports of States Parties to the Convention on the Elimination of All Forms of Discrimination Against Women (CEDAW)*. Dili: Secretary of State for the Promotion of Equality (SEPI) and United Nations.
Democratic Republic of Timor-Leste. 2016. *Orsamentu Geral Estadu 2017: RAEOA-ZEESM: Livru 3* [General state budget: RAEOA-ZEESM: Book 3]. Dili: Ministry of Finance, Democratic Republic of Timor-Leste.
De Sousa Shields, Marc. 2011. *Inclusive Finance for the Underserved Economy (INFUSE): Mid-term Evaluation*. Dili: United Nations Capital Development Fund (UNCDF).
Dichter, Thomas, and Malcolm Harper. 2007. *What's Wrong with Microfinance?* London: Practical Action.
Doornbos, Martin. 2006. *Global Forces and State Restructuring: Dynamics of State Formation and Collapse*. Edited by Timothy M. Shaw. Houndmills: Palgrave Macmillan.
Downer, Alexander. 2007. "Australia's Commitment to the Pacific." Biennial Sir Arthur Tange Lecture on Australian Diplomacy, Canberra, August 8.
Downie, Sue. 2007. "UNTAET: Statebuilding and Peacebuilding." In *East Timor: Beyond Independence*, edited by Damien Kingsbury and Michael Leach, 29–40. Melbourne: Monash Asia Institute.
Drolet, Julie. 2010. "Feminist Perspectives in Development: Implications for Women and Microcredit." *Affilia* 25 (3): 212–223.
Drysdale, Jennifer. 2007. "Sustainable Development or Resource Cursed? An Exploration of Timor-Leste's Institutional Choices." PhD diss., Fenner School for Environment and Society, Australian National University.
Duffield, Mark. 2001. *Global Governance and the New Wars: The Merging of Development and Security*. London: Zed Books.
Duffield, Mark. 2005. "Getting Savages to Fight Barbarians: Development, Security and the Colonial Present." *Conflict, Security & Development* 5 (2):141–159.
Duggan, Catherine S. M. 2016. "Doing Bad by Doing Good? Theft and Abuse by Lenders in the Microfinance Markets of Uganda." *Studies in Comparative International Development* 51 (2): 189–208.
Dunn, James. 2003. *East Timor: A Rough Passage to Independence*. Sydney: Longueville Media.
Elson, Diane. 1993. "Gender-Aware Analysis and Development Economics." *Journal of International Development* 5 (2):237–247.
Elyachar, Julia. 2002. "Empowerment Money: The World Bank, Non-governmental Organizations, and the Value of Culture in Egypt." *Public Culture* 14 (3):493–513.
Elyachar, Julia. 2005. *Markets of Dispossession: NGOs, Economic Development and the State in Cairo*. Durham, NC: Duke University Press.
Enloe, Cynthia. 2000. *Maneuvers: The International Politics of Militarizing Women's Lives*. Berkeley: University of California Press.
European Union Election Observation Mission. 2012. *Timor-Leste Final Report: Parliamentary Election 2012*. Dili: European Union.

Eves, Richard, and Joanne Crawford. 2013. *Do No Harm: The Relationship between Violence Against Women and Women's Economic Empowerment in the Pacific*. Canberra: Society & Governance in Melanesia State, ANU.

Eyben, Rosalind, Naila Kabeer, and Andrea Cornwall. 2008. *Conceptualising Empowerment and the Implications for Pro-poor Growth*. Brighton. Institute of Development Studies.

Ferguson, Lucy. 2010. "Interrogating 'Gender' in Development Policy and Practice." *International Feminist Journal of Politics* 12 (1):3–24.

Fernandes, Rita. 2015. *Policy Note: Assessing the Bolsa da Mãe Benefit Structure: A Preliminary Analysis*. Dili: UNDP.

Ferreira, Elizario. 2012. *Dezenvolve Ekonomia Komunitaria liu husi Cooperativa Credito* [Community economic development through credit cooperatives]. Dili: *Federacao Cooperativa Credita* [Federation of credit cooperatives] *Hanai Malu*.

Field, Annette. 2004. "Places Oof Suffering Aand Pathways Tto Healing: Post-Cconflict Life Iin Bidau, East Timor." PhD diss., School of Anthropology, Archaeology & Sociology, James Cook University.FIELD-Support. 2014. *Assessment of Financial Services for Agribusiness and Rural Farmers in Timor-Leste*. Washington, DC: Economic Leveraging USAID Financial Integration, Broad-Based Dissemination and Support.

Fishburne Collier, Jane. 1988. *Marriage and Inequality in Classless Societies*. Palo Alto, CA: Stanford University Press.

Fishburne Collier, Jane, and Michelle Rosaldo. 1981. "Politics and Gender in Simple Societies." In *Sexual Meanings: The Cultural Construction of Gender and Sexuality*, edited by Sherry Ortner and Harriet Whitehead, 276–329. Cambridge: Cambridge University Press.

Forman, Stephen. 1980. "Descent, Alliance and Exchange Ideology among the Makassae of East Timor." In *The Flow of Life: Essays on Eastern Indonesia*, edited by James J. Fox, 152–176. Cambridge, MA: Harvard University Press.

Fox, James J. 2006. "The Transformation of Progenitor Lines of Origin: Patterns of Precedence in Eastern Indonesia." In *Origins, Ancestry and Alliance in Austronesian Ethnography*, edited by James J. Fox and Clifford Sather, 133–156. Canberra: Australian National University.

Fox, James J. 2008. "Repaying the Debt to Mau Kiak: Reflections on Timor's Cultural Traditions and the Obligations of Citizenship in an Independent East Timor." In *Democratic Governance in Timor-Leste: Reconciling the Local and the National*, edited by David Mearns, 119–128. Darwin, Australia: Charles Darwin University Press.

Fox, James J., ed. 1980. *The Flow of Life: Essays on Eastern Indonesia*. Cambridge, MA: Harvard University Press.

Fox, James J., and Dionísio Babo Soares, eds. 2003. *Out of the Ashes: The Destruction and Reconstruction of East Timor*. Canberra: ANU E-Press.

Francillion, Gerard. 1980. "Incursions upon Wehali: A Modern History of an Ancient Empire." In *The Flow of Life: Essays on Eastern Indonesia*, edited by James J. Fox, 248–265. Cambridge, MA: Harvard University Press.

Freire, Maria Raquel, and Paula Duarte Lopes. 2013. "Peacebuilding in Timor-Leste: Finding a Way between External Intervention and Local Dynamics." *International Peacekeeping* 20 (2):204–218.

Gaffney-Rhys, Ruth. 2011. "Polygamy and the Rights of Women." *Women in Society* 1:2–17.

García-Moreno, Claudia, Henrica Jansen, Mary Ellsberg, Lori Heise, and Charlotte Watts. 2005. "WHO Multi-country Study on Women's Health and Domestic Violence against Women." Geneva: World Health Organization.

Garikipati, Supriya. 2010. "Microcredit and Women's Empowerment: Understanding the Impact Paradox with Particular Reference to South India." In *The International Handbook of Gender and Poverty: Concepts, Research and Policy*, edited by Sylvia Chant, 599–605. Cheltenham: Edward Elgar.

Gehlich-Shillabeer, Mareen. 2008. "Poverty Alleviation or Poverty Traps? Microcredits and Vulnerability in Bangladesh." *Disaster Prevention and Management* 17 (3):396–409.

Gender and Constitution Subcommittee. 2001. "Women's Charter of Rights." Available in the *La'o Hamutuk Bulletin*. Under "Campaign to Support Women's Rights in the Constitution." https://www.laohamutuk.org/Bulletin/2001/Aug/bulletinv2n5.html#Campaign.

George, Nicole, and Laura. J. Shepherd. 2016. "Women, Peace and Security: Exploring the Implementation and Integration of UNSCR 1325." *International Political Science Review* 37 (3):297–306.

Goetz, Anne-Marie. 2007. "Gender Justice, Citizenship and Entitlements: Core Concepts, Central Debates and New Directions for Research." In *Gender Justice, Citizenship, and Development*, edited by Maitrayee Mukhopadhyay and Navsharan Singh, 15–57. Ottawa: International Development Research Centre.

Goetz, Anne-Marie, and Rina Sen Gupta. 1996. "Who Takes the Credit? Gender, Power, and Control over Loan Use in Rural Credit Programs in Bangladesh." *World Development* 24 (1):45–63.

Goetz, Anne-Marie, and Rob Jenkins. 2016. "Agency and Accountability: Promoting Women's Participation in Peacebuilding." *Feminist Economics* 22 (1):211–236.

Goldstone, Anthony. 2013. "Building a State and Statebuilding: East Timor and the UN: 1999–2012." In *Political Economy of Statebuilding: Power after Peace*, edited by Mats Berdal and Dominik Zaum, 209–230. Abingdon: Routledge.

Gonzalez-Vega, Claudio. 1977. "Interest Rate Restrictions and Income Distribution." *American Journal of Agricultural Economics* 59 (5):973–976.

Goody, Jack, and S. J. Tambiah. 1973. *Bridewealth and Dowry*. Cambridge: Cambridge University Press.

Graeber, David. 2011. *Debt: The First 5000 Years*. Brooklyn, NY: Melville House.

Graydon, Carolyn Julie. 2016. "Valuing Women in Timor-Leste: The Need to Address Domestic Violence by Reforming Customary Law Approaches While Improving State Justice." PhD diss., Faculty of Law, University of Melbourne.

Grenfell, Damien, Meabh Cryan, Kathryn Robertson, and Alex McClean. 2015. *Beyond Fragility and Inequity: Women's Experiences of the Economic Dimensions of Domestic Violence in Timor-Leste*. Dili: The Asia Foundation Nabilan Programme. https://researchrepository.rmit.edu.au/esploro/outputs/report/Beyond-fragility-and-inequity-womens-experiences-of-the-economic-dimensions-of-domestic-violence-in-Timor-Leste/9921862668601341.

Grenfell, Damien, and Anna Trembath. 2007. *Mapping the Pursuit of Gender Equality Non-government and International Agency Activity in Timor-Leste*. Dili: Democratic Republic of Timor-Leste, Office for the Promotion of Equality.

Grenfell, Damien, Mayra Walsh, Anna Trembath, Carmenesa Moniz Noronha, and Kym Holthouse. 2009. *Understanding Community: Security and Sustainability in Four Aldeia in Timor-Leste*. Melbourne. RMIT University Press.

Grenfell, Laura. 2006. "Legal Pluralism and the Rule of Law in Timor-Leste." *Leiden Journal of International Law* 19:305–337.
Grenfell, Laura. 2013. *Promoting the Rule of Law in Post-conflict States*. Cambridge: Cambridge University Press.
Grindle, Merilee S. 2012. *Jobs for the Boys: Patronage and the State in Comparative Perspective*. Cambridge, MA: Harvard University Press.
Groves, Gabrielle Eva Carol, Bernadette P. Resurreccion, and Phillippe Doneys. 2009. "Keeping the Peace Is Not Enough: Human Security and Gender-Based Violence during the Transitional Period of Timor-Leste." *Journal of Social Issues in Southeast Asia* 24 (2):186–210.
Guérin, Isabelle. 2014. "Juggling with Debt, Social Ties, and Values: The Everyday Use of Microcredit in Rural South India." *Current Anthropology* 55 (S9):40–50.
Guérin, Isabelle, Santhosh Kumar, and Isabelle Agier. 2013. "Women's Empowerment: Power to Act or Power over Other Women? Lessons from Indian Microfinance." *Oxford Development Studies* 41 (1):76–94.
Guérin, Isabelle, Marc Labie, and Jean-Michel Servet. 2015. *The Crises of Microcredit*. London: Zed Books.
Gunn, Geoffrey. 1999. *Timor Loro Sa'e: 500 Years*. Macau: Livros do Oriente.
Gunn, Geoffrey. 2011. *Historical Dictionaries of Asia, Oceania, and the Middle East*. No. 78, *Historical Dictionary of East Timor*. Plymouth, UK: Scarecrow Press.
Gusmão, Alex. 2012. "Electing Community Leaders: Diversity in Uniformity." *Local-Global* 11:180–191.
Guterres, Francisco da Costa. 2006. "Elites and Prospects of Democracy in East Timor." PhD diss., Department of International Business and Asian Studies, Griffith University.
Haase, Dwight. 2013. *The Credibility of Microcredit: Studies of Impact and Performance*. Leiden: Brill.
Hägerdal, Hans. 2010. "The Slaves of Timor: Life and Death on the Fringes of Early Colonial Society." *Itinerio* 34 (2):19–44.
Hägerdal, Hans. 2012. *Lords of the Land, Lords of the Sea; Conflict and Adaptation in Early Colonial Timor 1600–1800*. Leiden: Brill.
Hall, Nina. 2009. "East Timorese Women Challenge Domestic Violence." *Australian Journal of Political Science* 44 (2):309–325.
Hall, Nina, and Jacqui True. 2008. "Gender Mainstreaming in a Post-conflict State: Toward Democratic Peace in Timor-Leste?" In *Gender and Global Politics in the Asia-Pacific*, edited by Bina D'Costa and Katrina Lee-Koo, 159–174. Basingstoke: Palgrave Macmillan.
Hameiri, Shahar. 2008. "Risk Management, Neo-Liberalism and the Securitisation of the Australian Aid Program." *Australian Journal of International Affairs* 62:357–371.
Hameiri, Shahar. 2010. *Regulating Statehood: Statebuilding and the Transformation of the Global Order*. Basingstoke: Palgrave Macmillan.
Hameiri, Shahar, Caroline Hughes, and Fabio Scarpello. 2017. *International Intervention and Local Politics: Fragmented States and the Politics of Scale*. Cambridge: Cambridge University Press.
Hameiri, Shahar, and Lee Jones. 2017. "Beyond Hybridity to the Politics of Scale: International Intervention and 'Local' Politics." *Development and Change* 48 (1):54–77.
Harris-Rimmer, Sue. 2010. *Gender and Transitional Justice: The Women of East Timor*. London: Routledge.

Hessing, Johan, and Ebenhaizer I. Nuban [translator] Timo. 1923. "*Kawin Belis dan Kawin Gereja* [Brideprice marriage and church marriage]." *De Timor-Bode* (86):1–23.

Hewison, Kevin, Richard Robison, and Garry Rodan. 1993. *Southeast Asia in the 1990s: Authoritarianism, Democracy and Capitalism*. Sydney: Allen and Unwin.

Hicks, David. 1983. "Unachieved Syncretism: The Local-Level Political System in Portuguese Timor, 1966–1967." *Anthropos* 78 (1/2):17–40.

Hicks, David. 2004. *Tetum, Ghosts and Kin: Fertility and Gender in East Timor*. Second ed. Long Grove, IL: Waveland Press.

Hicks, David. 2012. "Compatibility, Resilience and Adaptation: The *Barlake* of Timor-Leste." *Local Global* 11 (12):124–137.

Hicks, David. 2013. "Adat and the Nation-State: Opposition and Synthesis in Two Political Cultures." In *The Politics of Timor-Leste: Democratic Consolidation after Intervention*, edited by Michael Leach and Damien Kingsbury, 25–43. Ithaca, NY: Cornell University Press.

Hicks, David. 2015. *Rhetoric and the Decolonization and Recolonization of East Timor*. New York: Routledge.

Hill, Hal. 2001. "Tiny Poor and War Torn: Development Policy Challenges for East Timor." *World Development* 29:1137–1156.

Hodžić, Aida. 2009. "Unsettling Power: Domestic Violence, Gender Politics and Struggles over Sovereignty in Ghana." *Ethnos* 74 (1):331–360.

Hohe, Tanja. 2002a. "The Clash of Paradigms: International Administration and Local Political Legitimacy in East Timor." *Contemporary Southeast Asia* 24 (3):569–589.

Hohe, Tanja. 2002b. "Totem Polls: Indigenous Concepts and 'Free and Fair' Elections in East Timor." *International Peacekeeping* 9 (4):69–88.

Hohe, Tanja. 2003. "Justice without Judiciary in East Timor." *Conflict, Security & Development* 3 (3):336–357.

Hohe, Tanja, and Rod Nixon. 2003. *Reconciling Justice: "Traditional" Law and State Judiciary in East Timor*. Washington, DC: United States Institute for Peace.

Hohe, Tanja, and Sofi Ospina. 2002. *Traditional Power Structures and Local Governance in Timor-Leste: A Case Study of the Community Empowerment Project*. Geneva: Graduate Institute of Development Studies.

Hohe-Chopra, Tanja, Susan Pologruto, and Timotio de Deus. 2009. "Fostering Justice in Timor-Leste: Rule of Law Program Evaluation." Dili: USAid.

Holloh, Detlev. 1998. *Microfinance in Indonesia: Between State, Market and Self Organisation*. Hamburg: Lit Verlag.

Hoskins, Janet. 2004. "Slaves, Brides and Other 'Gifts': Resistance, Marriage and Rank in Eastern Indonesia." *Slavery and Abolition* 25 (2):90–107.

Hozić, Aida, and Jacqui True. 2016. *Scandalous Economics: Gender and the Politics of Financial Crises*. Oxford: Oxford University Press.

Hudson, Valerie M. 2016. WomanStats Project Database: Marriage Scale 3 (MARR-SCALE-3) Brideprice/Dowry/Wedding Costs (Type and Prevalence). WomanStats. http://www.womanstats.org.

Hudson, Valerie M., and Hilary Matfess. 2017. "In Plain Sight: The Neglected Linkage between Brideprice and Violent Conflict." *International Security* 42 (1):7–40.

Hughes, Caroline. 2009. *Dependent Communities: Aid and Development in Cambodia and East Timor*. Ithaca, NY: Cornell University Press.

Hughes, Caroline. 2011. "The Politics of Knowledge: Ethnicity, Capacity and Return in Post-conflict Reconstruction Policy." *Review of International Studies* 37 (4):1493–1514.

Hughes, Caroline. 2012. "Tackling the Legacies of Violence and Conflict: Liberal Institutions and Contentious Politics in Cambodia and East Timor." In *Routledge Handbook of Southeast Asian Politics*, edited by Richard Robison, 263–285. Oxon: Routledge.

Hughes, Caroline. 2015. "Poor People's Politics in East Timor." *Third World Quarterly* 36 (5):908–928.

Hughes, Caroline, Joakim Öjendal, and Isabell Schierenbeck. 2015. "The Struggle versus the Song: The Local Turn in Peacebuilding: An Introduction." *Third World Quarterly* 36 (5):817–824.

Human Rights Watch. 2019. *"Give Us a Baby and We'll Let You Go" Trafficking of Kachin "Brides" from Myanmar to China*. Amsterdam: Human Rights Watch, May 21. https://www.hrw.org/report/2019/03/21/give-us-baby-and-well-let-you-go/trafficking-kachin-brides-myanmar-china.

Hunt, Janet. 2008. "Local NGOs in National Development: The Case of East Timor." PhD diss., School of Global Studies, Social Science and Planning, RMIT University.

Hutchings, Kimberly. 2008. "Cognitive Short Cuts." In *Rethinking the Man Question: Sex, Violence and International Politics*, edited by Marysia Zalewski and Jane Parpart, 23–46. London: Zed Books.

Hutchison, Jane, Wil Hout, Caroline Hughes, and Richard Robison. 2014. *Political Economy and the Aid Industry in Asia*. Basingstoke: Palgrave Macmillan.

Hynes, Michelle, Jeanne Ward, Kathryn Robertson, and Chadd Crouse. 2004. "A Determination of the Prevalence of Gender-Based Violence among Conflict-Affected Populations in East Timor." *Disasters* 28 (3):294–321.

Ignatieff, Michael. 2003. *Empire Lite: Nation-Building in Bosnia, Kosovo and Afghanistan*. London: Vintage / Random House.

Inder, Brett, Katy Cornwell, and Gaurav Datt. 2015. *Measuring Poverty and Wellbeing in Timor-Leste*. Melbourne: Monash University.

Ingram, Sue, Lia Kent, and Andrew McWilliam. 2015. "A New Era? Timor-Leste after the UN. Timor-Leste Update." Canberra: Australian National University.

International Crisis Group. 2006. *Asia Report: Resolving Timor-Leste's Crisis*. Brussels: International Crisis Group.

International Crisis Group. 2013. *Asia Report: Timor-Leste: Stability at What Cost?* Brussels: International Crisis Group.

Isern, Jennifer, L. B. Prakash, Anuradha Pillai, Robert Peck Christen, and Richard Rosenberg. 2007. "Sustainability of Self-Help Groups in India: Two Analyses." Washington, DC: CGAP.

Isserles, Robin G. 2003. "Microcredit: The Rhetoric of Empowerment, the Reality of 'Development as Usual.'" *Women's Studies Quarterly* 31 (3):38–57.

Jackson, David, Faustino Cardoso Gomes, Jesper Steffensen, Jose Turquel de Jesus, Roger Shotton, and Tanja Hohe. 2003. *Local Government Options Study: Final Report*. Dili: Irish Aid UNDP. Copy on file with author.

Jakimow, Tanya. 2009. "Non-government Organisations, Self-Help Groups and Neo-liberal Discourses." *South Asia: Journal of South Asian Studies* 32 (3):469–484.

Jayasuriya, Kanishka, and Garry Rodan. 2007. "Beyond Hybrid Regimes: More Participation, Less Contestation in Southeast Asia." *Democratization* 14 (5):773–794.

Jolliffe, Jill. 1978. *East Timor: Nationalism and Colonialism*. Brisbane: University of Queensland Press.

Jolly, Margaret. 2015. "*Braed Praes* in Vanuatu: Both Gifts and Commodities?" *Oceania* 85 (1):63–78.

Jolly, Margaret, Christine Stewart, and Carolyn Brewer. 2012. *Engendering Violence in Papua New Guinea*. Canberra: ANU E-Press.

Jones, Lee. 2010. "(Post-)colonial State-Building and State Failure in East Timor: Bringing Social Conflict Back In." *Conflict, Security & Development* 10 (4):547–575.

Jones, Lee. 2013. "State Theory and Statebuilding: Towards a Gramscian Analysis." In *New Agendas in Statebuilding: Hybridity, Contingency and History*, edited by Robert Egnell and Peter Haldén, 71–91. New York: Routledge.

Joshi, Vijaya. 2005. "Building Opportunities: Women's Organizing, Militarism and the United Nations Transitional Administration in East Timor." PhD diss., Clark University.

Journal Independente. 2017. "17 Families without Compensation for Home Loss in Oecusse: Teme." February 17.

JSMP, PRADET, and ALFeLa. 2015. *Shadow Report: Timor-Leste Government's Progress in Implementing the United Nations Convention on the Elimination of All Forms of Discrimination Against Women (CEDAW)*. Dili: Psychosocial Recovery and Development in East Timor Judicial System Monitoring Program, Women and Children's Legal Aid.

Kabeer, Naila. 1991. "Gender, Production and Well-Being: Rethinking the Household Economy." *IDS Discussion Paper* 288.

Kabeer, Naila. 2000. *The Power to Choose*. London: Verso.

Kabeer, Naila. 2001. "Conflicts over Credit: Re-evaluating the Empowerment Potential of Loans to Women in Rural Bangladesh." *World Development* 29 (1):63–84.

Kabeer, Naila. 2003. *Gender Mainstreaming in Poverty Eradication and the Millennium Development Goals*. London: Gender Section Commonwealth Secretariat.

Kabeer, Naila. 2005. "Is Microfinance a 'Magic Bullet' for Women's Empowerment? Analysis of Findings from South Asia." *Economic and Political Weekly* 40 (44):4709–4718.

Kabeer, Naila. 2014. *Violence Against Women as "Relational" Vulnerability: Engendering the Sustainable Human Development Agenda*. New York. UNDP Human Development Report Office.

Kammen, Douglas. 1999. "Notes on the Transformation of the East Timor Military Command and Its Implications for Indonesia." *Indonesia* (67):61–76. https://www.jstor.org/stable/335137.

Kammen, Douglas. 2003. "Master-Slave, Traitor-Nationalist, Opportunist-Oppressed: Political Metaphors in East Timor." *Indonesia* 76:69–85. https://ecommons.cornell.edu/handle/1813/54301.

Kammen, Douglas. 2012. "The Armed Forces in Timor-Leste: Politicization through Elite Conflict." In *The Political Resurgence of the Military in Southeast Asia: Conflict and Leadership*, edited by Marcus Mietzner, 107–125. Abingdon: Routledge.

Kammen, Douglas. 2016. *Three Centuries of Conflict in East Timor*. Singapore: National University of Singapore Press.

Kammen, Douglas. 2017. "Fantasy and Fossilization in the Study of Timor-Leste." In *Fieldwork in Timor-Leste*, edited by Maj Nygaard-Christensen and Angie Bexley, 125–143. Copenhagen: Nias Press.

Karim, Lamia. 2008. "Demystifying Micro-credit: The Grameen Bank, NGOs, and Neoliberalism in Bangladesh." *Cultural Dynamics* 20 (1):5–29.

Karim, Lamia. 2011. *Microfinance and Its Discontents: Women in Debt in Bangladesh.* Minneapolis: University of Minnesota Press.

Karim, Lamia. 2014. "Analyzing Women's Empowerment: Microfinance and Garment Labor in Bangladesh." *Fletcher Forum of World Affairs* 38 (2):153–166.

Kelly, Liz. 2005. "Inside Outsiders." *International Feminist Journal of Politics* 7 (4):471–495.

Kent, Lia. 2004. *Unfulfilled Expectations: Community Views on CAVR's Community Reconciliation Process.* Dili: Justice System Monitoring Program.

Kent, Lia. 2006. *Independent Evaluation: Commission on Cadres of the Resistance (CAQR).* Dili: World Bank Timor Leste.

Kent, Lia. 2012a. *The Dynamics of Transitional Justice: International Models and Local Realities in East Timor.* Abingdon: Routledge.

Kent, Lia. 2016. "After the Truth Commission: Gender and Citizenship in Timor-Leste." *Human Rights Review* 17 (1):1–20.

Kent, Lia, and Naomi Kinsella. 2015. "*A Luta Kontinua*, The Struggle Continues." *International Feminist Journal of Politics* 17 (3):473–494.

Kent, Lia, and Joanne Wallis. 2013. *Timor-Leste's Veterans' Pension Scheme: Who Are the Beneficiaries and Who Is Missing Out?* Canberra: ANU Briefing Paper.

Kerstan, Birgit, and Jutta Berninghausen. 1992. *Forging New Paths: Feminist Social Methodology and Rural Women in Java.* London: Zed Books.

Khan, Nasrin, and Selma Hyati. 2012. *Brideprice and Domestic Violence in Timor-Leste: A Comparative Study of Married-In and Married-Out Cultures in Four Districts.* Dili: FOKUPERS and UNFPA.

Kingsbury, Damien. 2007. "Political Developments." In *Beyond Independence*, edited by Damien Kingsbury and Michael Leach. Melbourne: Monash University Press.

Kingsbury, Damien. 2008. "East Timor's Political Crisis: Origins and Resolution." In *Democratic Governance in Timor-Leste: Reconciling the Local and the National*, edited by David Mearns, 33–51. Darwin, Australia: Charles Darwin University Press.

Kingsbury, Damien. 2017. "Is East Timor Run by a 'Stable' Government or Conspiratorial Oligarchy?" *Deakin Speaking: A Deakin University Weblog*, January 27. https://blogs.deakin.edu.au/deakin-speaking/2017/01/27/is-east-timor-run-by-a-stable-govt-or-conspiratorial-oligarchy/.

Kirk, Tom. 2015. "Taking Local Agency Seriously: Practical Hybrids and Domestic Violence in Timor-Leste." *International Journal on Minority and Group Rights* 22 (3):435–458.

Kniepe, A. 2013. *Law Against Domestic Violence: Obstacles to Implementation Three Years On.* Dili: Justice System Monitoring Program.

Koichi, Fujita. 2015. "The Excess Funds Problem of the Savings Groups in Laos: Case Study of a Village in Vientiane Municipality." *Southeast Asian Studies* 3:135–155.

Kovar, Annika. 2012. "Approaches to Domestic Violence Against Women in Timor-Leste: A Review and Critique." *Human Rights Education in Asia-Pacific* 3:207–252.

Kronsell, Annica, and Erika Svedberg. 2011. *Making Gender, Making War: Violence, Military and Peacekeeping Practices.* Basingstoke: Routledge.

Kumar, Chetan, and Jos de la Haye. 2012. "Hybrid Peacemaking: Building National 'Infrastructures for Peace.'" *Global Governance* 18 (1):13–20.

Lao Hamutuk. 2013. *National Impact of Veterans' Payments.* BELUN Seminar, Dili, March 5.

Lao Hamutuk. 2016. *Submission to Timor-Leste National Parliament on the Proposed General State Budget for 2016.* Dili: Lao Hamutuk.

Lemay-Hébert, Nicolas. 2009. "Statebuilding without Nation-Building? Legitimacy, State Failure and the Limits of the Institutionalist Approach." *Journal of Intervention and Statebuilding* 3 (1):21–45.

Lemay-Hébert, Nicolas. 2011. "The 'Empty-Shell' Approach: The Setup Process of International Administrations in Timor-Leste and Kosovo, Its Consequences and Lessons." *International Studies Perspectives* 12 (2):190–211.

Lemay-Hébert, Nicolas. 2017. "Exploring the Effective Authority of International Administrations from the League of Nations to the United Nations." *Journal of Intervention and Statebuilding* 11 (4):468–489.

Leonardsson, Hanna, and Gustav Rudd. 2015. "The 'Local Turn' in Peacebuilding: A Literature Review of Effective and Emancipatory Local Peacebuilding." *Third World Quarterly* 36 (5):825–839.

Lieberman, Ira, Anne Anderson, Zach Grafe, Bruce Campbell, and Daniel Kopf. 2008. *Microfinance and Capital Markets: The Initial Listing / Public Offering of Four Leading Institutions*. N.p: Council of Microfinance Equity Funds.

Loney, Hannah. 2015. "'The Target of a Double Exploitation': Gender and Nationalism in Portuguese Timor, 1974–75." *Intersections: Gender and Sexuality in Asia and the Pacific* 37. http://intersections.anu.edu.au/issue37/loney.pdf.

Loney, Hannah. 2016. "In Women's Words: A New History of Violence and Everyday Life during the Indonesian Occupation of East Timor (1975–1999)." PhD diss., University of Melbourne.

Low, Alaine. 1995. *A Bibliographic Survey of Rotating Savings and Credit Associations*. Oxford: Oxfam, Centre for Cross Cultural Research on Women.

Lyman, Timothy, Leesa Shrader, and Olga Tomilova. 2015. *Inclusive Finance and Shadow Banking*. Washington, DC: CGAP.

Mac Ginty, Roger. 2010. "Hybrid Peace: The Interaction between Top-Down and Bottom-Up Peace." *Security Dialogue* 41 (4):391–412.

Mac Ginty, Roger. 2015. "Where Is the Local? Critical Localism and Peacebuilding." *Third World Quarterly* 36 (5):840–856.

Mac Ginty, Roger, and Oliver Richmond. 2013. "The Local Turn in Peace Building: A Critical Agenda for Peace." *Third World Quarterly* 29 (10):763–783.

Mader, Philip. 2014. "Financialisation through Microfinance: Civil Society and Market-Building in India." *Asian Studies Review* 38 (4):601–619.

Mader, Philip. 2015. *The Political Economy of Microfinance*. Houndmills: Macmillan.

Mader, Philip. 2016. "Card Crusaders, Cash Infidels and the Holy Grails of Digital Financial Inclusion." *Behemoth* 9 (2):50–81.

Malhotra, Anju, Sidney Ruth Schuler, and Carol Boender. 2002. *Measuring Women's Empowerment as a Variable in International Development*. Washington, DC: World Bank.

March, Stephanie. 2008. "East Timor Poor Missing Out on Subsidised Rice." Australia: Radio Australia, September 9.

Marino, Pascal. 2006. "Beyond Economic Benefits: The Contribution of Microfinance to Post-conflict Recovery in Asia and the Pacific." In *Aid in Conflict*, edited by Matthew Clarke. New York: Nova Science Publishers.

Martinus, Danial. 2020. *Indonesian Women Are Abducted and Forced to Marry Their Captors. But It Might Change Soon*. Jakarta: Mashable Southeast Asia, July 20. https://sea.mashable.com/culture/11586/indonesian-women-are-abducted-and-forced-to-marry-their-captors-but-it-might-change-soon.

Matsuno, Akihisa, and Jose-Luis Oliviera. 2016. *Luta ba Lia Loos no Justisia: Relatoriu Final ba Peskiza Konjunta Asosiasaun HAK-Koligasaun Japones sira ba Timor-Leste konaba Eskravidaun Seksual Militar Japones iha Timor-Leste, 1942–1945* [The struggle for truth and justice: The final report of the research between Asosiasaun HAK and East Timor Japan Coalition about the Japanese military's sexual slavery in Timor-Leste 1942–1945]. Dili: Asosiasaun HAK and East Timor Japan Coalition.

Maurer, Klaus. 1999. *Bank Rakyat Indonesia (BRI) Indonesia (Case Study).* Eschborn: CGAP Working Group on Savings Mobilization.

Mayoux, Linda. 2000. *Microfinance and the Empowerment of Women: A Review of the Key Issues.* Geneva: International Labour Organization.

Mayoux, Linda. 2001. "Tackling the Down Side: Social Capital, Women's Empowerment and Microfinance in Cameroon." *Development and Change* 32 (3):435–464.

McLeod, Laura. 2015. "A Feminist Approach to Hybridity: Understanding Local and International Interactions in Producing Post-conflict Gender Security." *Journal of Intervention and Statebuilding* 9 (1):48–69.

McWilliam, Andrew. 2007. "Introduction: Restorative Custom: Ethnographic Perspectives on Conflict and Local Justice in Timor." *Asia Pacific Journal of Anthropology* 8:1–8.

McWilliam, Andrew. 2011. "Exchange and Resilience in Timor-Leste." *Journal of the Royal Anthropological Institute* 17:745–763.

McWilliam, Andrew. 2012. "New Fataluku Diasporas and Landscapes of Remittance and Return." *Local Global* 11:72–85.

McWilliam, Andrew, Lisa Palmer, and Christopher Shepherd. 2014. "*Lulik* Encounters and Cultural Frictions in East Timor: Past and Present." *Australian Journal of Anthropology* 25 (3):304–320.

Meagher, Kate. 2012. "The Strength of Weak States? Non-state Security Forces and Hybrid Governance in Africa." *Development and Change* 43 (5):1073–1101.

Mearns, David. 2002. *Looking Both Ways: Models for Justice in East Timor.* Sydney: Australian Legal Resources International.

Mearns, David, and Steven Farram. 2008. *Democratic Governance in Timor-Leste: Reconciling the Local and the National.* Darwin, Australia: Charles Darwin University Press.

Meger, Sara. 2015. "Toward a Feminist Political Economy of Wartime Sexual Violence." *International Feminist Journal of Politics* 17 (3):416–434.

Meillassoux, Claude. 1975. *Maidens, Meal and Money: Capitalism and the Domestic Community.* Cambridge: Cambridge University Press.

Merry, Sally Engle. 2006. "Transnational Human Rights and Local Activism: Mapping the Middle." *American Anthropologist* 108 (1):38–51.

Millar, Gearoid. 2014. "Disaggregating Hybridity: Why Hybrid Institutions Do Not Produce Predictable Experiences of Peace." *Journal of Peace Research* 51 (4):501–514.

Mishra, Vijay, and Bob Hodge. 2005. "What Was Postcolonialism?" *New Literary History* 36:375–402.

Morgan, Anthony, and Hannah Chadwick. 2009. Research in Practice: Key Issues in Domestic Violence Summary Paper. Canberra: Australian Institute of Criminology.

Mosley, Paul, Blessing Chiripanhura, Jean Grugel, and Ben Thirkelll-White. 2012. *The Politics of Poverty Reduction.* Oxford: Oxford University Press.

Moxham, Ben. 2005. "The World Bank's Land of Kiosks: Community Driven Development in Timor-Leste." *Development in Practice* 15 (3–4):522–528.

REFERENCES   235

Murshid, Nadine S. 2016. "Men's Response to Their Wives' Participation in Microfinance: Perpetration and Justification of Intimate Partner Violence in Bangladesh." *Public Health* 141:146–152.
Musisi, Nakanyike B. 1991. "Women, 'Elite Polygyny,' and Buganda State Formation." *Signs* 16 (4):757–786.
Myrttinen, Henri. 2005. "Masculinities, Violence and Power in Timor-Leste." *Lusotopie* 7 (1–2):233–244.
Nakaya, Sumie. 2010. "Women and Gender Issues in Peacebuilding: Lessons Learned from Timor-Leste." In *Women, Peace And Security: Translating Policy Into Practice*, edited by Funmi Olonisakin, Karen Barnes, and Ikpek Eka, 155–170. Basingstoke: Routledge.
Narciso, Vanda, Pedro Damião De Sousa Henriques, and Mário Tilman. 2012. "Land and Gender in Matrilineal Timor-Leste." *Indian Journal of Gender Studies* 17 (1):49–72.
Nega, Berhanu, and Geoffrey Schneider. 2014. "Social Entrepreneurship, Microfinance, and Economic Development in Africa." *Journal of Economic Issues* 48 (2):367–376.
Nentwich, Julia C., and Elisabeth K. Kelan. 2014. "Towards a Topology of 'Doing Gender': An Analysis of Empirical Research and Its Challenges." *Gender, Work & Organization* 21 (2):121–134.
Nguyen, Nga Kim. 2015. *An Exploratory Study of Menstruation Management in Timor-Leste*. Dili: Australian Aid, BESIK Programme.
Niner, Sara. 2001. "A Long Journey of Resistance: The Origins and Struggle of the CRNT." In *Bitter Flowers, Sweet Flowers*, edited by R. Tanter, M. Selden and Stephan R. Shalom, 14–72. Washington, DC: Rowman and Littlefield.
Niner, Sara. 2011. "*Hakat Klot*, Narrow Steps." *International Feminist Journal of Politics* 13 (3):413–435.
Niner, Sara. 2012. "*Barlake*: An Exploration of Marriage Practices and Issues of Women's Status in Timor-Leste." *Local Global* 11:138–153.
Niner, Sara. 2016. "Effects and Affects: Women in the Post-conflict Moment in Timor-Leste: An Application of V. Spike Peterson's 'Gendering Insecurities, Informalization and War Economies.'" In *The Palgrave Handbook of Gender and Development*, edited by Wendy Harcourt, 495–512. Basingstoke: Routledge.
Nixon, Rod. 2008. "Integrating Indigenous Approaches into a 'New Subsistence State': The Case of Justice and Conflict Resolution in East Timor." PhD diss., Charles Darwin University.
Olsson, Louise. 2009. *Gender Equality and United Nations Peace Operations in Timor-Leste, International Peacekeeping*. Leiden: Martinus Nijhoff Publishers.
Ormhaug, Christin Marsh, Patrick Meier, and Helga Hernes. 2009. *Armed Conflict Deaths Disaggregated by Gender*. Oslo: PRIO.
Ospina, Sofi. 2006. *Participation of Women in Politics and Decision Making in Timor-Leste: A Recent History*. Dili: UNIFEM.
Ottendörfer, Eva. 2013. "Contesting International Norms of Transitional Justice: The Case of Timor-Leste." *International Journal of Conflict and Violence* 7 (1):24–35.
Paffenholz, Thania. 2011. "Civil Society beyond the Liberal Peace and Its Critique." In *A Liberal Peace? The Problems and Practices of Peacebuilding*, edited by Susanna Campbell, David Chandler, and Meera Sabaratnam, 138–156. London: Zed Books.
Paris, Roland. 2004. *At War's End: Building Peace after Civil Conflict*. Cambridge: Cambridge University Press.

Patterson, Orlando. 2012. "Trafficking, Gender and Slavery: Past and Present." In *The Legal Understanding of Slavery: From the Historical to the Contemporary*, edited by Jean Allain, 322–374. Oxford: Oxford University Press.

Peake, Gordon, Lia Kent, Andrey Damaledo, and Pyone Myat Thu. 2014. "Influences and Echoes of Indonesia in Timor-Leste." *SSGM Discussion Paper* 8.

Pearse, Rebecca, and R. Connell. 2016. "Gender Norms and the Economy: Insights from Social Research." *Feminist Economics* 22 (1):30–53.

Pearson, Ruth. 2004. "The Social Is Political." *International Feminist Journal of Politics* 6 (4):603–622.

Peletz, Michael G. 1995. "Kinship Studies in Late Twentieth-Century Anthropology." *Annual Review of Anthropology* 24:343–372.

Perry, Donna. 2002. "Microcredit and Women Moneylenders: The Shifting Terrain of Credit in Rural Senegal." *Human Organization* 61 (1):30–40.

Peterson, Jenny H. 2012. "A Conceptual Unpacking of Hybridity: Accounting for Notions of Power, Politics and Progress in Analyses as Aid-Driven Interfaces." *Journal of Peacebuilding & Development* 7 (2):9–22.

Piedade, Sisto Moniz. 2003. "Agriculture: New Directions for a New Nation: East Timor." Australian Centre for International Agricultural Research Conference, Sydney, August 18–20.

Pinghui, Zhuang. 2019. *Chinese City Caps "Bride Price" at US$7,450 to Reduce Wedding Pressure*. Hong Kong: South China Morning Post, February 1. https://www.scmp.com/news/china/society/article/2184757/chinese-city-caps-bride-price-us7450-reduce-wedding-pressure.

Porter, Doug, and Habib Rab. 2011. "Timor-Leste's Recovery from the 2006 Crisis: Some Lessons." Washington, DC: World Bank.

Poulantzas, Nicos. 1978. *Classes in Contemporary Capitalism*. London: Verso.

Prawiranata, Iwan. 2013. "Sustainable Microfinance in Indonesia: A Sociocultural Approach." PhD diss., Victoria University.

Rabinow, Paul. 1977. *Reflections on Fieldwork in Morocco*. Berkeley: University of California Press.

Rahman, Aminur. 1999. "Microcredit Initiatives for Equitable and Sustainable Development: Who Pays?" *World Development* 27 (1):67–82.

Randazzo, Elisa. 2016. "The Paradoxes of the 'Everyday': Scrutinising the Local Turn in Peace Building." *Third World Quarterly* 37 (8):1351–1370.

Ranjana, Sheel. 1997. "Institutionalisation and Expansion of Dowry System in Colonial North India." *Economic and Political Weekly* 32(28):1709–1718.

Rankin, Katharine. 2001. "Governing Development: Neoliberalism, Microcredit, and Rational Economic Woman." *Economy and Society* 30 (1):18–37.

Rankin, Katharine. 2002. "Social Capital, Microfinance, and the Politics of Development." *Feminist Economics* 8 (1):1–24.

Rankin, Katharine. 2004. *The Cultural Politics of Markets: Economic Liberalization and Social Change in Nepal*. London: Pluto Press.

Ravicz, Marisol R. 1998. *Searching for Sustainable Microfinance: A Review of Five Indonesian Initiatives*. Washington, DC: World Bank.

Rede Feto. 2001. *Public Figure Detained Again for Domestic Violence*. Dili: Lao Hamutuk.

Rees, Susan, Mohammed Mohsin, Alvin Kuowei Tay, Rosamund Thorpe, Samantha Murray, Elisa Savio, Mira Fonseca, Wietse Tol, and Derrick Silove. 2016. "Associations between Bride Price Obligations and Women's Anger: Symptoms of Mental Distress,

Poverty, Spouse and Family Conflict and Preoccupations with Injustice in Conflict-Affected Timor-Leste." *BMJ Global Health* 1:1–11.

Reille, Xavier, Sarah Forster, and Daniel Rozas. 2011. *Foreign Capital Investment in Microfinance: Reassessing Financial and Social Returns*. Washington, DC: CGAP.

Reille, Xavier, and Jasmina Glisovic-Mezieres. 2009. *Microfinance Funds Continue to Grow Despite the Crisis*. Washington, DC: World Bank Consultative Group to Assist the Poor.

Reinharz, Shulamit, and Lynn Davidman. 1992. *Feminist Methods in Social Research*. Oxford: Oxford University Press.

Republic of Indonesia. 1945. *Constitution of the Republic of Indonesia*. Jakarta: Republic of Indonesia.

Republic of Kenya. 2014. *Marriage Act*. Nairobi: Republic of Kenya.

Richmond, Oliver. 2005. *The Transformation of Peace*. Basingstoke: Palgrave Macmillan.

Richmond, Oliver. 2007. "Emancipatory Forms of Human Security and Liberal Peacebuilding." *International Journal* 62 (3):458–477.

Richmond, Oliver. 2011. "De-romanticising the Local, Demystifying the International: Hybridity in Timor-Leste and the Solomon Islands." *Pacific Review* 24 (1):115–136.

Richmond, Oliver. 2014. "The Impact of Socio-Economic Inequality on Peacebuilding and Statebuilding." *Civil Wars* 16 (4):449–467.

Richmond, Oliver, and Jason Franks. 2008. "Liberal Peacebuilding in Timor-Leste: The Emperor's New Clothes?" *International Peacekeeping* 15 (2):185–200.

Richmond, Oliver, and Jason Franks. 2009. *Liberal Peace Transitions*. Edinburgh: Edinburgh University Press.

Richmond, Oliver, and Audra Mitchell, eds. 2012. *Hybrid Forms of Peace from Everyday Agency to Post-Liberalism* Basingstoke: Palgrave Macmillan.

Rihi, Ular. 2009. "Interview with FALINTIL Commander Ular Rihi (Virgílio dos Anjos)." Edited by Zelda Grimshaw. East Timor and Indonesia Action Network. http://www.etan.org/et2010/01january/16/14intrvw.htm.

Rittich, Kerry. 2006. "The Future of Law and Development: Second Generation Reforms and the Incorporation of the Social." In *The New Law and Economic Development: A Critical Appraisal*, edited by David M. Trubek and Alvaro Santos, 203–251. Cambridge: Cambridge University Press.

Robinson, Marguerite S. 2002. *The Microfinance Revolution*. Volume II: *Indonesia*. Washington, DC: World Bank.

Robinson, Marguerite S. 2004. *Why the Bank Rakyat Indonesia Has the World's Largest Sustainable Microbanking System and What Commercial Microfinance Means for Development*. BRIs International Seminar on BRIs Microbanking System, Bali, Indonesia, December 1.

Rocamora, Joel. 1980. "FRETILIN: The Struggle Continues." *Southeast Asian Chronicle* 74:18–23.

Rodan, Garry, Kevin Hewison, and Richard Robison, eds. 2006. *The Political Economy of South-East Asia: Markets, Power and Contestation*. Third ed. Melbourne: Oxford University Press.

Rodan, Garry, and Caroline Hughes. 2012. "Ideological Coalitions and the International Promotion of Social Accountability: The Philippines and Cambodia Compared." *International Studies Quarterly* 56 (2):367–380.

Roll, Kate. 2014. "Encountering Resistance: Qualitative Insights from the Quantitative Sampling of Ex-combatants in Timor-Leste." *Political Science & Politics* 47 (2):485–489.

Roll, Kate. 2015. "Inventing the Veteran, Imagining the State: Post-conflict Reintegration and State Consolidation in Timor-Leste, 1999–2012." PhD diss., Oxford University.

Roosa, John. 2007. "How Does a Truth Commission Find Out What the Truth Is? The Case of East Timor's CAVR." *Pacific Affairs* 80:569–580.

Rosaldo, Michelle. 1980. "The Use and Abuse of Anthropology: Reflections on Feminism and Cross-Cultural Understanding." *Signs* 5 (3):389–417.

Rosaldo, Michelle. 1982. "Review: The Flow of Life, James J. Fox (ed)." *Journal of Asian Studies* 42 (1):213–214.

Rosaldo, Michelle, Louise Lamphere, and J. Bamberger. 1974. *Woman, Culture, and Society*. Palo Alto, CA: Stanford University Press.

Rosenberg, Richard, Scott Gaul, William Ford, and Olga Tomilova. 2013. "Microcredit Interest Rates and Their Determinants." Washington, DC. CGAP.

Ross, Melody-Ann. 2016. "Attitudes toward Tetun Dili, A Creole Language of East Timor." PhD diss., University of Hawai'i at Mānoa.

Rotberg, Robert. 2004. "The Failure and Collapse of Nation-States: Breakdown, Collapse and Repair." In *When States Fail: Causes and Consequences*, edited by Robert Rotberg, 1–46. Princeton, NJ: Princeton University Press.

Rothschild, Amy. 2017. "Victims versus Veterans: Agency, Resistance and Legacies of Timor-Leste's Truth Commission." *International Journal of Transitional Justice* 11 (3):443–462.

Rozario, Santi. 2002. "Grameen Bank–Style Microcredit: Impact on Dowry and Women's Solidarity." *Development Bulletin* 57:67–70. https://crawford.anu.edu.au/rmap/devnet/devnet/db-57.pdf.

Rubin, Gayle. 1975. "The Traffic in Women: Notes on the 'Political Economy' of Sex." In *Towards an Anthropology of Women*, edited by Rayna Reiter, 157–210. New York: Monthly Review Press.

Saad-Filho, Alfredo. 2015. "Social Policy for Neoliberalism: The *Bolsa Família* Program in Brazil." *Development and Change* 46 (6):1227–1252.

Sabaratnam, Meera. 2013. "Avatars of Eurocentrism in the Critique of the Liberal Peace." *Security Dialogue* 44 (3):259–278.

Scambary, James. 2009a. "Anatomy of a Conflict: The 2006–2007 Communal Violence in East Timor." *Conflict, Security & Development* 9 (2):265–288.

Scambary, James. 2009b. *Groups, Gangs and Armed Violence in Timor-Leste: The Timor-Leste Armed Violence Assessment*. Canberra: AusAid.

Scambary, James. 2013. "Conflict and Resilience in an Urban Squatter Settlement in Dili, East Timor." *Urban Studies* 50 (10):1935–1950.

Scambary, James. 2015. "In Search of White Elephants: The Political Economy of Resource Income Expenditure in East Timor." *Critical Asian Studies* 47 (2):283–308.

Scott, James. 1976. *The Moral Economy of the Peasant: Rebellion and Subsistence in Southeast Asia*. New Haven, CT: Yale University Press.

Seeds of Life. 2016. *Savings and Loans Activities of Two Commercial Seed Producer Groups*. Dili: Australian Aid Ministry of Agriculture and Fisheries.

Sepulveda, Magdalena. 2011. *Special Rapporteur on Extreme Poverty and Human Rights: Mission to Timor-Leste from 13 to 18 November 2001: Preliminary Observations and Recommendations*. Geneva: Office of the High Commissioner on Human Rights.

Sharp, Rhonda, and Ray Broomhill. 1990. "Women and Government Budgets." *Australian Journal of Social Issues* 25 (1):1–14.

Shepherd, Christopher J., and Andrew McWilliam. 2013. "Cultivating Plantations and Subjects in East Timor: A Genealogy." *Bijdragen tot de Taal-, Land- en Volkenkunde* 169 (2–3):326–361.

Shepherd, Laura J. 2011. "Sex, Security and Superhero(in)es: From 1325 to 1820 and Beyond." *International Feminist Journal of Politics* 13 (4):504–521.

Shiffman, Jeremy. 2002. "The Construction of Community Participation: Village Family Planning Groups and the Indonesian State." *Social Science & Medicine* 54 (8):1199–1214.

Shoesmith, Dennis. 2008. "Legislative-Executive Relations in Timor-Leste: The Case for Building a Stronger Parliament." In *Democratic Governance in Timor-Leste: Reconciling the Local and the National*, edited by David Mearns, 71–84. Darwin, Australia: Charles Darwin University Press.

Silva, Kelly. 2011. "*Foho* versus Dili: The Political Role of Place in East Timor National Imagination." *REALIS—Revista de Estudos Anti-Utilitaristas e Pos Coloniais* 1 (2):144–165.

Silva, Kelly, and Daniel Simião. 2012. "Coping with 'Traditions': The Analysis of East-Timorese Nation Building from the Perspective of a Certain Anthropology Made in Brazil." *Vibrant* 9 (1). https://www.scielo.br/j/vb/a/9cBRLcjW8CJhkFdmzXVHsff/?lang=en.

Simião, Daniel. 2007. "Representations of Body and Violence: The Invention of 'Domestic Violence' in East Timor." *Revista Brasileira de Ciências Sociais* 3:1–19.

Smith, Sarah. 2015a. "Gender in United Nations Peacebuilding: A Case Study of Timor-Leste." PhD diss., Swinburne University of Technology.

Smith, Sarah. 2015b. "'When "Gender" Started': The United Nations in Post-occupation Timor-Leste." *Global Change, Peace & Security* 27 (1):55–67.

Soederberg, Susanne. 2014. *Debtfare States and the Poverty Industry: Money, Discipline and the Surplus Population*. London: Taylor and Francis.

Soetjipto, Ani. 2014. *The Role of the Parliamentary Women's Caucus in Promoting Women's Participation and Representation: A Case Study in Indonesia and Timor-Leste*. Jakarta: Kemitraan Bagi Pembaruan Tata Pemerintahan.

Solano, Laura Silva. 2013. *Drivers and Determinants of Sustainability and Development of Savings and Loans Groups*. Dili: Australian Aid Ministry of Agriculture and Fisheries.

Staschen, Stephan. 2002. *Regulatory Requirements for Microfinance: A Comparison of Legal Frameworks in 11 Countries Worldwide*. Eschborn: Deutsche Gesellschaft für Technische Zusammenarbeit.

Stewart, Ruth, Carina van Rooyen, Kelly Dickson, Mabolaeng Majoro, and Thea de Wet. 2010. *What Is the Impact of Microfinance on Poor People? A Systematic Review of Evidence from Sub-Saharan Africa*. London: University of London.

Stivens, Maila. 1990. "Thinking about Gender, State and Civil Society in Indonesia." In *State and Civil Society in Indonesia*, edited by Arief Budiman, 99–114. Melbourne: Monash University Press.

Stoler, Ann Laura. 2001. "Tense and Tender Ties: The Politics of Comparison in North American History and (Post) Colonial Studies." *Journal of American History* 88 (3):829–865.

Strathern, Marilyn. 1988. *The Gender of the Gift: Problems with Women and Problems with Society in Melanesia*. Berkeley: University of California Press.

Streicher, Ruth. 2011. "The Construction of Masculinities and Violence: 'Youth Gangs' in Dili, East Timor." PhD diss., Center for Middle Eastern and North African Politics, Free University Berlin.

Su-Lyn, Boo. 2013. *Till Debt Do Us Part*. Kuala Lumpur: Malay Mail, December 24. https://www.malaymail.com/news/malaysia/2013/12/24/till-debt-do-us-part/586823.

Suradisastra, Kedi. 2006. "Agriculture Cooperatives in Indonesia." Agricultural Cooperatives in Asia: Innovations and Opportunities in the 21st Century, Seoul, Korea, September 11–15.

Suryakusuma, Julia. 2011. *State Ibuism: The Social Construction of Womanhood in the Indonesian New Order*. Depok: Komunitas Bambu / Institute of Social Studies.

Swaine, Aisling. 2003. *Traditional Justice and Gender Based Violence*. Dili: International Rescue Committee.

Sweetman, Caroline. 2008. *Feminist Economics: From Poverty to Power: How Active Citizens and Effective States Can Change the World*. London: Oxfam.

Syamsiyatun, Siti. 2007. "Advancing Their Gender Interests: A Case-Study of Nasyiatul Aisyiyah in Indonesian New Order Era." *Al-Jami'ah: Journal of Islamic Studies* 45 (1):57–89.

Tanter, Richard, Desmond Ball, and Gerry Van Klinken, eds. 2006. *Masters of Terror: Indonesia's Military and Violence in East Timor*. Lanham, MD: Rowman and Littlefield.

Taylor-Leech, Kerry. 2007. "The Ecology of Language Planning in Timor-Leste: A Study of Language Policy, Planning and Practices in Identity Construction." PhD diss., School of Languages and Linguistics, Griffith University.

Teerawichitchainan, Bussarawan, and John Knodel. 2012. "Tradition and Change in Marriage Payments in Vietnam, 1963–2000." *Asian Population Studies* 8(2):151–172.

Therik, Tom. 2004. *Wehali, The Female Land: Traditions of a Timorese Ritual Centre*. Canberra: Pandanus Books.

Thomas, Cheryl, Rosalyn Park, Mary Ellingen, Mary C. Ellison, Beatriz Menanteau, and Laura Young. 2011. *Developing Legislation on Violence Against Women and Girls*. New York. UNIFEM.

Thongyoojaroen, Tanyalak. 2017. *It's Time to Stop Paying "The Bride's Price."* Bangkok: UN Women, October 11. https://asiapacific.unwomen.org/en/news-and-events/in-focus/youth-voice/2018/tanyalak-thongyoojaroen/its-time.

Thu, Pyone Myat, Steffanie Scott, and Kimberly P. Van Niel. 2007. "Gendered Access to Customary Land in East Timor." *GeoJournal* 69:239–255.

Tickner, J. Ann. 2006. "Feminism Meets International Relations: Some Methodological Issues." In *Feminist Methodologies for International Relations*, edited by Brooke Ackerly, Maria Stern, and Jacqui True, 19–41. Cambridge: Cambridge University Press.

Tilley, Lisa. 2017. "The Condition of Market Emergence in Indonesia: Coloniality as Exclusion and Translation." PhD diss., University of Warwick and L'Université Libre de Bruxelles.

Tilman, Mateus. 2012. "Customary Social Order and Authority in the Contemporary East Timorese Village: Persistence and Transformation." *Local Global* 11:192–204.

Timor Post. 2015a. "Budget 2016: Government Approves Paying 60% to Veterans." September 15.

Timor Post. 2015b. "Cooperatives in Timor-Leste Develop." July 26.

Timor Post. 2015c. "Don Norberto: Life Pensions Injustice." September 5.

Timor Post. 2015d. "FALINTIL Resisted, but the People Determined Independence." September 1.
Timor Post. 2015e. "Prime Minister Taur Matan Ruak: Problems with Veterans Could Bring Down Nation." June 28.
Timor Post. 2015f. "This Year the Government Allocates 70 Percent of Monies to Basic Infrastructure." June 24.
Timor Post. 2015g. "Xanana and Alkatiri Are the Ones to Control the Destiny of Politician Life Pensions." September 7.
Traube, Elisabeth. 1980. "Mambai Rituals of Black and White." In *The Flow of Life*, edited by James J. Fox, 290–316. Cambridge, MA: Harvard University Press.
Trembath, Anna, Damian Grenfell, and Carmenesa Moniz Noronha. 2010. *Impacts of National NGO Gender Programming in Local Communities in Timor-Leste: A Collaborative Research and Evaluation Project*. Melbourne. RMIT University.
Trindade, Josh. 2008. "Reconciling Conflicting Paradigms: An East Timorese Vision of the Ideal State." In *Democratic Governance in Timor-Leste: Reconciling the Local and the National*, edited by David Mearns, 160–188. Darwin, Australia: Charles Darwin University Press.
True, Jacqui. 2009. "The Unfulfilled Mandate: Gender Mainstreaming and UN Peace Operations." *Georgetown Journal of International Affairs* 10:41–50.
True, Jacqui. 2010. "The Political Economy of Violence Against Women: A Feminist International Relations Perspective." *Australian Feminist Law Journal* 32:39–59.
True, Jacqui. 2012. *The Political Economy of Violence Against Women*. Oxford: Oxford University Press.
True, Jacqui. 2014a. "Are War and Violence Really in Decline?" *Australian Journal of International Affairs* 68 (5):487–494.
True, Jacqui. 2014b. "Winning the War on War but Losing the Battle: A Feminist Perspective on Global Violence." The Fay Gale Lecture, Monash University, June 19.
True, Jacqui. 2015. "A Tale of Two Feminisms in International Relations? Feminist Political Economy and the Women, Peace and Security Agenda." *Politics & Gender* 11 (2):419–424.
Turner, Barry. 2005. "*Nasution*: Total People's Resistance and Organicist Thinking in Indonesia." PhD diss., Swinburne University of Technology.
Ulrichs, Martina, and Keetie Roelen. 2012. "Equal Opportunities for All? A Critical Analysis of Mexico's *Oportunidades*." *IDS Working Papers* 2012 (413):1–23.
UNCDF. 2014. *Inclusive Finance for the Under-served Economy Final Report: Reporting Period: 1 January 2008–31 December 2014*. Dili: AusAid, United Nations Capital Development Fund, and UNDP.
UNDP. 2013. *Breaking the Cycle of Domestic Violence in Timor-Leste: Access to Justice Options, Barriers and Decision-Making Processes in the Context of Legal Pluralism*. Dili. United Nations Development Program Justice System Monitoring Program.
UNHCR. 2004. *Report of the United Nations High Commissioner for Human Rights on the Situation of Human Rights in Timor-Leste E/CN.4/2004/107*. Geneva. United Nations Economic and Social Council.
UNIFEM. 2009. *UNIFEM's Work on Gender Responsive Budgeting*. New York: UNIFEM.
United Nations. 1976. *Decolonisation: Issues on East Timor*. New York: United Nations Department of Political Affairs Trusteeship and Decolonization.
United Nations ECOSOC. 1997. *Agreed Conclusions of the 1997 Coordination Segment of the Economic and Social Council on Mainstreaming the Gender Perspective into All*

Policies and Programmes of the United Nations System. New York: United Nations Economic and Social Council.

United States Department of State. 2013. *Country Reports on Human Rights Practices*. Washington, DC: Bureau of Democracy, Human Rights and Labor.

UNMIT. 2008. *United Nations Peacekeeping Operations in Timor-Leste*. Dili: UN Integrated Mission in East Timor and UN Department of Peacekeeping Operations. https://peacekeeping.un.org/mission/past/unmit/.

UNMIT. 2009. *Timor-Leste Development Partners Meeting*. Dili: United Nations Integrated Mission in Timor-Leste.

UN Women. 2013. *Ending Violence Against Women and Girls: Programming Essentials*. New York. United Nations. http://www.endvawnow.org/uploads/modules/pdf/137 2349234.pdf.

UN Women. 2015a. *2016 State Budget of Timor-Leste: A Gender Analysis*. Dili. UN Women.

UN Women. 2015b. *CEDAW in Action*. UN Women. http://cedaw-in-action.org/en/timor-leste/. https://asiapacific.unwomen.org/en/countries/timor-leste/cedaw.

USAID and Mendez England. 2013. *Performance Evaluation of the USAID / Timor-Leste Consolidating Cooperative and Agribusiness Recovery Project*. Maryland. USAID.

Vik, Elisabeth. 2013. "In Numbers We Trust: Measuring Impact or Institutional Performance." In *The Credibility of Microcredit: Studies of Impact and Performance*, edited by Dwight Haase, 17–50. Leiden: Brill.

Walby, Sylvia. 1989. *Patriarchy at Work*. Cambridge: Polity Press.

Wallis, Joanne. 2012. "A Liberal-Local Hybrid Peace Project in Action? The Increasing Engagement between the Local and Liberal in Timor-Leste." *Review of International Studies* 38 (04):735–761.

Wallis, Joanne. 2015. *Assessing the Implementation and Impact of Timor-Leste's Cash Payment Schemes*. Timor-Leste Update. Canberra: Australian National University.

Wallis, Joanne, Renee Jeffery, and Lia Kent. 2016. "Political Reconciliation in Timor-Leste, Solomon Islands and Bougainville: The Dark Side of Hybridity." *Australian Journal of International Affairs* 70 (2):159–178.

Wandelt, Ingo. 2007. "Prabowo, Kopassus and East Timor: On the Hidden History of Modern Indonesian Unconventional Warfare." In *Indonesia—The Presence of the Past: A Festschrift in Honour of Ingrid Wessel*, edited by Eva Streifeneder and Antje Missbach, 121–147. Berlin: Regiospectra.

Weber, Heloise. 2002. "The Imposition of a Global Development Architecture: The Example of Microcredit." *Review of International Studies* 28 (3):537–555.

Weber, Heloise. 2004. "The 'New Economy' and Social Risk: Banking on the Poor?" *Review of International Political Economy* 11 (2):356–386.

Weber, Heloise. 2014. "Global Politics of Microfinancing Poverty in Asia: The Case of Bangladesh Unpacked." *Asian Studies Review* 38 (4):544–563.

Wieringa, Saskia. 1992. "*Ibu* or the Beast: Gender Interests in Two Indonesian Women's Organizations." *Feminist Review* 41:98–113.

Wieringa, Saskia. 1993. "Two Indonesian Women's Organizations: Gerwani and the PKK." *Bulletin of Concerned Asian Scholars* 25 (2):17–30.

Wigglesworth, Ann. 2010. "Becoming Citizens: Civil Society Activism and Social Change in Timor-Leste." PhD diss., School of Social Sciences, Victoria University.

Wigglesworth, Ann, Sara Niner, Dharmalingam Arunachalam, Abel Boavida dos Santos, and Mateus Tilman. 2015. "Attitudes and Perceptions of Young Men towards Gender

Equality and Violence in Timor-Leste." *Journal of International Women's Studies* 16 (2):312–329.

Williams, Paul D., and Alex J. Bellamy. 2007. "Contemporary Peace Operations: Four Challenges for the Brahimi Paradigm." *International Peacekeeping* 11 (1):1–29.

Wilson, Ian Douglas. 2006. "Continuity and Change: The Changing Contours of Organized Violence in Post–New Order Indonesia." *Critical Asian Studies* 38 (2):265–297.

Wise, Amanda. 2011. *Exile and Return among the East Timorese*. Philadelphia: University of Pennsylvania Press.

World Bank. 2013. *Timor-Leste Social Assistance Public Expenditure and Program Performance Report*. Bangkok: Human Development Sector Unit, East Asia and Pacific Region.

World Bank. 2017. *Timor-Leste Update*. Washington, DC: World Bank.

Wronka, Silvia. 2015. *Mobilizing Social Business to Accelerate MDGs Achievement in Timor-Leste: Access to Finance Consultancy Report*. Dili: UNDP.

Yoder, Laura S. Meitzner. 2005. "Custom, Codification, Collaboration: Integrating the Legacies of Land and Forest Authorities in Oecusse Enclave, East Timor." PhD diss., Yale University.

Yoder, Laura S. Meitzner. 2016. "The Formation and Remarkable Persistence of the Oecusse-Ambeno Enclave, Timor." *Journal of Southeast Asian Studies* 47:281–303.

Young, Iris Marion. 2003. "The Logic of Masculinist Protection: Reflections on the Current Security State." *Signs* 29 (1):123–154.

Zorn, Jean 2012. "Engendering Violence in the Papua New Guinea Courts: Sentencing in Rape Trials." In *Engendering Violence in Papua New Guinea*, edited by Margaret Jolly, Christine Stewart, and Carolyn Brewer, 163–196. Canberra: ANU E-Press.

Index

For the benefit of digital users, indexed terms that span two pages (e.g., 52–53) may, on occasion, appear on only one of those pages.

acar (slave), 133*t*, 197
accumulation, 112–15, 122, 136–40, 137*f*, 139*f*
adat (tradition), 80–81, 97–98, 107–9, 116–17, 129–30, 173–74, 197, 212n.3
administrator, 23, 50, 51, 52*t*, 54, 55*t*, 130, 197
adultery, 105
advocacy, against brideprice, 123–25
affine (relative by marriage), 120, 131–32, 197
Africa, 56–57, 101. *See also specific countries*
akan (commoner/farmer), 133*t*, 197
akanu (slave caste), 59, 197
aldeia (hamlet), 97, 197
a luta continua (the struggle continues), 197
amaf naek (noble), 197
Amaral, Xavier do, 56
Anderson, Siwan, 120–21
Angola, 56–57, 59–61
Angotta DPR, 197
animal husbandry, 110–11
anthropology, 25, 37, 40–42, 98, 107–9, 125–29, 187
APODETI. *See* Timorese Pro-Indonesian Integration Party
Araújo, Guilhermina, 209n.30
Araújo, Rui, 77
arisan (lottery finance), 156, 159–60, 173, 197
Armed Forces for the National Liberation of Timor-Leste (FALINTIL), 54, 56–57, 62–63, 67, 71–73, 74, 77, 78–79
armed masculinity, 63
Asia, 7–11, 56–57, 106–7, 195. *See also specific countries*

Asian Development Bank, 13–14, 16*t*, 144, 157, 158, 167
asuliars (servants), 60*t*, 197
atan (slave), 14*t*, 55*t*, 60*t*, 124, 133*t*, 197
Australia, 2, 27, 56–57, 157–58
authority, 25, 31, 37, 42, 67
autonomy, 1–3
auxiliar, 51, 61–62, 197

babinsa (noncommissioned guidance officer), 55*t*, 197
Badan Koordinasi Keluarga Berencana Nasional (BKKBN), 156
baikeno/baiqueno (language of Oecusse), 133*t*, 197
baino (noble), 133*t*, 197
Banco Nacional Commerçio de Timor-Leste (BNCTL), 147, 158, 161–62, 168–71
Banco Nacional Ultramarino, 216n.15
Bank Rakyat Indonesia (BRI), 154, 155
bapak (man/mister), 67, 137, 197
barlake (brideprice), 116–17, 126, 131, 197
barlaque (common-law marriage), 116–17, 197
bee manas ai tukan (hot water and firewood), 197
belak (chest jewelry), 128, 138, 197
belis (brideprice), 197, 213n.4
Bhabha, Homi, 21
biological sex, 35–36
BKKBN. *See* Badan Koordinasi Keluarga Berencana Nasional
BNCTL. *See* Banco Nacional Commerçio de Timor-Leste
BNU. *See* National Overseas Bank
Boaventura Dom, 48–50
Bolsa da Mãe, 70, 83–86, 94*f*

Bougainville, 2
BRI. *See* Bank Rakyat Indonesia
brideprice
   accumulation through, 136–40, 137*f*, 139*f*
   advocacy against, 123–25
   in anthropology, 125–29
   authority for, 42
   costs, 118*t*
   in culture, 129
   debts, 184–85
   in divorce, 131
   domestic violence and, 140–43
   economics of, 131–32, 139*f*, 139–40
   exchange of women and, 42, 116–20, 117*t*, 118*t*
   female status from, 130–31
   history of, 209n.27
   interest rates and, 143
   kinship and, 41–42
   LADV and, 123
   marriage and, 10, 66–67
   negotiation ceremonies, 214n.6
   in patriarchy, 185
   rural impoverishment and, 129–30
   social forces and, 132–36, 133*t*, 135*f*
   in society, 120–23
   support for, 214n.14
   traditional dispute resolution and, 141
   wealth transfer, 136, 137*f*
   of women, 65
bridetoken, 117*t*
bua malus (areca nut and betel leaf), 111, 197
budak (slave), 55*t*, 197
buibere (woman), 197
bupati (district head), 53–54, 197

camat (subdistrict head), 53–54, 197
Cambodia, 2, 120–21
capitacão (head tax), 51, 197
Carrascalão, João, 208n.9
Carrascalão, Mario, 208n.9
Carroll, Toby, 43
cash transfers, 70–73, 82–86, 211n.17
CAVR. *See* Commission for Reception, Truth, and Reconciliation
Charlesworth, Hilary, 27

chattel slavery, 57–58, 60*t*, 66, 197
children, in Timor-Leste, 167
China, 120–21, 154–55
clandestinos (clandestine nationalist front), 62–63, 197
class. *See also* liurai-dato class
   bias, 78–79
   Bolsa da Mãe and, 83–86
   fractions, 5, 8, 205n.3
   gender and, 45, 69, 85–86
   GRB and, 92–93
   identity and, 76–77
   local turn and, 194–95
class formation
   conflict-related SGBV from, 64–67
   in Indonesia, 52–57
   militarization and, 59–64
   in Portugal, 48–52
   slavery and, 47–48, 57–59
   in Timor, 68
CNRM. *See* Council Nacional Resistance Maubere
CNRT. *See* National Council for the Reconstruction of Timor
Cold War, 12
collateralization, 175
Collier, Jane Fishburne, 40–41, 45, 120, 121, 122, 138, 141, 214n.8
colonization
   bureaucracy and, 9
   colonial encounters, 21
   in Estado do India, 207n.3
   from Europe, 48–50, 123
   history of, 64
   resistance to, 52–57
   resources in, 65
   of Timor, 59–64
commercialized culture, 57–58
Commission for Reception, Truth, and Reconciliation (CAVR), 15–19, 82–83, 106, 208n.10, 209n.27
Conceição, Ilda Maria da, 92–93
conditional cash transfer programs, 211n.17
conflict-related SGBV, 64–67
conscientization, 56, 63, 153, 208n.19
control, in political economies, 112–15
Convention on the Elimination of All Forms of Discrimination against

Women, 15, 16t, 89, 100, 101, 103, 105, 125
Cooke, Bill, 43
cooperativa credito (credit cooperative), 197
Cornwall, Andrea, 29–30, 35–36
corruption, 92
corvée (labor tax), 51, 58, 60t, 197
Costa, Maria Maia dos Reis e, 92–93
Costa, Monica, 96
Council Nacional Resistance Maubere (CNRM), 56–57, 208n.22
court decisions, 112–14
crises, in microfinance, 158–59
Cruz, Antonia da, 211n.22

Da Silva, Francesco, 23, 209n.24
data, 86, 187
dato (noble), 51–52, 52t, 53–56, 58, 61, 76–78, 106–7, 197. *See also* liurai-dato class
debt
 bondage, 60t, 77–78, 122, 138–39, 197
 brideprice debts, 184–85
 debtfare, 164
 domestic violence and, 176–77
 labor and, 138–40
 from microfinance, 176–77
 pressure of, 174–77
 social, 165
 violence and, 165–66
Defense Forces of Timor-Leste (F-FDTL), 72–73, 77, 209n.1
demobilization programs, 70, 71–72
democracy, 23
deportardu (deported political prisoners), 197
deputada (female parliamentarian), 197
desa (village), 53–54, 197
differend (colonial injustice), 197
distribution, 69, 76–82, 182, 183
distriktu (district administrative area), 197
divorce, 131, 141
dom (king), 197
domestic violence. *See also* Law Against Domestic Violence
 brideprice and, 140–43
 debt and, 176–77

gender intervention and, 98–101
legal pluralism with, 112–15
local turn and, 104–7
political economies of, 97–98, 214n.8
programming, 104–7
scholarship on, 107–9
in traditional dispute resolution, 25–26, 110–12
in villages, 97
domestic work, 206n.10
Domingues-Alves, Maria, 82–83
double exploitation, 68
Downer, Alexander, 2
dowry, 117t, 123
Durkheim, Émile, 117–19, 126

East Timor. *See also specific topics*
 autonomy in, 1–3
 GAU in, 15–19, 16t, 27–29, 124–25
 Indonesia and, 61, 216n.14
 INTERFET, 13
 material outcomes in, 63
 Portugal in, 116
 Timor-Leste and, 205n.1
 UNMIT, 73, 157–58
 UNTAET, 13, 15–19, 22, 27–29, 70–72, 99–100, 105, 124–25
East Timorese Women's Communication Forum (FOKUPERS), 15–19, 16t, 99–101, 102–3, 124
economics. *See specific topics*
ekonomia (national economy), 197
elections, 71, 74, 80
elitism, 38, 51–52, 56–57, 78–79, 97–98, 164
Elson, Diane, 69
Elyachar, Julia, 161
ema bai bain (ordinary class), 194
ema boot (important person), 194, 197
ema kiik (ordinary person), 81, 197
ema reino (commoner), 52t, 55t, 133t, 197
ema susar (poor people with difficulties), 130, 167, 197
endogamous (clan marriage), 47–48, 197
Estado do India (Indian state), 197, 207n.3
ethnicity, 31–32, 34
Europe, 48–50, 116, 123, 194–95

exchange, of women, 42, 116–20, 117t, 118t, See also brideprice

FALINTIL. See Armed Forces for the National Liberation of Timor-Leste
family law
 hierarchies in, 132, 133t
 household bargaining, 36
 kinship and, 35
 marriage in, 34–35
 power in, 128–29
 property and, 54
 psychology of, 130–31
 wealth and, 183–84
family planning, 156
Family Welfare Movement, 156, 173
female status, 130–31
femininity, 63–64
feminism
 feminist methodology, 187
 feminist political economies, 114
 gender mainstreaming in, 45
 international, 126
 Marxism and, 120
 scholarship and, 2–3
 in Western culture, 108–9
 to women, 90
feto nia folin (brideprice), 116–17, 197
feto nona, 209n.29
F-FDTL. See Defense Forces of Timor-Leste
finance institutions, 155, 158, 159–60, 163, 184–85
financial inclusion, 151–52
financial intermediaries, 150–51
financialization, of development, 150–52
financial liberalization, 159–60
The Flow of Life, review of, 214n.10
FOKUPERS. See East Timorese Women's Communication Forum
folin (price, brideprice), 116–17, 125–26, 131, 197
forced marriage, 100
forsa la iha, 174
free trade, 215n.22
Freire, Paulo, 208n.19
FRETILIN. See Revolutionary Front for Independent Timor-Leste

Freycinet, Louis de, 64

gang rape, 65
gatekeepers, in field work, 193
gatekeeping, 32–33, 75–76
GAU. See Gender Affairs Unit
gender. See also specific topics
 bias, 107–9
 biological sex and, 35–36
 cash transfers and, 82–86
 class and, 45, 69, 85–86
 critical approaches to, 12–14, 14t, 27–34, 44–46
 development and, 3
 divisions of labor, 35–38
 equity, 88
 Gender Affairs Unit, 15–19, 16t, 27, 28, 29, 124–25
 gender-based violence, 91–92, 121, 141
 gender-disaggregated data, 86
 ideology, 63–64, 92, 183–84
 justice, 6–8, 34–35, 42–43, 96, 143
 mainstreaming, 3–4, 6, 27, 29–30, 45, 88, 205–6n.3
 marginality, 29
 New Order gender legacies, 173–74
 peace and, 181–85
 politics, 22–27, 42–43
 power imbalances, 106–7
 quotas, 33
 reform and, 10–11
 relational positioning with, 63–64
 relations, 27, 29–30, 35–36, 40–42, 90–91, 181–82
 SGBV, 40, 64–67, 82–83, 93–94, 99–100, 104–5, 156
 in Timor-Leste, 193–95
 Timor-Leste interviewees by, 188t
 to UN, 2–3
 UN Gender and the Law Working Group, 15, 16t, 30–31, 88–89, 91–92, 100
 violence and, 2–3, 194–95
Gender Affairs Unit (GAU), 15–19, 16t, 27–29, 124–25
gendered circuits
 debt pressure and, 174–77
 microfinance and, 165–66
 microfinance risks in, 177–80

New Order gender legacies, 173–74
in village political economy, 166–72
gender intervention
　analysis of, 44
　domestic violence and, 98–101
　gender justice and, 6–8
　history of, 16t
　LADV and, 103, 110
　legitimacy of, 20–22
　microfinance and, 19
　political economy of, 7–11
　scholarship on, 5–7
　structural feminist political economy of, 31–43
　structural political economies and, 31–34
　in Timor-Leste, 3, 9–11, 14–19, 27–31, 38–40, 44–45
　with women, 36
　women's empowerment and, 181–85
gender-responsive budgeting (GRB)
　class and, 92–93
　to government, 30
　in international affairs, 95–96
　LADV and, 7–8
　men and, 90–91
　omissions from, 93–95
　perception of, 92
　politics of, 28, 89–96
　in postconflict states, 182
　state resources and, 86–89
　technical constraints in, 91–92
　in Timor-Leste, 91
genocide, 12–13
German Technical Cooperation, 14
Ghana, 101, 177–78
globalization, 16t, 37, 42–43, 45–46, 86, 184–85
GMPTL. See Group of Women Parliamentarians in Timor-Leste
Goetz, Anne-Marie, 33–34
gotong royong (mutual cooperation), 153–54, 197, 216n.10
grau (military grade/rank), 77–78, 197
GRB. See gender-responsive budgeting
gross domestic product, 84
Group of Women Parliamentarians in Timor-Leste (GMPTL), 15–19, 16t, 86–87, 88–89, 90–91, 93–95

guerrilla armies, 71
Gusmão, Xanana, 29, 56–57, 71, 73–74, 77

haan hamutuk, 111
hafolin (to appreciate), 116–17, 197, 213n.4
Hameiri, Shahar, 23
Hanai Malu, 157–58, 163–64
HANSIP, 61–62
harmful practices, 207n.12
Henriques, Pedro, 131
Hicks, David, 126, 212n.3
household bargaining, 36
Hudson, Valerie, 121
Hughes, Caroline, 5, 23, 32–33, 44, 72, 160–61, 163–64
human rights, 6
Hutching, Kimberly, 63–64
hybridity, 20–22, 25, 26, 107, 109
hypogamous (marriage type), 136, 197

ianjo (military brothel), 66, 197
identity, 76–77
ideology, 37, 38–40, 63–64, 92, 109, 183–84
impunity, for men, 112
Inclusive Finance for the Underserved Economy, 158–59
income, 213n.2
India, 123, 171, 177–78
Indonesia
　APODETI, 51–52, 53–54, 210n.5
　China and, 154–55
　class formation in, 52–57
　culture of, 120–21
　East Timor and, 61, 216n.14
　Indonesian language, 6
　Indonesian West Timor, 1–2
　microfinance in, 10–11
　New Order ideology, 109, 153–54
　occupation, 68
　as occupiers, 161
　Portugal and, 55t
　resistance to, 79
　social rankings in, 55t
　Suharto in, 1, 154
　Sukarno for, 154
　Timor and, 1–7, 38, 59–64, 65
　West Timor and, 75–76

informal economies, 138–40
Institute for Social and Cultural Anthropology, 187
Integrated Mission in East Timor (UNMIT), 73, 157–58
interest rates
    brideprice and, 143
    microfinance and, 144–45, 147, 149–50, 152, 155–56, 158–59
    wealth and, 165, 169t, 172, 175
INTERFET. *See* International Force for East Timor
international affairs, 2, 22, 27, 95–96, 184
international feminism, 126
international finance institutions, 155, 158, 159–60, 163
International Force for East Timor (INTERFET), 2, 13
international humanitarianism, 12–13
International Labour Organization, 13–14
International Monetary Fund, 1
international NGOs, 100
International Organization for Migration (IOM), 13–14, 71–72, 74
interventions. *See specific topics*
IOM. *See* International Organization for Migration

Japan, 66
Jayasuriya, Kanishka, 43
Jolly, Margaret, 125–26
Jones, Lee, 23
Joshi, Vijaya, 27

kadeira (political chair), 197
Kammen, Douglas, 50
kampung (village), 197
katuas/ketuas (male leader/male elder), 128, 197
kelas menengah atas, 194
Kent, Lia, 70
kepala desa (head of village), 55t, 197
ketua adat (male spiritual leader), 197
ketuas/katuas (leader/leaders), 197
King, Angela, 27
kings, 197
Kinsella, Naomi, 70
kinship
    accumulation and, 122

affiliations, 194
brideprice and, 41–42
critical approaches to, 40–42
dualisms in, 214n.10
economics of, 138–40, 139f
family law and, 35
hierarchies from, 176–77
language of, 121
in *liurai-dato* class, 8
marriage and, 6, 47–48
microfinance and, 166–67, 166f
scholarship on, 124
structural feminist political economies, 40–42, 45
kios (small shop), 167, 168, 197
Kodim (district military command), 55t, 197
Kooperasi Unit Desa (KUD), 154–56
kooperativa (cooperative), 152–53, 197
koramil (subdistrict military command), 55t, 197
kore metan (death ceremony), 127–28, 140–41, 142, 197
koremetan naçional (national memorial ceremony), 197
korperasi simpan pinjam (savings and loans cooperative), 152–53, 197
kostumes (customs), 197, 212n.3
KUD. *See* Kooperasi Unit Desa
kultura (culture), 197, 212n.3

labor
    debt and, 138–40
    division of, 35–38
    domestic work, 206n.10
    gender divisions of, 35–38
    International Labour Organization, 13–14
    manual, 56
    rank and, 137–38
    SEFOPE, 81–82
    suffering and, 82–83
    unfree, 60t
    women's, 35–38, 44–46, 69, 110–11, 127–28, 130, 131, 137–38, 185
LADV. *See* Law Against Domestic Violence
lafurana hi kare (hearth and knife), 197
Lao Hamutuk, 78

Law Against Domestic Violence (LADV)
  brideprice and, 123
  consequences of, 97, 98–101, 112–15
  gender intervention and, 103, 110
  GRB and, 7–8
  history of, 104
  microfinance and, 188
  politics of, 9–10, 29
  reform with, 30–31
  resistance to, 101–3
  in Timor-Leste, 35, 183
  traditional dispute resolution and, 98
  UN Gender and the Law Working Group and, 91–92
  VPU and, 92
  for women, 15–19
legal frameworks, 16t
legal pluralism, 112–15, 184
leten, 166–67
Lévi-Srauss, Claude, 41
lia loos (truth), 197
lia nain (elder), 22, 111, 138, 197
liberal-local hybrid systems, 106
liberal peace, 20–27
Liquiça Church massacre, 216n.13
lisan (customary practice), 25, 97, 197, 212n.3
liurai (landowner)
  leadership, 25, 47–64, 112
  marriage to, 138
  power of, 49f, 52–53, 52t, 60t, 68, 138, 166–67, 185
  reputation of, 75–80, 92–93, 106–7, 116, 124, 134, 177, 197
liurai-dato class
  history of, 8, 47–52
  leadership of, 56, 97–98
  lineages in, 138
  local turn and, 23
  pension eligibility in, 77–80
  politics of, 10–11
  Portuguese conflict with, 56
  power of, 80–82
  rank in, 124
  Richmond on, 23–24, 26
  in Timor-Leste, 25
  veteran status, 75–82
  women in, 181–82
Lobo, Sérgio, 102–3

local turn
  class and, 194–95
  domestic violence and, 104–7
  gender bias in, 107–9
  hybridity and, 20–22
  liurai-dato class and, 23
  local societies, 25
  microfinance and, 160–64
  in scholarship, 22, 23, 44, 181
  World Bank and, 26
lulik (sacred or taboo), 197, 212n.3
Luta Hamutuk, 75
lutu-hum (dwellers at the bottom of the pale), 58, 197

Mac Ginty, Roger, 20, 26
mahar, 213n.4
Malaysia, 120–21
manual labor, 56
Manufahi rebellion, 50
Manufahi village, 166–72
marriage
  adat and, 80–81, 97–98, 107–8, 109, 116–17, 129–30, 173–74
  brideprice and, 10, 66–67
  choice in, 141–42
  in family law, 34–35
  forced, 100
  hierarchies from, 138
  kinship and, 6, 47–48
  to liurai, 138
  male mediators and, 110–11
  matrilateral cross cousin, 134, 135f
  payments, 117t, 214n.12
  polygynous, 66, 122–23
  rape in, 109
  servile, 55t, 58–59, 60t, 65, 197
  in Timor, 41–42
Marxism, 120, 205n.3
masculinity, 63–64, 70
mate rasik (die alone), 174, 197
material relations, 31–34
Matfess, Hilary, 121
matrifocality, 127
matrilateral cross cousin marriage, 134, 135f
matrilocal residence (married couple residing with wife's family), 128–29, 131, 197

maubere (male Timorese farmer), 56–57, 197, 208n.22
maun-alin, 133
Mauss, Marcel, 117–19
Maya Declaration on Financial Inclusion, 161–62
McLeod, Laura, 26
McWilliam, Andrew, 127–28
Mearns, David, 126–27
mediation, 110–11
Meillassoux, Claude, 41
Mello, Sergio Vieira de, 27
men. *See also* gender intervention
　adultery by, 105
　in aristocracy, 51
　armed masculinity, 63
　in authority, 25
　children and, 6
　in FRETILIN, 102–3
　GRB to, 90–91
　impunity for, 112
　leadership by, 104
　male authority, 37
　male elitism, 97–98
　male mediators, 110–11
　patriarchy, 93
　power of, 124
　state resources for, 182
　in Timor, 41, 53–54
　in war, 39–40
　women and, 143, 185
meo (noble warrior class), 133*t*, 197
Merry, Sally, 90–91
mestiço (ethnic description), 48, 50, 51–52, 197, 207n.4
microfinance
　crises in, 158–59
　debt from, 176–77
　gendered circuits and, 165–66
　gender intervention and, 19
　in Indonesia, 10–11
　interest rates and, 144–45, 147, 149–50, 152, 155–56, 158–59
　kinship and, 166–67, 166*f*
　LADV and, 188
　loans with, 178
　local turn and, 160–64
　microcredit, 145
　militarization of, 152–56
　for moneylending, 172
　neoliberal globalization and, 45–46
　to NGOs, 159, 179–80
　NGOs and, 164, 178
　policy for, 7–8
　politics of, 145–52
　poverty and, 175
　poverty reduction with, 148–50, 160–61
　risks of, 177–80
　SHGs and, 144–47, 146*t*, 151–53, 157–58, 159–60, 165, 166*f*, 171, 178, 179, 216n.8
　in Timor, 144–45, 160–64
　Timorese microfinance organizations, 92–93
　in Timor-Leste, 44, 146*t*
　visible hand of, 157–60
　women and, 7–8
　World Bank, 26, 43
Middle East, 123
migration, 13–14, 71–72, 74
mikrokredit (microcredit), 197
militarization, 47–48, 59–64, 77, 152–56
militarized conflict, 14, 38–40, 45
military, 82, 83
militias, 59, 67, 71
Millar, Gearoid, 104
Ministry of Social Solidarity (MSS), 84–85, 91, 93–94, 211n.22
Mission of Support, 72, 73
monetization, 131–32
moneylending, 152, 172
The Moral Economy of the Peasant (Scott), 215n.27
moris naroman (enlightenment), 129–30, 197
Moris Rasik, 157–59, 168–71, 169*t*, 173, 174–75
Mota, 166–72
Mozambique, 56–57, 59–61
MSS. *See* Ministry of Social Solidarity
Myanmar, 120–21
Myrttinen, Henri, 62

naizuf (king), 81, 197
NAP. *See* National Action Plan on Domestic Violence

Narcisco, Vanda, 131
natal family, 127–28
National Action Plan on Domestic Violence (NAP), 103
national budget, 84–85, 94f
National Council for the Reconstruction of Timor (CNRT), 73–76
National Overseas Bank (BNU), 54, 216n.15
National Police Force of Timor-Leste (PNTL), 16t, 72, 92
National Program for Village Development (PNDS), 94
neoliberal globalization, 42–43, 45–46, 184–85
New Deal, 74–75, 83–84
New Order gender legacies, 173–74
New Order ideology, 109, 153–54
NGOs. *See* nongovernmental organizations
Nixon, Richard, 114
nongovernmental organizations (NGOs)
 with banks, 157
 from Europe, 194–95
 international, 100
 Lao Hamutuk, 78
 leadership in, 92–93
 Luta Hamutuk, 75
 MFI and, 164, 178
 microfinance to, 159, 179–80
 research with, 187–88
 Seeds of Life, 159, 169t, 172, 175, 177–78
 SHGs and, 147
 in Timor, 163–64
 as transnational actors, 33
 women and, 85, 193
non-liberal politics, 20
Nucleos de Resistencia Popular, 78–79
Nunes, Liurai Gaspar, 208n.15

Öjendal, Joakim, 23
Olsson, Louise, 27
OMT. *See* Organização Popular da Mulher Timorense
OPMT. *See* Popular Organization of Timorese Women
ordinença (ordnance), 56, 197

Organização Popular da Mulher Timorense (OMT), 68, 99
orphans, 68

paca (noble), 133t, 197
patriarchy, 37. *See also specific topics*
patrilineages (kin groups related by males), 41, 42, 118t, 128–29, 131, 133–34, 141–42, 197
patrilocal residence (married couple residing with husband's family), 133–34, 197
peace/peace building. *See specific topics*
Peake, Gordon, 65
pembantu (maid), 137, 197
pensaun veteranus (veteran's pension), 70, 84–85, 94f, 197
pensaun vitalisia (life pension), 70, 197
pension eligibility, 70, 77–80, 84
pensions, 78, 79–80
Pereira, Maria do Céu, 209n.30
perlawanan rakyat. *See* wanra
petani (farmer), 55t, 197
Peterson, Jenny, 21
Petroleum Fund, 72, 73–74
piastres (Portuguese currency), 197
Pires, Milena, 102
plantations, 48–51, 52t, 54, 57–58, 59–60, 60t, 154–55
PNDS. *See* National Program for Village Development
PNTL. *See* National Police Force of Timor-Leste
policymakers, 107
political economy. *See also* structural feminist political economy
 in Asia, 195
 control in, 112–15
 of domestic violence, 97–98, 214n.8
 feminist, 114
 of gender intervention, 7–11
 with liberal-local hybrid systems, 106
 structural, 7–11
 of Timor, 143
 of traditional dispute resolution, 110–12
 village political economy, 166–72
political elite, 78–79
political hybridity, 25

political order, 80–82
polygynous marriage, 66, 122–23
Popular Organization of Timorese Women (OPMT), 68, 99
Portugal
  Angola and, 56–57
  BNU, 54, 216n.15
  citizenship, 207n.6
  class formation during Portuguese colonization, 48–52
  in East Timor, 116
  Indonesia and, 55t
  language from, 101–2
  Portuguese National Republican Guard, 14
  social rankings in, 52t
  Timor and, 47–48, 60t, 68
  trade with, 59–61
poverty, 79, 85, 148–50, 160–61, 175, 182–83, 217n.2
power
  authority and, 31
  economic, 168–71
  in family law, 128–29
  FRETILIN in, 77
  gender power imbalances, 106–7
  hierarchies of, 214n.10
  in hybrid peace, 26
  of liurai, 49f, 52–53, 52t, 60t, 68, 138, 166–67, 185
  of liurai-dato class, 80–82
  of men, 124
  peace and, 32–33
  of state resources, 171
  in UN, 28–29
  wealth and, 7–8
  women's empowerment, 5, 7, 144, 148–50, 152–53, 181–85
preman (gangsters), 59, 197
Presidential Decree No. 13/2010, 87–88
public violence, 185
public war, 39

qualitative data, 8

race, 34
rai lulik (spiritual world), 197
Ramos-Horta, José, 77, 87–88

Randazzo, Elisa, 24
rank, 121–22, 124, 130–31, 132, 133t, 135–36, 137–38
rape, 114, 209n.28
ratih (trained civilians), 55t, 197
ratu (king), 133t, 197
reform, 10–11, 30–31, 182–83
regulo (petty king), 50, 52t, 197
reino (peasant, kingdom, realm, tribe, subjects, commoners, people), 52t, 55t, 133t, 197
relational positioning, 63–64
repossession, 175
reproduction, 37–38
reproductive economies, 138–40
research methods, 6–8, 187–88, 189t, 193–95
resistance, 52–57, 61–62, 68, 79, 101–3
Resolution No. 12/2010, 87–88
resources, 65, 69, 182–83. *See also* state resources
Revolutionary Front for Independent Timor-Leste (FRETILIN)
  history of, 51–57, 207–8n.8, 208n.18, 210n.5, 216n.9
  leaders of, 32–33, 77, 92–93, 94–95, 102–3
  in politics, 71–73, 144, 153, 160–61, 210n.9
  women in, 68, 99, 124
Richmond, Oliver, 20, 23–24, 26
risks, of microfinance, 177–80
Robinson, Fiona, 150
Rodan, Garry, 43
Roll, Kate, 63, 75, 81, 82, 85–86
Rosaldo, Michelle, 120, 127–28, 214n.10
rotating savings and loans associations, 216n.8
Ruak, Taur Matan, 23, 63, 77
Rubin, Gayle, 37, 41, 42, 120, 128
rubrica orçamental separada (separate budget lines), 87–88, 197
rukun tetangga (neighborhood association), 55t, 197
rukun warga (administrative unit), 55t, 197
rural communities, 85
rural impoverishment, 129–30

Rwanda, 12–13

Sabaratnam, Meera, 24
safety, of women, 39–40
Santos, Jacinta dos, 163–64
saun (material world), 197
Schierenbeck, Isabell, 23
scholarship
    from anthropology, 25, 37, 40–42, 98, 107–9
    on domestic violence, 107–9
    explanations in, 4–5
    feminism and, 2–3
    on gender intervention, 5–7
    on gender marginality, 29
    on gender relations, 181–82
    on kinship, 124
    on liberal-local hybrid systems, 106
    local turn in, 22, 23, 44, 181
    on male elitism, 97–98
    from Marxism, 205n.3
    Marxist-feminism, 120
    on monetization, 131–32
    on peace, 24
    peace scholars, 43, 126–27
    research and, 6–8
    on society, 59
    from structural feminist political economies, 44
    on structural political economy, 7–11
    on Timor-Leste, 3–4, 75–76, 187–88, 188*t*, 189*t*, 193–95
    on traditional dispute resolution, 98
    on traditional slavery, 58
    on violence, 6
    on women's rights, 127–28
Scott, James C., 215n.27
second-generation neoliberalism, 42–43
secretaria suko (secretary of the suku), 197
Secretariat of State for the Support and Socio-Economic Promotion for Women, 15, 16*t*, 88–89, 162, 206n.4
Secretariat of State for Vocational Training and Employment (SEFOPE), 81–82
Seeds of Life, 159, 169*t*, 172, 175, 177–78
SEFOPE. *See* Secretariat of State for Vocational Training and Employment

self-help groups (SHGs)
    MFI and, 165, 166*f*, 171, 178, 179, 216n.8
    microfinance and, 144–47, 146*t*, 151–53, 157–58, 159–60
serfdom, 47, 50, 52*t*, 55*t*, 58, 60*t*, 64, 197
serralhos (harem), 64–65, 197
servile marriage, 55*t*, 58–59, 60*t*, 65, 197
servo, servi, servidor (serf), 60*t*, 197
sexual and gender-based violence (SGBV), 40, 64–67, 82–83, 93–94, 99–100, 104–5, 156
sexual slavery, 47, 60*t*, 64–67, 209n.27
SGBV. *See* sexual and gender-based violence
SHGs. *See* self-help groups
Silva, Kelly, 126
sirih pina (areca nut and betel leaf), 130, 197
slavery
    chattel, 57–58, 60*t*, 66, 197
    class formation and, 47–48, 57–59
    psychology of, 57–59, 208–9n.23
    sexual, 47, 60*t*, 64–67, 209n.27
    traditional, 58, 68, 209n.25
    unfree labor and, 60*t*
Smith, Sarah, 26
Soares, Rosa Bonaparte, 209n.30
social conflict, 80–81
social debt, 165
social forces, 31–34, 59–64, 132–36, 133*t*, 135*f*
social inclusion, 42
social rankings, 52*t*, 55*t*
socioeconomics, 67
Solomon Islands, 2
Southeast Asia, 7–11
Special Zone of Social Market Economy (ZEESMs), 74–75, 79, 80–81, 94–95, 162, 162n.19, 217n.19
Srebrenica massacre, 12–13
state resources
    by CNRT, 73–76
    distribution of, 69, 76–82, 182
    GRB and, 86–89
    for men, 182
    politics of, 77–82
    power of, 171
    in Timor, 70–73
    veteran status and, 80

structural feminist political economy
   critical approaches to, 31–43
   gender divisions of labor and, 35–38
   gender justice and, 34–35
   ideology of, 38–40
   kinship to, 40–42, 45
   in neoliberal globalization, 42–43
   scholarship from, 44
   social forces in, 31–34
structural political economy, 7–11, 31–34
subdistriktu (subdistrict administrative area), 54, 55*t*, 130, 197
subsistence economies, 138–40
suffering, 82–83
Suharto, 1, 154
Sukarno, 154
suku, suco, suko (village), 53–54, 197, 207n.5
Suku Mota, 166–67

tais (traditional Timorese woven cloth), 138, 197
tama (enter/interfere), 116–17, 197
tara bandu (official prohibition), 116–17, 130, 197, 212n.3
tau korenti, tau morteen (engagement ceremony), 66, 197
TBO. *See* Tenaga Bantuan Operasi
temukung (head of lineage), 55*t*, 197
Tenaga Bantuan Operasi (TBO) (military operation assistants), 61–62, 67, 197
Tetun language, 6
Thailand, 120–21
Tilman, Mário, 131
Timor. *See also specific topics*
   APODETI, 51–52, 53–54, 210n.5
   class formation in, 68
   colonization of, 59–64
   economics of, 6, 69
   elitism in, 38
   government of, 43
   history of, 57–59
   income in, 213n.2
   Indonesia and, 1–7, 38, 59–64, 65
   marriage in, 41–42
   Maya Declaration on Financial Inclusion in, 161–62
   men in, 41, 53–54
   MFI in, 144–45, 160–64
   militarization in, 47–48
   militarized conflict in, 45
   NGOs in, 163–64
   OMT, 68, 99
   policymakers in, 107
   political economy of, 143
   Portugal and, 47–48, 60*t*, 68
   reputation of, 126
   resources in, 182–83
   slavery in, 57–59
   social forces in, 7–11, 59–64
   society of, 37
   state resources in, 70–73
   Timorese Democratic Union, 51–54, 56–57
   Timor-Leste context, 9–11
   transparency in, 75
   West Timor, 75–76, 116, 187, 188*t*, 193
   women's liberation, 68
Timorese Pro-Indonesian Integration Party (APODETI), 51–52, 53–54, 210n.5
Timor-Leste
   average income in, 116
   Banco Nacional Ultramarino in, 216n.15
   children in, 167
   culture of, 6
   domestic work in, 206n.10
   East Timor and, 205n.1
   FALINTIL in, 54, 56–57, 62–63, 67, 71–73, 74, 77, 78–79
   F-FDTL, 72–73, 77, 209n.1
   gender in, 193–95
   gender intervention in, 3, 9–11, 14–19, 27–31, 38–40, 44–45
   gender mainstreaming in, 29–30
   GMPTL, 15–19, 16*t*, 86–87, 88–89, 90–91, 93–95
   GRB in, 91
   history of, 7
   interventions in, 2
   LADV in, 35, 183
   liurai-dato class in, 25
   map of, 49*f*

microfinance in, 44, 146*t*
New Deal in, 74–75, 83–84
Nixon on, 114
qualitative data from, 8
scholarship on, 3–4, 75–76, 187–88, 188*t*, 189*t*, 193–95
trade in, 48
UN in, 13, 14*t*, 95–96, 105–6, 181–85
West Timor and, 187
women in, 132–34, 133*t*, 172
tob, tobe (noble), 133*t*, 197
toos nain (farmer), 52*t*, 55*t*, 133*t*, 194, 197
topasses (Portuguese-speaking people), 48, 197
trade, 48–50, 59–61, 138–40, 215n.22
traditional dispute resolution
  brideprice and, 141
  divorce in, 141
  domestic violence in, 25–26, 110–12
  LADV and, 98
  legal pluralism and, 184
  political economy of, 110–12
  scholarship on, 98
traditional slavery, 58, 68, 209n.25
Transformation of Peace (Richmond), 24
transnational actors, 33
transparency, 75, 92, 93–95
True, Jacqui, 27, 31, 44, 214n.8
tua haraki (palm liquor), 197
tuur hamutuk (sit together), 141–42, 197

ulun-houris (chattel slave), 52*t*, 55*t*, 58, 60*t*, 197
uma (house, lineage group), 197
umane (wife's family), 110–11, 112–13, 197
UN. *See* United Nations
UNAMET. *See* United Nations Mission in East Timor
UN Capital Development Fund (UNCDF), 106, 144, 151–52, 157–58, 162–63, 216n.7
unfree labor, 59, 60*t*
United Nations (UN). *See also specific programs*
  after Cold War, 12

Development Fund for Women, 15–19, 16*t*, 28, 100, 101
Development Program, 172
Gender and the Law Working Group, 15, 16*t*, 30–31, 88–89, 91–92, 100
gender in, 2–3
on harmful practices, 207n.12
interventions, 12–13, 16*t*
Millennium Development Goals, 148–49, 210n.3
peacekeepers, 144
Population Fund, 15–19, 16*t*, 28, 100
power in, 28–29
in Timor-Leste, 13, 14*t*, 95–96, 105–6, 181–85
on violence, 206–7n.11
women and, 19, 39, 87, 100, 101
United Nations Mission in East Timor (UNAMET), 1, 2, 14*t*, 206n.5
United States, 155–56, 162–63
UNMIT. *See* Integrated Mission in East Timor
UN Transitional Administration in East Timor (UNTAET)
  efforts of, 13, 22, 70–72, 99–100, 105
  GAU in, 15–19, 16*t*, 27–29, 124–25
Usaha Bersama Simpan Pinjam, 147
usif (king), 197

value, 130–31
VAW. *See* violence against women
veteran status, 70, 75–82, 84
villages
  domestic violence in, 97
  elections in, 80
  leadership in, 104, 111, 130
  Manufahi village, 166–72
  mediation in, 110–11
  patrilineality in, 41, 42, 128–29, 133–34, 135*f*, 141–42
  PNDS, 94
  rank in, 135–36
  village administrative areas, 197
  Village Development Councils, 106–7
  village political economy, 166–72
  women in, 137

violence. *See also specific topics*
  crimes of, 109
  critical approaches to, 38–40
  debt and, 165–66
  domestic, 25–26, 39
  effects of, 135–36
  fines for, 110–11
  gang rape, 65
  gender and, 2–3, 194–95
  gender-based, 91–92, 121, 141
  globalization of, 37
  in Indonesian West Timor, 1–2
  Liquiça Church massacre, 216n.13
  masculinity and, 70
  militia, 59
  moneylending and, 152
  public, 185
  scholarship on, 6
  SGBV, 40, 64–67, 82–83, 93–94, 99–100, 104–5, 156
  socioeconomics of, 67
  Srebrenica massacre, 12–13
  UN on, 206–7n.11
  violensia bai-bain, 113, 197
violence against women (VAW), 39–40, 82–83, 100–2, 104–5, 108–9, 145–49, 185, 194–95
violensia bai-bain (normal violence), 113, 197
violensia boot (serious violence), 113, 197

Vulnerable Person's Unit (VPU), 92

wanra (*perlawanan rakyat*) (people's resistance), 55*t*, 197
war, 38–40
wealth, 7–8, 136, 137*f*, 165, 169*t*, 172, 175, 183–84
Western culture, 101, 108–9, 127, 145
West Timor, 75–76, 116, 187, 188*t*, 193. *See also specific topics*
Whittington, Sherrill, 27
wife giver, 110–11, 122, 126, 136, 137*f*, 142, 197
wife taker, 122, 126, 136, 137*f*, 197
women. *See specific topics*
Women, Peace and Security (WPS) policy agenda, 2–3
Wood, Mary, 27
World Bank, 26, 43, 144, 157, 163, 164
World Bank Community Empowerment Program, 106, 109, 157, 158, 163
World War II, 66
WPS policy agenda. *See* Women, Peace and Security policy agenda

xefe aldeia (hamlet chief), 97, 197
xefe posto (chief of the post), 51, 197
xefe suku, 51, 166–67

ZEESM. *See* Special Zone of Social Market Economy